William Dean Howells

AMERICAN CULTURAL HERITAGE SERIES 8
Jack Salzman, *General Editor*

WILLIAM
DEAN
HOWELLS

The Realist as Humanist

by

William Alexander

Burt Franklin & Company

Published by Burt Franklin & Co.
235 East Forty-fourth Street
New York, New York 10017

©1981 by Burt Franklin & Co., Inc.

Library of Congress Cataloging in Publication Data

Alexander, William Raymond Hall.
William Dean Howells, the realist as humanist.

(American cultural heritage; 8)
Bibliography: p.
Includes index.
1. Howells, William Dean, 1837–1920.   2. Novelists,
American — 19th century — Biography.   I.   Title.
II.   Series.
PS2033.A69   813^1.4[B]   80–26137
ISBN 0–89102–171–X

Designed by Bernard Schleifer
Manufactured in the United States of America

For my mother and father

Contents

Acknowledgments

I WISH TO EXPRESS my gratitude to the following persons and institutions: Edmund Berkeley, Jr., for permission on behalf of Mr. Barrett to quote from a letter by Hjalmar Boyesen in the Barrett Library at the University of Virginia; Frederick V. L. Brokaw, Howard P. Brokaw, Elliot L. Morris, Martha Harrison Pyle, and Davis L. Rianhard for permission to quote from letters by Howard Pyle; Rodney G. Dennis for permission of the Houghton Library at Harvard to quote from correspondence and manuscripts by William Dean Howells and other writers (MS-H in the notes); Rosamund Gilder for permission to quote from letters by her father, Richard Watson Gilder; James Holsaert and the Massachusetts General Hospital for permission to quote from letters by Thomas Sergeant Perry; John N.M. Howells for permission to quote, on a one-time-only basis, from *Life in Letters of William Dean Howells,* edited by Mildred Howells (copyright 1928); Professor William White Howells for permission to quote from William Dean Howells manuscripts at the Houghton Library, from letters by William Dean and Elinor Howells at the Houghton Library and in other collections, and from letters by William Dean Howells that appear in texts cited in the notes (all of this material is under the control of the heirs of William Dean Howells and may not be used again without express permission by Professor Howells); Alexander R. James for permission to quote from letters by Henry, Robertson, and William James; James Parton for permission to quote from letters by his grandfather James Parton; Professor John P. Pickard for permission to quote from letters by John Greenleaf Whittier; Mrs. James Sherman Pitkin for permission to quote from a letter by John William de Forest; the Trustees of the Boston Public Library for permission to quote from the manuscript of William Dean Howells's article "Execution by Electricity"; and Neda

Westlake for permission on behalf of the Charles Van Pelt Library at the University of Pennsylvania to quote from letters by S. Weir Mitchell and, by agreement between the University of Pennsylvania and the Estate of Theodore Dreiser, for permission to quote from a letter by Theodore Dreiser.

Introduction

I HAVE CHOSEN to limit this study to a period of fourteen years for two reasons. First, these are the years of Howells's effort to face honestly the economic injustice he, more than most others of his class, was willing to acknowledge in his own country. This effort did not by any means cease in 1895, but by then its parameters were firmly established, and it is these parameters that concern me. Second, by focusing on these major years and not tracing the subject in detail into its antecedents and into its subsequent manifestations in Howells's life, I am able to give close analysis to all his relevant writing of the period. I can investigate not only the novels but also the published and unpublished letters, articles, editorials, critical essays, poetry, stories, and sketches, in order to reach some depth of understanding of Howells's experience.

Underlying my story are two particular goals. One is to present the humane and democratic values in Howells's realistic theory and practice. It is a truism that Howells believed in responsibility toward one's fellow man, in altruism and common kindness, but too seldom has it been shown how this belief informed his aesthetics and art and how this belief was tested and strained during these years. The other goal is the creation of a better understanding of Howells himself. I hope to convey to today's reader a sense of how Howells as a humane liberal (sometimes a radical) felt a profound social responsibility and felt himself painfully limited and inadequate for the carrying out of that responsibility. I hope to convey how he was in fact limited and inadequate and yet how he worked within and beyond his limitations and was in the end admirably much more adequate than most of us in his effort to carry his perceptions into practical activity. His commitment to a kind of realism that is intended to make a difference in his readers' lives, his struggle with the problem of whether words can make any difference at all, his commitment to social reform, and his consciousness of the rationalizations and lies by which he sometimes evaded responsibility give him an honesty, strength, and tenacity as man and writer that make it difficult for those who know him and his work to remain unaffected.

This view of Howells puts me in a position different from that of apologists who argue that a given group of Howells's best novels gives him the right to our attention. I agree that his books are good and are worth reading, but I feel that in the total panorama of American literature, not to mention world literature, his books by themselves do not give him the right to very much of our attention. I think it is the man trying, within and outside of his fiction and criticism, to be worthy of his art, of his humanity, and of the best in his country that establishes his real claim upon us. And it is that Howells whom I am attempting to present.

While I cannot speak for other Howells scholars of recent years, I suspect that for them as for me Howells has had an important personal effect and it is that response that has brought him much of the critical and admiring attention he has received in the past two decades and more. This particular effect is of a tamer sort than the practical political commitment he excites in some who know him. (His own degree of commitment is clearly one that must be surpassed.) Yet it is an effect he would have treasured. In experiencing both his treatment of his fictional characters and his manner of living with those around him, that is, in experiencing his gentleness, richness of understanding, and depth of sympathy, we grow significantly in our own tolerance and kindliness. For myself, at least, the years spent with Howells have been important in this way.

Anyone writing now about Howells has a number of important debts to acknowledge: to Edwin Cady for his assiduous, detailed, and incisive biography, to Olov Fryckstedt and Kermit Vanderbilt for their excellent biographical-critical works, to Clara and Rudolf Kirk for their illuminating discoveries and analyses through the years, to Vito J. Brenni, Clayton L. Eichelberger, William M. Gibson, and George Arms for their thorough and indispensable bibliographic work, to Don L. Cook and David Nordloh and the people who have worked with them on the *Selected Edition of W. D. Howells* for their dedicated attention to texts without losing sight of the significance of content and of critical biography, and to many of the other recent Howells scholars and critics, I very gratefully acknowledge those debts here and in the pages to follow.

Most of my research and the initial draft of my manuscript were done at the end of the 1960s and at the beginning of the 1970s, while I was a graduate student and then junior faculty member at Harvard University. Thanks to a half-time fellowship from the Charles Warren Center there in 1968–69, I was able to gain some relief from the stimulating demands of the tutorial system and of my first lectures to research the Howells family letters just then becoming accessible and to deepen my reading of Howells.

I will always be grateful to Walter Jackson Bate and David Perkins for the encouragement they gave to my work, and to Alan Heimert for his support in backing me for the Warren Fellowship and for the kind of probing, frank dialogue about American literature he encouraged in lectures and discussions. I thank Kenneth Lynn for insights gained in our discussions both before and during the writing of his own work on Howells. Perhaps most important to me then were the discussions of American literature carried on by a number of faculty and graduate-student colleagues and close friends: I think especially of Bruce Bennett, Steve Botein, Ann Douglas, Brooke Hopkins, John McWilliams, Barry O'Connell, Gail Parker, and Gordon Taylor. Later, Warner Berthoff and Morton Bloomfield generously gave careful readings to portions of the manuscript at a time when the research and writing had become over-wrought, and their sensitive advice helped me to create a more readable tale. I am grateful, finally, to Jack Salzman for his patience and support and for the insight with which he has suggested improvements in the final version.

1

A Starting Point

I

WITH THE PUBLICATION of *A Modern Instance* in 1882, William Dean
Howells appeared to have abandoned his earlier fictional method. No
longer writing in the conventional frame of courtship, he had composed a
serious and critical study of the ordinary contemporary American environment and thereby had become the most prominent and promising
American novelist. Not that his commitment and potential had previously lacked acknowledgment. *The Nation*, for example, had announced in
1880, with far from complete approval of the fact, that "Mr. Howells's
realism is . . . a definitely held creed," and Henry James, with a high if
qualified sense of Howells's capabilities, had conceived of his "mission" as
being "to Americanize and to *realize*" and thus to become the "Zola of the
U.S.A." or the "American Balzac."[1] Nor had his reputation as a writer
previously been small: Since the writing of his earliest books, he had been
read widely by critics and public alike in America and, increasingly, in
England.

A Modern Instance, however, was hailed as a significant step forward.
While the reviews were by no means entirely favorable, few critics could
disagree that it was a book to be reckoned with. Horace Scudder, while
wishing for a more hopeful novel, called it a great work of art and the
"weightiest novel of the day," Howells's "greatest achievement, not in an
artistic, but in an ethical apprehension." It showed a "distinct advance in
the author's conception of the life which lies behind the novel, and the
foundations are laid deeper in the heart of things." *The Critic*, if dissatisfied with the lack of noble heroines and ideal characters generally,
recognized Howells's "growing power of portraying the higher passions"

and his presentation of the "serious aspect of some very serious questions"; whereas Howells hitherto had "reflected only the surface of life," the new volume showed greater promise. John Hay wrote to Howells that if *A Modern Instance* had appeared anonymously, everyone would have cried out, "Here is the fellow who is to write a great American Novel at last." Clarence King heartily congratulated Howells "on what seems to be a sudden acquisition of power."[2] And other competent critics, such as Hamilton Wright Mabie and Edmund Gosse, were to pay tribute to Howells's growing sense of purpose.[3] Richard Watson Gilder, editor of *Century Magazine*, in which *A Modern Instance* was serialized in 1881–82, reported to Howells, "You must know what an immense and strongly moved audience you are drawing along with you in this powerful story. It is a success in every way — both as literature and as 'magazine literature.'"[4]

Many of the younger realists considered, or came to consider, *A Modern Instance* the great revolutionary work in American literature. Although with *The Undiscovered Country* (1880) Howells had "reached the full stature of a novelist," according to Hamlin Garland, with *A Modern Instance* he "took his place among the wisest and the best of the world's novelists." Later critics have for the most part agreed on the significance of this novel. Olov Fryckstedt, for example, chose to end his excellent study of the early Howells with a discussion of *A Modern Instance* because, among other reasons, "with it he reached the high-water mark of his artistic achievement." Howells's firm grasp of American reality and character and his ability to penetrate the surface of American life demonstrated that "his long apprenticeship in the craft of fiction had finally come to its conclusion."[5]

There are additional reasons, as Fryckstedt knows, to end, or begin, a study of Howells in the year 1882. On February 1, 1881, Howells had resigned the editorship of the *Atlantic Monthly*, where he had worked for fifteen years, as assistant editor until 1871, then as editor in chief. Thomas Wentworth Higginson may have stimulated the resignation with his suggestion that the editorship protected Howells from the wholesome ordeal of honest criticism of his fiction. Another, more definite factor was disagreement over the magazine's policies. Howells wrote to the owner, H. O. Houghton, that he felt himself "unable to meet your wishes in some features of management. I have been making a magazine that is neither your ideal nor mine." Whitelaw Reid, offering Howells a job in New

York, was sure the work would "be free from some embarrassments" Howells had known on the *Atlantic*, and Helen Hunt Jackson hinted knowledge of underlying differences: "Very well we know what would happen to the Atlantic if you go out of it."

During the eight years of Houghton's ownership, Howells's salary had remained the same. And Howells had long regretted the strain of editorial work and its diversion of time from his writing. In the late 1870s he was often "minded to jump out and take the consequences — to throw myself upon the market" — and it is likely that by late in 1880 he felt enough confidence in his ability, and in America as a source of material, to be willing to take his chances. If the result for *A Modern Instance* was the more severe criticism that Higginson had predicted, it is true also that the move was hailed as one that promised great gains for American fiction. Henry James wrote of his pleasure in learning of Howells's resignation: "Honestly I feel a thrill of almost physical satisfaction in the thought of that genius of yours now having its ease and its leisure to go and do one great thing after another through all the coming years."[6]

Howells's widening acclaim as a novelist was certainly sufficient to increase his confidence. Late in 1879, he learned that Turgenev had spoken of his works "as superior to those of any one now living." In the spring of 1881, his "life and works" were made the subject of study in a school in Jefferson, Ohio, one of his boyhood hometowns. And in June 1881 the man whose Harvard and Yale had been a printer's shop received an honorary M.A. from Yale and was introduced at a dinner by the university president in terms that made him, as he later said, "blush for pride and pleasure." In the summer of 1882, Howells departed for a year in Europe, where, following in an American tradition that had begun with Benjamin Franklin, he was to gather in foreign plaudits, including a summons to meet the crown princess of Germany in Venice and so many invitations during a London fortnight, he said, that he could have boarded around for a year. "Certain little books seemed to be known in quarters where their author never expected to find them; and from the bookstalls he had to turn his modest eyes away." He also achieved some international notoriety in 1882 through an article on Henry James in which he confidently announced that the methods of the modern realistic school had outmoded the fiction of such English masters as Dickens and Thackeray. The article, which Howells was never allowed to forget, became a central document in the history of nineteenth-century realism, principally for the outcry it stimulated on both sides of the Atlantic from the opponents of the new fiction.

By 1882, Howells had become the leader of an American school of realism. He had freed himself from editorial work to concentrate on his career as a novelist and on his increasing commitment to America. He had achieved international fame. He had written a significant novel and showed promise of even better works in the years ahead. He would also be spurred by the counterattacks on his theoretical pronouncements to formulate and enunciate more clearly his literary beliefs. Henry James wrote to him in November 1882, "You have only to go on."[7]

II

By this time, Howells was in fact well on his way to formulation of his general aesthetic purpose, a purpose worth stating at the outset.

In 1887, Howells was to receive a letter from an anxious reader of the "Editor's Study," his column in *Harper's Monthly*. This reader, a self-aware Emma Bovary one might say, traced to his reading of fiction the wild, visionary, untrue, and injurious parts of his mental makeup. He found that fiction begot such high-strung, supersensitive ideas of life that everyday industry, poverty, and distress met with no sympathy from readers at all. All of this was very true, Howells replied; not of realism, however, but of the fiction of the recent past and, unfortunately, of some contemporary nonrealistic fiction. Most people do not read the great realistic novels, and thus fail to gain much good from fiction; they read poor little novels that tickle their prejudices, coddle their sensibilities, pamper their gross appetite for the marvelous, and exalt the passions above the principles of life. They read novels by Rider Haggard:

> The kind of novels he likes, and likes to write are intended to take his reader's mind, or what the reader would probably call his mind, off himself; they make one forget life and all its cares and duties. . . . No sordid details of verity here, if you please; no wretched being humbly and weakly struggling to do right and to be true, suffering for his follies and his sins ... nothing of all this, but a great whirling splendor of peril and achievement, a wild scene of heroic adventure, and of emotional ground and lofty tumbling, with a stage "picture" at the fall of the curtain, and all the good

characters in a row, their left hands pressed upon their hearts, and kissing their right hands to the audience, in the good old way that has always charmed and always will charm, Heaven bless it!

Such writers are not entirely to blame, for it is all too true that the average reader prefers falsehood to truth and wishes to have his mind taken off himself.[8]

The best fiction, on the other hand, the kind that gives us insight into the world in which we actually live and implicates us in the lives of characters like ourselves, can do us great good in a number of ways. It reveals, first of all, the moral universe in which we live and teaches us that the evil we do will sooner or later recoil upon us. Second, it may simply show us "things we have passed / Perhaps a hundred times nore cared to see" — the charm, interest, and spirit underlying our everyday existence. Looking back from 1914, Howells recalled how the Russian novelists had impressed him as a young man: "They opened to me what seemed to be a new world — and it was only the real world."[9]

Third, realistic fiction, by definition, tells what is really there; it cuts through all the habits, conventions, and interests that lie to us about our lives. It throws us back on ourselves. Through becoming implicated in the lives of its characters, we learn motives, emotions, and experiences of substantial importance for our own lives. What the realist "can and must do ethically"

> . . . is to make us take thought of ourselves, and look to it whether we have in us the making of this or that wrong, whether we are hypocrites, tyrants, pretenders, shams conscious or unconscious; whether our most unselfish motives are not really secret shapes of egotism; whether our convictions are not mere brute acceptations; whether we believe what we profess; whether when we force good to a logical end we are not doing evil. . . . If we find ourselves all right we can go ahead with a good conscience, but never so cocksure afterwards.

When realism becomes critical realism, it also elucidates our civilization. Dickens, in his Christmas literature, put the comfortable and refined in mind of the savagery and suffering all about them; and all literature, as Howells came to see it, must confront its readers with themselves and with the growing problems within our social and political systems. If this troubled some readers, there was an answer:

> A great many good, elderly minded people think it dreadful Ibsen should show us that the house we have lived in so long is full of vermin, that its drainage is bad, that the roof leaks and the chimney smokes abominably; but if it is true, is it not well for us to know it? It is dreadful because it is so, not because he shows it so; and the house is no better because our fathers got on in it as it is.[10]

What fiction can and should do, then, is make the reader think and question, and thus initiate change in our adverse conditions.

Fourth, and perhaps most important, realistic fiction may humanize the reader. That is, besides making him aware of his own egoistic, corrupt behavior and attitudes that break down sympathy and understanding, it can also make him more respectful, kindly, compassionate, and humane, more united with others in common brotherhood. This it can do by bringing him into close contact with his fellow men.

Howells consciously belonged to what might be called the humanistic school of realism, the school Eugène Melchior Vogüé wrote of when opposing the Russian novelists to the French, the school that fosters democracy and Christianity in human relations. This affiliation is not often noted, and when it is noted, it is rarely given sufficient status; yet it represents the aspect of his critical theory and fiction he would most probably wish brought out. "Humanist" is a valid term for Howells, one he would readily accept, and one that is used advisedly. It should not be taken to mean the Christian humanism that unites within itself the paradoxes of man's great powers and great weaknesses or to mean the Arnoldian humanism that advocates a full and rounded development of individuals and of society toward perfected being. The term is taken as deriving primarily from "humane"; it is used as Howells himself uses it in writing about the Russian authors:

> They are all so very much more than realists that this name, never satisfactory in regard to any school of writers, seems altogether insufficient for them. They are realists in ascertaining an entire probability of motive and situation in their work; but with them this is only the beginning; they go so far beyond it in purpose and

effect that one must cast about them for some other word if one would try to define them. Perhaps humanist would be the best phrase in which to clothe the idea of their literary office if it could be limited to mean their simply, almost humbly, fraternal attitude toward the persons and conditions with which they deal, and again extended to include a profound sense of that individual responsibility from which the common responsibility can free no one.

Humanity, Howells says, is as much a part of realism as the truth itself, and he quotes from *Some Aspects of Humanity* E. Hughes's effort to make us realize the "greatness of its mission as a humanizing influence."[11]

It is true that Howells writes about humanism for the most part after his discovery of Tolstoy in 1886, but his interest in it dates from much earlier. No writer's ethical appeal had been stronger for him than that of George Eliot, whose literary goals are strikingly close to his and whom he first read in 1859.[12] In 1873 he wrote of Turgenev's *Rudin* that although we do not wholly understand Rudin's character at the end, "in the mean time we are taught a merciful distrust of our own judgments, and we take Leschnieff's forgiving and remorseful attitude towards him. It may be safely surmised that this was the chief effect that Turgénieff desired to produce in us." In his 1877 article on Carlo Goldoni, Howells expressed gratitude that he had come upon Goldoni's memoirs early and read them together with his comedies, "so that the romantic city [Venice] became early humanized to me through the life and labors of the kindly dramatist." Goldoni himself, he said, had learned mercifully early the "lesson that humanity is above literature."[13]

Although Howells's humanism can be traced to his contact with Eliot, Björnson, Turgenev, Tolstoy, and other European writers, a strong case may be made for its simultaneous derivation from a native tradition, emanating for the most part, but not entirely, from New England. The case may be made by reference to Howells's opinions on a number of friends and acquaintances from the preceding generation of American writers. Longfellow, whom he found "noble and perfectly democratic" for all his stateliness of manner, "had not only great faith in men, but patience as vast and kindly as Lincoln's. Neither the foibles nor the sins of his fellow-mortals shut his heart against them, or inclined him to distinguish himself from them." Although Howells's relations with Emerson were never very fortunate and although, accordingly, he had some reservations about him, in at least one place he expresses high appreciation of this characteristic in his writing:

> In humanity as in his theories of what literature should be to us, Emerson is still the foremost of all our seers, and will be so a hundred years hence.... Every new thing, every new thought, challenged him: abolition, Brook Farm, Walt Whitman: he was just to each, and, with Emerson, as with all high souls, to be just was to be generous.

Howells tells of how he, as a young Ohioan, had worshiped George William Curtis for his writing, and how, when Curtis took a strong anti-slavery stand, he suddenly learned that that dazzling talent, that traveled and accomplished gentleman, "was a man with the heart to feel the wrongs of men so little friended then as to be denied all the rights of men." Howells had difficulty writing of him merely as a man of letters, "for humanity was above the humanities with him, and we all know how he turned from the fairest career in literature to tread the thorny path of politics because he believed that duty led the way, and that good citizens were needed more than good romancers." Speaking as one of James Russell Lowell's successors as editor of the *Atlantic*, he said that Lowell gave the magazine "literary conscience and human responsibility, and the best that his successive successors could do was to keep it true to his conception of its mission." A line from one of Lowell's memorial poems "sums up and utters the best that America means for the race, where he says — 'That none can breathe her air nor grow humane' — a truth that broadens and deepens as you think of it."[14]

America, indeed, was peculiarly the location for realism to achieve its humane and democratic potential, for realism is the material of democracy, and no great art, Howells says, can arise outside of democracy. In America, realism is to reach its highest, most effective form, for the American writer's upbringing and civilization give him an inherent perception of "equality running through motive, passion, principle, incident, character, and commanding with the same force his interest in the meanest and the noblest, through the mere virtue of their humanity." For this reason, humanity has a claim upon the American writer and "upon America beyond all other lands"; humanity once again looks to America, the city on the hill, for a way of life:

The gods have taken us at our word, and have responded to us with a civilization in which there is no distinction perceptible to the eye that loves and values it. Such beauty and such grandeur as we have is common beauty, common grandeur ... these conditions invite the artist to the study and the appreciation of the common, and to the portrayal in every art of those finer and higher aspects which unite rather than sever humanity, if he would thrive in our new order of things.[15]

This is Howells at his most hopeful, the Howells who, whatever his doubts, never entirely gave up hope that the American realist might, by his particular humanizing conscience, appeal to and develop in Americans, against insidious countercurrents of class distinctions and material values, the underlying knowledge of equality and fraternity bred into every one of them.

III

In 1882, then, Howells was an artist of stature, of increasing depth, and of great promise, an artist with a clear, strong purpose. And he was to remain for his contemporaries over the next decades a major novelist. Yet, as we know, time has not served him well. In this century, attention has been paid him, more in some decades than in others, but he has never attained the universal respect accorded his friends and contemporaries Mark Twain and Henry James. It is, in fact, very easy now to meet intelligent, educated Americans who have never read Howells, and it is not at all difficult to find those who have not even heard his name. His sort of fiction does not now much engage us, and the limits he set himself deprive his work of the dimensions that make novels survive as major works of art.

Still, Howells remains, for those who turn to him, a large and significant figure. Both his writing and his character, as Lionel Trilling argues, make it difficult to place him in a minor position as a merely transitional personage in American literature, an early exponent and practitioner of realism, clearing the way for the greater writers to follow. In Trilling's words, there is something "indomitable" about Howells. We must have the grace to see

> ... that in resisting Howells, in rejecting him, we are resisting and rejecting something more than a literary talent or temperament or method. There is in Howells ... an odd kind of muted, stubborn passion which we have to take account of, and respect, and recognize for what it is, the sign of a commitment, or an involvement in very great matters — we are required to see that in making our judgment of him we are involved in considerations of a way of life, of quality of being.

Although Howells was not a "man of heroic moral intensity," he was a "man of principle." Hamlin Garland applies the same point of view to the fiction: Howells's method "does not secure great emotional tension, but it is fraught with great good to the reader."[16]

The pages that follow are a quest for the sources of Howells's strength, those qualities that make for his tenacity and refusal to become merely a figure in the background of our literature. They represent an effort to understand the nature of his commitment, expressed by himself and his contemporaries in the early 1880s and still compelling to Lionel Trilling in 1955. And they are an exploration of his struggle to make his art a force in the America he discovered.

2

From
A Modern Instance
to
The Minister's Charge

I

HOWELLS, like most writers after the Civil War, had been full of confidence in the future of America. Like James and Mark Twain, Howells was
young and hopeful, and thus less quick to become disillusioned with the
direction of American civilization than such older writers as Lowell,
Norton, Whitman, and Melville. He was shocked in 1874 at Lowell's
calling America the "Land of Broken Promise." The labor uprisings of
1877, however, penetrated to the quiet seclusion of Cambridge, and
Howells was moved by personal and editorial responsibility to take an
interest in economic and social conditions. The result was an increasing
number of *Atlantic* articles devoted to issues connected with the
depression. These included J. B. Harrison's studies of the conflict
between labor and capital — which contained detailed observation of
working-class lives — and Henry Demarest Lloyd's famous exposé of
Standard Oil, which Howells approved for publication just before he left
the magazine.[1]

Harrison's studies, which had considerable influence on *A Modern
Instance*, were entitled "Certain Dangerous Tendencies in American
Life." Their conservative bias reflected Howells's own belief in laissez-
faire government and economics, in the at least partial culpability of the
prodigal poor, and in elitest responsibility. At the same time, however,
Harrison called attention to the poor conditions of the laborer under unrestricted capitalism and planted a seed of doubt in the minds of some of
his conservative readers — readers who found themselves rather close to
Atherton, one of the major commentators in *A Modern Instance*.

According to Atherton, it does not make much difference to a society
if undisciplined, uneducated country people like Bartley and Marcia

Hubbard go wrong, but if a Ben Halleck of Boston does so, it is calamitous. "It 'confounds the human conscience,' as Victor Hugo says. All that careful nurture in the right since he could speak, all that life-long decency of thought and act, that noble ideal of unselfishness and responsibility to others, trampled underfoot and spit upon — it's horrible!" The natural man, says Atherton, is a wild beast, and

> . . . it's the implanted goodness that saves, the seed of righteousness treasured from generation to generation, and carefully watched and tended by disciplined fathers and mothers in the hearts where they have dropped it. The flower of this implanted goodness is what we call civilization, the condition of general uprightness that Halleck declared he owed no allegiance to.[2]

Some caution is necessary before asserting that Howells is speaking through one of his characters, but Atherton's social philosophy is not directly challenged or undercut.[3] Furthermore, the novel has shifted by this point, disproportionately, to a concentration upon Ben Halleck and his overwrought and somewhat perverse struggles with the moral problems of his relationship to Marcia Hubbard. Howells, in the course of the book, touches on a number of negative factors in American civilization: the breakdown of spiritual values in rural communities; the sad results of a lack of family discipline; the counting-room morality of the press and the pandering to the public in print, in the theater, and in the church; election betting; the tasteless and dangerous tendency of Americans to respect men who dress and talk "smart" more than men of real honesty and character; and other defects and corruptions. Painful as these things are, and painful as the decline of Bartley and Marcia is, perhaps the real torment in the novel is in the breakdown of Halleck, who had been trained as a member of the elite (though not of the hereditary Boston elite) to hold high standards and values and to be of an honest and socially responsible character.[4]

Howells has not here abandoned his native, western belief in the equality of all persons regardless of class and schooling, and echoes of that belief may be found in the book. But that he subscribes here to the more aristocratic, if still somewhat democratic, elitist values of some Easterners as well as to western egalitarian values creates a certain minor tension. It stems from the conflict he felt as a younger man between the rich culture of Europe and the thin American heritage, and it may be traced as well to his close relations with such men as James Russell Lowell, Charles Eliot Norton, and Oliver Wendell Holmes. This elitist viewpoint underlying *A Modern Instance* is a clear indication of where Howells stood, if not entirely steadily, in 1881.

If Atherton's social philosophy goes unchallenged, Howells does contrive to undercut him in another way. After the words quoted above, seated in his "luxurious dining room" on Beacon Street overlooking the Back Bay,

> Atherton lifted, with his slim, delicate hand, the cup of translucent china, and drained off the fragrant souchong, sweetened, and tempered with Jersey cream to perfection. Something in the sight went like a pang to his wife's heart. "Ah!" she said, "it is easy enough for us to condemn. *We* have everything we want!"

Atherton admits this and says that sometimes when he thinks of it, he is ready to renounce all judgment of others: "The consciousness of our comfort, our luxury, almost paralyzes me at those times, and I am ashamed and afraid even of our happiness."[5]

Norton wrote to Lowell in 1874 that Howells had grown "plump and with ease shining out from his eyes" — the image of a man rapidly becoming a popular American writer. By 1881, Howells was a very successful author. He had held for over a decade the prominent position of *Atlantic* editor. And he had moved upward from house to house, from Sacramento Street to Berkeley Street to a house built for him on Concord Avenue (where he made his prospective brother-in-law "wonder at the comfort and splendor of our house — carpeted through the first floor with one pattern of Brussels!" and where he tried "not to be proud," and which he advertised as "one of the finest estates in Cambridge") to a home designed for him by McKim, Mead, and White on the hill above Belmont. In 1882 he could write a letter to Henry James moralizing, as James paraphrased it in reply, "about middle-age and this inevitable *embourgeoisment.*"[6]

The reference to Atherton's comforts and subsequent unease reflects Howells's growing sense of how his own economic and social position was tending to isolate him from important aspects of American life. Howells is not Atherton, but that he remarks such a conflict in Atherton's situation — and also in Clara Kingsbury's — reveals at the least a degree of interest in it. Swedenborgian instruction in the pitfalls of egoism and a background in Heinesque irony were enough to make Howells conscious of his propensity to arrogate himself above his fellow men, a propensity that worried him considerably.[7] From the early 1860s on, he makes references to his desire for "worldly success," to his "restless ambition . . . evil thoughts . . . scornful hopes . . . sinful deeds," to his egoistic forgetfulness of the family he left behind in Ohio, and to the poor example being set his children by a man whose life "has been too much given to the merely artistic and to worldly ambition" and whose "morality has been a hand to mouth affair."

A short story, written in 1880 and based on an experience of his son's, suggests how he was now feeling about the ease with which he had detached himself from any sense of complicity in the evil around him. The Boy had, after long unsuccess, finally managed to catch a squirrel in his trap, but his triumph was fatally marred by finding the animal dead, probably from terrified efforts to escape. "He walked slowly and sadly home, thinking of the life lost, the freedom wronged, the small squirrely joys and hopes blotted out." When his father found him in his room grieving in the dusk,

> . . . the Boy opened his sore and heavy heart to him. . . . His father, who had encouraged and patronized the trap, felt guilty, too; but he knew better how to hide his sense of culpability. He consoled the Boy, as if from a clear conscience, and told how a great poet had bidden us
>> Never to blend our pleasure or our pride
>> With sorrow of the meanest thing that feels.
> In this way, he put it all on the Boy.

The popular author and editor, the man who subscribed to Atherton's elitist views while wondering at Atherton's right to judge those whose circumstances he had not known, probably put some personal feeling into Ben Halleck's assertion that

> . . . character is a superstition, a wretched fetish. Once a year wouldn't be too often to seize upon sinners whose blameless life has placed them above suspicion, and turn them inside out before the community, so as to show people how the smoke of the Pit had been

quietly blackening their interior. That would destroy character as a cult.[8]

II

One morning in July 1880, within a few months of the squirrel story, Howells caught an early train from Belmont into Boston to attend a session of the police court. A year later, he repeated the visit to confirm his impressions for an article, which he first published as "Police Report" in the *Atlantic* for January 1882. What whim led him to the police court, he said, he did not know. It may have been the lack of other summer amusements in the city. It may have been that in his revolt against the unreality of the novel he was working on, he "was in the humor to see life whose reality asserts itself every day in the newspapers with indisputable force." Here, as elsewhere in the article, Howells indicates that he is attempting, with his considered approach to the police court, to counteract the sordid, tasteless, and harmful publicity of the police reports in the daily newspapers. He is also, however, setting a precedent for later excursions into police courts, jails, tramps' lodgings, and slums. This pattern was already asserting itself in his visits to the Soldiers' Home — "a sad metropolis of sickness and suffering" — in Dayton, Ohio, and down into the coal mines in Danville, Illinois, in the summer of 1881. It was a pattern that would repeat itself through the next two decades of his life.

There are a number of reasons for this first excursion and those that followed. In the late 1870s, Harrison had stimulated his interest in the "other Americans," and an initial, reasonably safe way of observing them was through the police court. Howells had been impressed with Harrison's realistic method, and if he too was to write realistically about the common man, the police court offered promising material. Here he might find both some answers to problematic aspects of America and some help in his more or less conscious effort to close the gap he now saw widening between himself and the lower economic classes in America.

He was also motivated by a sense of opportunities missed. He later wished that as a boy he had spent less time in his study in Ashtabula, Ohio, and more time involved in the life around him. He was sorry that he had quit his Cincinnati newspaper job after a single night's round of the police stations had convinced him he was not cut out for such work; had he suffered fewer qualms, he would have known "many phases of life that I have always remained ignorant of."

In his youth and as a reporter such haunts would have been more natural, but now he feels self-conscious and somewhat out of place. His references to his fellow policemen and fellow spectators and his passing himself off as a plainclothes detective to get a seat on his second visit are not entirely in fun. He believes at first it is himself being addressed when an officer approaches and says to one of his fellow habitués, "No room for you here today, my friend. Go up on the Common."[9]

The "Police Report" has two primary purposes: conveying to readers an understanding of, and a merciful justice toward, the minor and even major criminal — a purpose shared with *A Modern Instance*[10]— and an arraignment of a judicial and penal system that serves only to perpetuate the criminal instinct. In studying the courtroom spectators and the demoralizing effect on them of the proceedings, Howells is questioning the attitudes of his readers as well. To this end, he distinguishes the gloating, obscene delight of the onlookers from his own recognition of the human qualities of the prostitute, her procurer, and the old fool they robbed. He describes his merciful impulses toward some of the accused, recognizes to an extent some of the conditions that made them what they are, and dwells upon the conditions that will make them what they are to be. The House of Correction, he argues with force, is not purgatory but hell, and the future of an offender sent there is entirely hopeless.

Perhaps most interesting, however, and justification for dwelling on "Police Report" before following Howells into the 1880s are the attitudes it reveals. We find self-satire upon the author's incipient, somewhat justifiable arrogance toward his fellow spectators at the beginning, upon his falling into sympathy with their reactions, and upon his "light mind" shifting easily from one case to another. He uses a theatrical metaphor for the setting and gives cases such names as "a little Police Pastoral" and "a laughable little interlude of Habitual Drunkenness." He emphasizes the comedy of some interchanges and dwells with amusement and slightly annoying superiority on the thickheadedness of those on the stand. However, he moves from the predominating comedy into reflections and pleas that are sober and even indignant. His awareness of his method is clear from the following passage:

> I have tried to treat my material lightly and entertainingly, as a true
> reporter should, but I would not have my reader suppose that I did

not feel the essential cruelty of an exhibition that tore its poor rags from all that squalid shame, and its mask from all that lying, cowering guilt, or did not suspect how it must harden and deprave those whom it daily entertained.[11]

There àre at least three reasons for the humorous approach. Howells is attempting to parody the usual police report. He also desires to sugar-coat his message, entertaining his readers so they will accept his more serious lessons and indictments; the moralizings, which increase toward the end, cast a pathos over some of the earlier laughable scenes. The third reason is more personal and very human: Howells's humor and light touch, as he partially realizes, keep the unpleasant and distressing at a distance and serve as a defense. "I could not refuse my sympathy to the general content; I took another respite from thought of my poor thief, and I too lent myself to hope of enjoyment from this Laughable After-piece."[12] As a realist, of course, Howells felt he could not observe well or depict accurately if he was too emotionally involved in his scene or characters, and humor is an aid to detachment. But more is involved than realism.

A reporter for the *New York Tribune*, after a visit to Howells in 1880, reported his conversation to be as facile, bright, and graceful as his style, abounding in delicate humor and gentle cynicism: "He avoids serious subjects, and cannot be betrayed into argument, but illustrates whatever he touches with a picturesque lightness." Edwin Cady notes that other alert observers in the 1880s recognized in Howells this use of wit and gentleness as defensive weapons. His delicate humor had been early remarked by Lowell and encouraged by Edwin L. Godkin, who in hiring Howells for *The Nation* in late 1865 found one of those rare Americans he had been seeking who could "handle any subject with a light touch." Such humor could add grace to a story and serve to deflate the bombastic rhetoric and romance Howells opposed, but it could also undercut involvement and belittle serious concerns. It increases the entertainment of "Police Report" and also weakens its appeal. Hamilton Wright Mabie thinks this is a key defect in Howells's fiction:

Is Mr. Howells ashamed of life in its outcries of pain and regret? Does he shrink from these unpremeditated and unconventional revelations of character as vulgar, provincial, inartistic; or does he fail to comprehend them? . . . Whenever the reader begins to warm a little, a slight turn of satire, a cool phrase or two of analysis, a faint suggestion that the writer doubts whether it is worth while, clears the air again.[13]

A rather startling passage occurs at the end of "Police Report." Howells tells of having seen a Black Maria driving away from the high portal of the courthouse, probably on its way to the House of Industry, the House of Correction, Deer Island, "or some of those places where people are put to go from bad to worse." He cannot help thinking

> . . . that for all reasonable hope as to the future of its inmates the Black Maria might as well have been fitted with one of those ingenious pieces of mechanism by which some of our adoptive citizens propose to disable English commerce, and driven out to some wide, open space where the explosion could do no harm to the vicinity, and so when the horses and driver had removed to a safe distance —

This violent suggestion is, of course, extravagance for the sake of Howells's indictment of the penal system. When he argues that criminal trials should be kept private, he is stating the matter seriously on behalf of both the criminals and the onlookers.[14] It is probable, however, that in both cases he is, consciously or not, attempting to shut out unpleasantness he has forced himself to see and does not enjoy.

"The hurt is past all surgery," he writes about the poverty, injustice, and immorality he touches on in his "Letters from Venice"; "let us hide it, and be deceived in peace." In *A Chance Acquaintance* he looks askance on Arbuton's "personal dislike, as I may call it, of poverty" and on Kitty's enjoyment of it "because it was strange and suggestive," but he scarcely does either of them better in his brief treatment of it. In *A Modern Instance* he knows that Clara Kingsbury "was all the more anxious to perform her whole duty, because she confessed that indigent children were personally unpleasant to her," and Olive Halleck can say about the trip to the Indiana divorce court: "Our coming off, in this way, on such an errand, is something so different from the rest of our whole life! And I *do* like quiet, and orderly ways, and all that we call respectability! . . . But I've concluded that we mustn't care. It's right, and we must do it."

This wish for orderly existence is common in Howells's writing, and some of his artistic ideals — simplicity, repose, restraint — correspond to a desire for a society composed of similar qualities. Yet Olive Halleck *is* going on the errand for the sake of her seriously upset friend, and Howells *is* attending the police court and doing *his* best to improve the lot of the prisoners. While such efforts are difficult for a man of his years, position, and temperament, a temperament unhappy with the disturbing and sordid, still he writes with conviction at this time that one cannot read the life of Charles Kingsley "without feeling the brotherhood of a soul that has suffered and has learned through suffering that there is but one great thing for men to do in this world, and that is to do right."[15]

III

At forty-four, planning to take his family to Europe on January 1, 1882, for eighteen months or more, Howells, in order to finish *A Modern Instance* by Thanksgiving, began in the late summer of 1881 to work at an exhausting pace. Mid-November brought a fever; complications ensued and put him in bed, seriously ill "for seven incredible weeks," and it was not until mid-March that he felt entirely well. After spending May in the better air of Lexington, the family returned to Boston and Belmont before traveling in July, probably via Niagara Falls, to Toronto and Quebec, where they finally set sail for Europe.[16]

Other causes may have added to the strain, but the prime source of the illness was overwork.[17] The most significant result — signaled by the grayish beard that sprouted while he lay in bed — was a realization of the vulnerability of his years. He felt, he said, "much older than before," a feeling aggravated by a weakened heart, which made it impossible for him to think of living on the Belmont hill any longer. This forty-five-year-old man had to grapple for the first time with middle age, and he began to do so in a sketch he worked at on shipboard. The Marches, who as a relatively young couple visited the falls in *Their Wedding Journey*, decide in "Niagara Revisited" to return twelve years later with their children. They now live comfortable if fairly expensive middle-class lives and resemble the Howellses in other ways. Basil March, for instance, his last name the month of Howells's birth, "was now forty-two, and his moustache was well sprinkled with gray.... He had grown stouter." They wish to "find their lost second-youth" on the trip, but through the way they now see Niagara, their sense of age is reinforced, and they react by resolving to feel and behave as youthfully as possible. Isabel catches herself wondering in a reverie whether marriage and the day-to-day had not vulgarized them both. Breaking free from the thought, she runs remorsefully and acceptingly toward her husband, "whose broad, honest back with no visible neck or shirt-collar, was turned towards her, as he stood, with his head thrown up, studying a time-table on the wall."[18]

The Howellses had last been in Europe in 1865, and their return would have some of the same quality as the Marches' return to Niagara. *Indian Summer*, a novel conceived during their stay in Italy, would parallel "Niagara Revisited" in its explorations of the timetable of middle age.

What we have, then, is Howells the successful, well-to-do, middle-class novelist who had recently been praised by Turgenev, whose "life and works" were being studied in his boyhood town, who had received an honorary degree from Yale, and who was now headed to Europe for even more lionization. Yet this successful, well-to-do, middle-class Howells of elitist sympathies could also be found sitting in the police court temperamentally ill at ease and a little uncertain about his right to be there. This writer on American life was realizing his distance from some of the important aspects of that life, and he was a man in tension, tension increased by the fact that he was also a forty-five-year-old man wondering how to handle middle age.

He was worried too about how to deal with Europe, for "Lexington," composed in London, may be read as a stand for older American values and for spare, honest American realism against the European temptations he must have felt in his recent walks and talks with Henry James. His respect for the Lexingtonians embattled against great odds at the outset of the Revolutionary War may derive at least partially from his awareness that his attack on Thackeray and Dickens was to explode out of the pages of the November *Century*, setting him, although he could not have known this, on the path to being the foremost American exponent of realistic fiction. Apologist for, and successful practitioner of, realism as Howells was, however, "Lexington" reveals a writer unsure of his own and old Lexington's relation to the America of the 1880s, in a kind of agony over his awareness of complicity and corruptibility. Horse races, he learns, are held at Lexington. Having driven out to one, he goes "about bewildered at this transformation of my poor New England, and fearfully hoping there was nothing wicked in so much apparent enjoyment with no apparent useful purpose, till I heard myself indicated in a whisper as 'one of the horsemen.' Then I desperately abandoned myself to the common dissipation, for it was idle to be better than one seemed."[19]

Howells was as yet unaware that his daughter was fatally ill. He had hoped that the year abroad would be beneficial for eighteen-year-old Winifred, whose health had noticeably weakened in 1880 and who was a source of constant worry. She had spent the fall of 1880 exercising in a gymnasium and in July 1881 had gone to Dr. James Jackson Putnam to undergo a rest cure for what was diagnosed as a nervous disorder. After the first week of treatment, not yet an adequate test of its efficacy, Howells wrote his father that nothing really seemed to do her any good, "and she is a burden on my heart. I see these days of her beautiful youth slipping away, in this sort of dull painful dream, and I grieve over her. 'Oh, papa, what a strange youth I'm having!' she said once with a burst of tears that wrung my soul."

The treatment continued — Winny was "bathed, rubbed, and *lunched* continually" — but without much apparent success; in fact, Howells thought, there were some adverse effects: "The privation has thrown her thoughts back upon her, and made her morbid and hypochondriacal." By October there had been some improvement, although Howells now saw ahead of him "Winny's expensive invalidism." In the spring she seemed nearly herself, and in Europe the family would seek climates they believed conducive to her good health. She was a very talented young girl; her poetry, written at this time and earlier, is extraordinarily mature and sensitive. It is often bleak and painful too, and Howells, looking it over years later, found that

> ... these pathetic breaths of rhyme, with the surprise, the bewilderment in them of the doom she could not escape, whisper to me out of a misery of thwarted and foregone endeavor running far back of the time when we began to fear even temporary arrest in her beautiful achievement. I remember one twilight, while she seemed as yet quite well, she was driving home with her mother and me, when something in the talk made us speak with hope of what she might do in literature. She broke suddenly into a wild grief of tears, and sobbed into her hands, and besought us, "Oh, don't expect anything of me — *don't* expect anything!" We comforted her with

what was the truth — that we were not ambitious for her, and only glad in the gift which she would know best how to use to the best end — and she was gay again in her gentle way; but the prescience in her appeal struck us with the first chill of the sorrow that advanced fitfully but certainly upon us, with many a pause but no backward step.[20]

This was written in retrospect, and father and mother sometimes suspected Winny of hypochondria, were sometimes impatient, and were defensively anxious to avoid a dire outlook on her condition. But as these passages indicate, they were living with a real grief and a burden of painful possibilities.

IV

The family was to spend late July to mid-September in London, mid-September to early December in Switzerland, December to May in Italy, June and early July in London, and would arrive once more in Quebec on July 13, 1883. Most of Howells's experience was that of the tourist, the vacationer by the shores of Lake Geneva, the writer of travel sketches, of *A Little Swiss Sojourn* and *Tuscan Cities*. But the concerns that took him to the Boston police court persisted. His sightseeing visit to the Harlot Market in London seems to have been for diversion after a play, rather than for any more serious purpose. One friend, however, possibly Edmund Gosse, was "much concerned" that Howells know the underside of the city, and he took Howells

> . . . to some dreadful purlieu where I saw and heard and smelled things quite as bad as any that I did long afterwards in the over-tenanted regions of New York. My memory is still haunted by the vision of certain hapless creatures who fled blinking from one hole in the wall to another, with little or nothing on, and of other creatures much in liquor and loudly scolding and quarreling, with squalid bits of childhood scattered about underfoot, and vague shapes of sickness and mutilation, and all the time a buying and selling of loathsome second-hand rags.[21]

From Switzerland Howells wrote James about middle age and *embourgeoisment*. He considered himself, he said,

> . . . especially fictionable, and I am sorry you are not here to study me in the character of a thoroughly bourgeois American: a man who had once some poetical possibilities, but who finds himself more and more commonplace in surroundings that twenty years ago appealed not in vain to something fine in him. I daily put on more *sitzfleisch*, and feel hopelessly middle-aged, when I meet the pretty girls walking the Chillon to gather the crimson leaves of the Virginia creeper, which hangs its splendor from all the wall here.

Beyond what he learned in his lodgings, he later wrote, he was able to learn little about the political and social life at Villeneuve. He noted what the pastor's wife said about pauperism but confessed he had seen little of it. He discussed Swiss politics, felt a certain premonitory fascination with the "practical socialism" of the community, took an interest in (and opposed) an attempt to nationalize the school system, and felt that the Swiss radicals resembled the U.S. Democrats in being sometimes the retrograde party in regard to the labor situation.[22]

In Florence he intended to write a travel sketch which would draw on the historical past of this part of Italy and portray realistically what had been too much sentimentalized. This intention was carried out in *Tuscan Cities*. He also meant to write about social conditions, perhaps a serious novel dealing with a member or members of the lower classes, perhaps something in the vein of *The Minister's Charge*. "In pursuance of an intention of studying Florence more seriously than anything here represents," he writes in *Tuscan Cities*, "I assisted one morning at a session of the police court, which I was willing to compare with the like tribunal at home." Again self-conscious about his presence there, he noted that the crowd was as shabby as that in Boston, but not so truculent-looking or dirty, "and my respectability was consoled when I found myself shoulder to shoulder with an *abbate* in it."

Much of his time in Florence was taken up with finishing *A Woman's Reason*, with visiting neighboring cities with his illustrator Joseph Pennell, with making a start on *Tuscan Cities*, and with an immense amount of flattering but "absolutely enraging" socializing. He found lionization "the very most insubstantial of all pleasures," if one he had "so long longed for!" He found time in the midst of all this to visit the Pia Casa di Ricovero, a refuge for paupers, "the helpless and hapless of our own species," and took notes on the city's sanitation policy, its food, and the work the paupers were taught to do — the same kind of notes he would take during his later visit to Boston's City Lodging for tramps on Hawkins Street. He also went to most of the Florentine schools, giving special attention to those run by charity.[23]

Arriving in Venice, Howells was stunned by the poverty, which, he realized, he had not begun to see when he lived there in 1861–65. He wrote to Mark Twain that Winny "takes the deadly romantic view of Venice, and doesn't hesitate to tell me that I did the place great injustice in my books . . . she thinks it is *all* beauty and gayety." His son John, on the other hand, "was dismayed by the misery and squalor everywhere," and he himself, sickened by the rags and dirt he witnessed in a morning walk, found Venice "forlorner and shabbier than ever." The shock of being in Venice again eighteen years after he spent his early twenties there, the continued socializing, and especially this startling look at poverty stopped Howells's head "like a watch that's been dropped," and he was totally unable to write.[24]

Venice was the city of Winny's birth, and Howells in his pain years later thought that "something of that unearthly loveliness might have entered into her life and estranged it at the beginning from the world in which we lived with her, apart from her." He later recalled that in 1883,

> . . . when the slow martyrdom of her malady had begun, but while we were still buoyantly incredulous of any end but happy youth and health, the air of Venice seemed to work a miracle for her, as if the mother city had taken pity on her child . . . at the first breath of the lagoons the tortured nerves began to calm themselves.

Kept close to St. Mark's Square and away from the misery, Winny, in contrast to her miserable experience elsewhere in Italy, was feeling better in Venice than she had felt anywhere else on the Continent. She was sleeping eleven hours a night and was very active: "The sea-air does her good, and the novel beauty fills her romantic soul."[25]

The upshot of this year for Howells was a certain disillusionment with Europe. His middle-aged responses were no longer the enchanted ones of twenty years before, and scenes like those in Venice contrasted sharply with his memory of the great potential and vitality of America. Although on leaving Italy he felt some nostalgia and could write glowingly of the Italians and almost wish to pass his days there, he wrote to Charles Dudley Warner in March that the idea of the Colosseum made him sick, that the dome of the State House was good enough for him, and that he wished he "could see it, this minute." He wrote to Thomas Sargeant Perry that he had been putting himself in rapport with Italy again: "But I'm not sure that it pays. After all, *we* have the country of the present and the future."

While he would not have forgotten the aspects of America that had troubled him in his review of Harrison and in *A Modern Instance*, *A Woman's Reason*, and "Police Report," it is likely that during his absence he had built up an ideal of America, one that might not long sustain itself against the reality he would find on his return. That Howells had confronted his readers' sentimental preconceptions of Venice with a realistic description of Venetian life, that he had confronted Kitty Ellison's ideal of Boston with Miles Arbuton, and the ideals of idyllic America and of married life with Equity, Maine, and the Hubbards, and that he had excused Dickens for his early remarks on America because he "came here in the glow of very lively sympathies with democracy in the ideal, and was shocked and outraged by the vulgarity, the vanity, the dulness, the timidity which belong to the American, as well as to all human experiments, whether in republicanism or monarchy"[26] — all proved him well versed in testing the ideal against the real.

Howells also was to return home with a writer's determination to prove himself, for he had been strongly and cruelly challenged on his critical pronouncements on the realistic novel and had even been asked why he did not write as well as Dickens and Thackeray. That he was feeling this is evident in a note of November 23, 1882, to his publisher and literary agent, James Ripley Osgood, telling him, on second thought, not to send "Niagara Revisited" to the *Atlantic*: "I don't care, just now, to challenge criticism by an inferior thing in a prominent place. *Please don't sell it to anybody.*" He intended to write an article on Dickens and Thackeray to clarify his critical stance, and he had refused the tempting offer of a professorship of literature at Johns Hopkins, thus keeping himself free for dedication to his fiction.[27] He was, if anything, more aware of human misery now and perhaps more concerned about his own relation to it, and Europe had increased his need for sources of vitality at age forty-six.

V

Beacon Steps, a small street on Beacon Hill where the Harknesses of *A Woman's Reason* (1883) had their home, was of "blameless social tradition," and when the house was auctioned off, the bidders were appealed to by an enumeration of its social advantages. Howells, who just before leaving for Europe had been living grandly enough at 16 Louisburg Square on Beacon Hill, returned to live at Number 4 for his first year home. One side of him clearly called for this kind of location, comfort, and standing. Another side, equally clearly, was demanding that he and his readers, his Helen Harknesses and David Sewells, become acquainted with other sides of Boston life.

With *The Minister's Charge* already in mind, he came down off Beacon Hill on the night of September 9, 1883, and with his cousin-in-law Edwin Mead, visited the Boston Young Men's Christian Union and the Boston Young Men's Christian Association, Sullivan's barroom, with its lewd painting and blackguardly crowd, and the police station up Elliott Street, where he inquired about the working of the station, the kinds of prisoners, and their accommodations. Six days later, at four o'clock in the morning, he went with Mead to see Irving Market, noting such items as the "poor fellow asleep in doorway on Cornhill," the drunk on South Street, the relatively busy market scene, the early-morning restaurant.

Although *The Minister's Charge* was germinating, he was still uncertain what kind of writing he should for the time devote himself to. Until sometime before the November election, he did "nothing but begin stories, and tear them up, after I had written fifty or sixty pages on each," although now, he said, he was onto something practical. Probably this "practical" work was practical for his reputation and for sales and was therefore *Indian Summer* and not *The Minister's Charge*. But Howells was clearly wondering what would happen to a country boy who came to Boston without Bartley Hubbard's newspaper training, Silas Lapham's money, or Helen Harkness's friends. "Think," said Mrs. Butler, "if you had really been some poor girl, with nothing, and had met with such a disappointment!"[28]

After the long depression of the 1870s and the violence of the "Great Strike" of 1877, the early 1880s had been prosperous and had seen an immense amount of railway building and financial speculation. Howells, who had invested, or was shortly to invest, in railway stock, had warned in his 1880 review of Harrison that the returning prosperity might be only a temporary alleviation of basic economic problems. The nation shared with him, despite the optimism of its speculators, a continuing uneasiness about its economic stability. The 1883 crops were poor, and rate wars took place in the East, West, and South. The Knights of Labor and the organization soon to be known as the American Federation of Labor were growing in membership and activity. Richard Watson Gilder, editor of the *Century*, wrote to Howells in August that he thought *A Woman's Reason*, then running in the *Century*, a seasonable treatment of a widely diffused trouble.[29] The July *Century* had carried an editorial advising laborers to cease striking for higher wages and to learn to spend their present incomes more wisely and tastefully. The August *Century* carried the first installment of John Hay's antilabor novel *The Bread-Winners*. These were uneasy times, and there was much discussion. The year 1884 would bring unnerving business failures. That of former President Grant in particular would register painfully for those concerned with upholding the best of the Republican tradition. Market crashes and bank closures and a general panic followed in rapid succession, and by the end of the year the country was in the midst of another depression.

By the beginning of 1884, Howells was ready to pick up his critical tools again and had written to Gilder about use of the *Century* as his forum. Gilder answered on January 3 that he would be willing to try the plan Howells had suggested (probably that Howells contribute to the "open letter" section). In a January 7 letter to John Hay, Howells approved of Hay's treatment of the working class, remarking that were he to defend the book he would insist on its courageous expression of "a fact not hitherto attempted: the fact that the workingmen *as* workingmen are no better or wiser than the rich *as* the rich, and are quite as likely to be false and foolish." It had not struck him, he said, as it had struck other critics, that Hay was assailing them as a class.

The defense Howells was contemplating appeared in the May *Century*. He listed questions that had been troubling the public and, to an extent, himself: What did Hay intend by making his rich and well-to-do people happy and his poor the opposite? Are his sympathies, then, with the rich against the poor? Does he think all workingmen vicious? Does he think it wrong for the starving laborer to strike? He thought it of first importance that the reader realize Hay "shows no strong antipathy to strikers till they begin to burn and rob and propose to kill," and he thought this an entirely proper attitude. Whether the qualifying and damaging adjective "strong" indicates an acquiescence in, or even approval of, a certain antipathy toward strikers or whether it simply indicates a tacit admission that Hay does have some such antipathy is indeterminable. Howells does assert that underpaid workers have a right to strike, an unpopular assertion at this time and one clearly divorced from Hay, although he does not so clearly present it as such.[30]

Announcing that "we are all workingmen in America, or the sons of workingmen, and few of us are willing to hear them traduced," Howells repeats what he had written to Hay: "But for our own part, they do not seem to us preeminent for wisdom or goodness, and we cannot perceive that they derive any virtue whatever from being workingmen." His attitude is meant to be realistic, yet it is also somewhat conservative, indeed antipathetic, and reveals a certain concern over the workingman's potential for disorder:

> Let us be just before we are generous, even to the workingman. Let us recognize his admirable qualities in full measure; but let us not make a fetich of him, impeccable, immaculate, infallible.... Workingmen are in no bad way among us. They have to practice self-denial and to work hard, but both of these things used to be thought good for human nature. When they will not work, they are as bad as club men and ladies of fashion, and perhaps more dangerous. It is quite time we were invited to consider some of them in fiction as we saw some of them in fact during the great railroad strike.

Although Howells pokes at the idle rich as maleficent factors, his mild complacence about laboring-class conditions and his call from Louisburg Square for self-denial echo the tone of the July editorial in the *Century* on "The Greatest Need of the Working Class." If his perceptions are changing, his responses are lagging a little behind.

Howells is here also serving notice to other novelists, to the public, and to himself. *The Bread-Winners* caused agitated discussion of Hay's intentions and attitudes, a sign that "the novelist is hereafter to be held to account as a public teacher" and "must expect to be taken seriously." Howells was impressed with Hay's courage to face unpleasant facts about American civilization: "If the result is not flattering, or even pleasing, that is not his fault, and neither his art nor his morality is to blame for it." He might be read here as addressing his own public, and Henry Mills Alden in particular, and wondering how far he himself would be allowed to go. Alden had expressed delight with *Indian Summer* in March and would take it for *Harper's Monthly* but was unenthusiastic about what he had seen and heard of *The Minister's Charge*, which he would not take. Howells may have had in mind letters from Osgood in 1882 and 1883 attempting to explain why *A Modern Instance* was not selling better: "It is almost universally acknowledged your *strongest* book, but is generally thought your least pleasant one. It is undeniable that the average novel-reader takes unkindly to it."

Howells's attestation as to Hay's courage, however, is also self-urging (or self-castigation) by a novelist who had recently been told by James that he did not "go far enough," a novelist who in December had published a popular farce, who was working on a comic opera and a comedy, and who in March had finished *Indian Summer*, which, for all its virtues as a novel, was not concerned with the American scene, was not the study of Florence he had at first intended, and was not *The Rise of Silas Lapham* or *The Minister's Charge*. Howells wrote in May 1884 that he considered life a very serious affair and that Lemuel Barker's story was likely to grow tragical. In April, he had written to E. W. Howe in praise of the remarkable realism, the sincerity, frankness, and courage, and the moving impression of simple, naked humanness in *The Story of a Country Town* (points he would repeat in an August "open letter" in the *Century*). In that month he had also written to Twain about "the shabby motives which I always find at the bottom of my soul if I examine."[31]

All of this suggests a Howells aware of his failure to make the best of his freedom from editorial work, feeling himself caught in a rut, wishing to take risks, to challenge his audience and himself, and to explore unsettling factors in American life. It is Howells at a potential turning point in his career as citizen and writer, knowing in mid-life that he can continue to do well by writing and behaving as before, but suspecting that to succumb to such a temptation is to fare less than well.

VI

In the spring of 1884, the Howellses were in search of a house and were thinking of Cambridge. Elinor Howells, according to Edwin Cady, was determined to exploit their Boston contacts and prestige for their children's benefit, and it was time to prepare for Winny's debut. Late June found Howells requesting from Twain a payment of $2,000 for his part of the *Library of Humor.* Twain replied that he was now "like everybody else — everything tied up in properties that cannot be sold except at fearful loss." On July 2, Howells wrote to explain:

> It is all right about that payment. I shouldn't have thought of turning to you if it hadn't been for the shameful behavior of C. B. & Q., which seized the moment of my buying a house to go down 13 points below where I bought; but I have got the money here, and you must simply forget that I asked you.[32]

The foreshadowing was perfect: The uncertain value of Howells's capital investments would be recorded not only in the stock market but also in his own outlook, and his commitment to high society would fall below the point at which he required a prestigious Beacon Street address.

The house at 302 Beacon, possibly similar to the one the newly married Athertons had bought in *A Modern Instance,* needed renovation, and the Howellses were not to move in until the fall. In early August, Howells left his family in Kennebunkport, Maine, and came to the house alone to put his books in order and to do some writing. On August 10 he wrote to Elinor about the immense labor of putting the books up and about the brief attack of diarrhea it had brought on. She was not to wonder that he had done little since he had been there, for "I've been sick nearly the whole time, and several days I only went out of the house to meals, having a bad 'pain across me' most of the time. O dear! If I could only get a little real rest." He wrote to Twain, also on August 10, that he had "a mighty pretty house." His reflections in a letter to his father, written on the same day, were more telling:

> And here I have been hard at work, and lonesome of course. There is not only nobody else in the house, but nobody else I know sleeps in

town. Altogether the effect is queer. There are miles of empty houses all round me. And how unequally things are divided in this world. While these beautiful, airy, wholesome houses are uninhabited, thousands upon thousands of poor creatures are stifling in wretched barracks in the city here, whole families in one room. I wonder that men are so patient with society as they are.

That insight may have contributed to the illness, because Howells was experiencing a general personal crisis. The writing he was now "hard at work" on was a story "in which the chief personage builds a house 'on the water side of Beacon,'" and he expected to use all his experience, "down to the quick." "Sometimes I feel it an extraordinary thing," he added in this letter to James, "that I should have been able to buy a house on Beacon str."

He soon returned to Maine and went from there to Campobello, New Brunswick, and was back at 302 Beacon, to be alone for ten more days, at the end of the month. There he was to have further unsettling experiences and at least one occasion to question his "shabby motives." He told Owen Wister of a "religious experience" he had undergone through two contrasting impulses. The first was, as owner of the Beacon Street house, to call in and thank the policeman who had chased people off his back fence, on which they had climbed to see the rowers racing on the bay. The second occurred after the policeman had left: "It came over me, what better right had I than they to sit comfortably in this room when they were out on the fence?" Wister protested that Howells had earned it by his gift and hard work: "He gave a baffled sigh. 'Yes, yes, but it oughtn't to be.'"[33] That he could describe this as a religious experience suggests how seriously he took it. It also suggests how a man without religion, one who recently had acknowledged his entrance into middle age and who kept himself working at a heavy pace, was casting about for a new lease on life and a new outlook.

It is possible that Howells's knowledge of the wretched barracks of the poor was by this time direct knowledge. The Fourth Annual Report of the Associated Charities, in November 1883, called for more male visitors to the poor, and expressed the hope that all would read *How to Help the Poor,* a little book just published by Howells's friend Annie (Mrs. James T.) Fields and intended to "awaken a wider interest in the hearts of well-to-do people — an interest strong enough to increase the number of visitors to the homes of the poor." Mrs. Fields believed that "only by creating a feeling of relationship and connection between different classes of society . . . can we ever bring about any great and permanent melioration of the condition of the poor." The Fifth Annual Report, in November 1884, listed Howells among its donors for the first time. Unfortunately, the reports ceased listing visitors after the Second Annual Report in 1881, and it is difficult to know whether Howells also began his visiting in 1884. With his usual integrity, Howells did not, as he was told he should not, develop any of his visits into literary material, and in his writing he seldom referred to his work for the Associated Charities.

In January 1884, he suggested through Norton that Harrison write up his experience as a humanitarian under the title "Giving: when it Helps and when it Hurts," which may indicate his having confronted the Associated Charities' oft enunciated admonition against giving alms to the poor when one should be helping them to help themselves. In "Tribulations of a Cheerful Giver" (1895), Howells wrote that in both New York and Boston he had lent himself, "sparingly and grudgingly, I'll own," to organized efforts to relieve the poor,[34] although the Boston reference may simply be to 1889 and 1890, when we know he did such work. With his own complex inclination to visit police courts and precincts, paupers' refuges, charity schools, bars, and slums, however, it is as likely as not that by August 1884 he had begun his charitable visits to the tenements. And he probably made them with the self-consciousness of a man who was purchasing a house for his daughter's debut.

Other events were conspiring in 1884 to trouble Howells. In early June, the Republicans nominated James Blaine over Chester A. Arthur, and Blaine was first suspected and then, to the satisfaction of many, proved to have been unprincipled in his public life. His record in Congress was marred by corrupt relations with railway corporations, and he could not explain a communication written to a man named Fisher with the postscript "Burn this letter." Because of such disclosures, the Mugwumps, including Twain, Perry, Higginson, Curtis, and other friends of Howells's, broke with the party and went over to Democratic candidate Grover Cleveland, where most of them would remain despite Cleveland's admission that he had fathered an illegitimate child by a widow who had been his mistress. They argued that for the national interest an honest political life was more essential than an irreproachable personal life.

Howells did not join the Mugwumps, and in late August, from his

Beacon Street windows, he could see the sun spread "a glory over the Back Bay that is not to be equalled by the blush of a Boston Independent for such of us Republicans as are going to vote for Blaine." He wrote to Twain that "what I want to do is to vote for Cleveland's *widow*. She's the one who ought to be elected": His vote would protest a double standard that condemned the woman and not the man. Being at best "but a very drab-colored sheep" in the eyes of his Mugwump friends, he received plenty of fire. Thomas Sergeant Perry asserted that to vote for Blaine "is equivalent not merely to pardoning but to rewarding the most serious crimes that can stain a public officer," adding that Blaine was attracting all the corruption in the country while men of honor, undesirous of office, were turning to Cleveland: "What stronger proof is there of the path of the just citizen?" That the charges against Blaine were proved, Twain wrote, "bars you & and all other honest & honorable men . . . from voting for him." But Howells could not vote for Cleveland with "that harlot and her bastard in the background."

He was troubled and not terribly happy about his decision. On first reading, he thought the telltale correspondence innocent, but he began to find Blaine, if not a rogue, a great ass and certainly a selfish politician. Two weeks before the election he was "much perplexed politically. When I read Blaine's letters, I see no wrong in them, though they are not very inspiring, but when I get them rearranged by the Independents, I am quite bewildered." But, he rationalized, Blaine had been outraged "by the publication of his private, business correspondence, and that makes me indignant."[35] And he went on to vote for Blaine.

Howells may have used Cleveland's indiscretions as a cover for another factor involved in his vote. He wrote Edmund Gosse in January 1884 that America had wrongly meddled in the just hanging of the Irishman Patrick O'Donnell for murder. It had meddled because the Democratic Congress was trying to capture Irish votes, "and by making a Republican president its instrument it could foist any disagreeable consequences upon *us*." In reply to a statement by Howells, Twain argued that allegiance to the country and party was very good, "but as certainly a man's *first* duty is to his own conscience & honor — the party & the country come second to that, & never first." Howells's vote, then, was at least partly determined by his strong identification with the party of Lincoln, the party that had represented the idealism of his father and his New England friends at the time of the Civil War, the party whose past three elected Presidents he had known personally, even intimately, and had much admired. Howells was not an uncritical supporter of the Republican Party — he felt the party had deserved its defeats in 1874, was critical of Hayes and Garfield when he felt they were lagging on civil service reform, and was ashamed at the thought of having Arthur as President — but he was a strong and loyal supporter. Continuity was important to him, and in his campaign biography of Hayes and in his obituary for Garfield he was eager to draw parallels between these later Presidents and Lincoln and Grant. If the Republicans now were established as the party of conservative business, it was not this that aligned Howells with the party. If he was troubled by the rising number of Irish in the Boston and national Democratic Party politics, this was not his principal reason for voting against that party.[36] His alignment and opposition lay mainly in his wish to believe that the old liberalism and idealism of the Republicans continued. His decision, however, left him ill at ease.

VII

The first two chapters of *The Rise of Silas Lapham* appeared in the November *Century*. Bartley Hubbard's interview of Colonel Lapham in his office, which opens the story, made it clear to the reader that Howells had a continuing interest in American business values. A reader who knew the author might have noticed a certain physical resemblance between him and his Colonel Lapham. In personal appearance, Lapham

> . . . is a fine type of the successful American. He has a square, bold chin, only partially concealed by the short reddish-grey beard, growing to the edges of his firmly closed lips. His nose is short and straight; his forehead good, but broad rather than high; his eyes blue, and with a light in them that is kindly or sharp according to his mood. He is of medium height, and fills an average arm-chair with a solid bulk, which on the day of our interview was unpretentiously clad in a business suit of blue serge. His head droops somewhat from a short neck, which does not trouble itself to rise far from a pair of massive shoulders.

Howells, according to an 1887 description by Harriet E. Monroe, "is about five feet four inches in height, quite stout, with a short neck, large head carried a little in front...pleasant blue eye, iron-gray hair and moustache, colorless Napoleonic face." Most of those who had never seen Howells, Franklin Smith remarked, "have an idea that he has the frame of a giant.... But Mr. Howells is no giant, although he is no pigmy. He is quite stout, and while he is less than five feet six in height, his accumulation of flesh gives him the appearance of being shorter than he really is."[37] The reader who knew Howells might also have noticed a certain congruity in other respects: Colonel Lapham, Hubbard told his Boston readers, is a liberal subscriber to the Associated Charities, is and always has been a staunch Republican, and "is building a house on the water side of Beacon Street." The second chapter reveals that Mrs. Lapham thought the house would serve to place their daughters in Boston society and that Colonel Lapham agreed; it would also serve as an agreeable symbol of business success. A policeman, probably continuous in Howells's mind with the one who had seemed to be ousting him from the crowded Boston police court in 1880, and probably continuous with the one he had thanked for removing people from his back fence, appears in the novel as well, at first taking Lapham for a tramp and intruder and threatening to evict him from his own house.

The novel was under way, was causing a great deal of talk and controversy, and promised to substantiate Howells's growing reputation as the first among American novelists. His prospects could not have been better. Yet sometime in late November or early December, he underwent another seemingly crucial "religious" crisis. According to an interviewer more than eleven years later, Howells was confronted at this time with grave questions, which would eventually lead to *A Traveler from Altruria*, and which refused to be curtly dismissed:

> They made their demand — these questions and problems — when Mr. Howells was writing *Silas Lapham*. His affairs prospering, his work marching as well as heart could wish, suddenly, and without apparent cause, the status seemed wholly wrong. His own expression, in speaking with me about that time, was "The bottom dropped out."

This crisis took place close to December 1, the date of Edmund Gosse's arrival in Boston to stay with the Howellses for twenty days while lecturing in the area. Gosse later wrote to Howells, "I constantly think of what you so affectionately confided to me at Concord, and without any curiosity of a vulgar kind, I am solicitous to know as much as you ever feel inclined to tell me of your troubles and anxieties." Howells in an evasive reply said, "Gosse, I suppose I shall never have as good a time again as I had with you. You just suited my complaint. These laughs at nothing, these senseless giggles, what intellectual pleasure ever equalled them?" An idea of some of the fun may be gathered from a poem the two possibly collaborated on at this time. "The Masque of Diseases," written in something approaching the measure of Milton's "L'Allegro," celebrates a dance led by Jocund Palsy and followed by Ague, Delirium, Malaria, Fever, Obesity, Rheumatism, and Bright's Disease.

Two passages in *The Rise of Silas Lapham*, both unusually bleak for Howells and both written after the crisis, suggest how low he must have felt in December. "Each one of us," he wrote, "must suffer long to himself before he can learn that he is but one in a great community of wretchedness which has been pitilessly repeating itself from the foundation of the world." And, "This thing that is embittered to us, so that we may be willing to relinquish it; the world, life itself, is embittered to most of us, so that we are glad to have done with them at last."[38]

By late November, several kinds of strain were adding up to a crisis. As before his illness in November 1881, he had been working at a devilish pace ("a frightful year of work"), and looking forward to a visit with his father in Virginia, he wrote to him on November 9, "I am feeling fagged with the last year's work, and shall be glad of a complete rest." At the same time he was planning a schedule for the coming year that he would later call "appalling."

He had reasons to so burden himself. The house, while perhaps a good investment, had cost a great deal of money, and interior carpentry and painting were still going on at the end of September. By December he may have had an intimation of the impending business failure of his agent, Osgood, and been uncertain as to how he himself would come out. He felt harassed by his father's farming troubles, and his mid-November visit must have brought prescience of new outlays for support of several family members. He wrote to James Parton in March 1885, "I must give my daughter her chance in this despicable world — where I'm so much better for having had none; I must get my boy through school and into college — where I'm so much wiser for not having been!... I wish," he added, "I could see you and talk with you sometimes."

Parton, a close and sensitive friend, read between the lines of Howells's list of recent publications and his laments over heavy work and saw related frustrations: Howells was upset over his compromises with the marketplace. Parton replied soothingly that pure literature had no chance to be self-sustaining until the long-sought international copyright was attained. Nor could he recall any author "who did no task or hack work, that could safely live in the style of a prosperous grocer, unless he had property or a pension." Financial concerns, then, were behind Howells's excessive industry, but he was also laboring so hard to keep his mind off other unpleasant aspects of his existence. By late November, this was not serving.[39]

He was doing fairly well — he knew how to bargain and later recalled that at this time "I used to make people pay shocking prices for my things" — but he was not sure he was going to have enough. The failure of three dramatic enterprises in the fall had depressed him somewhat, although he reassured his father on November 9 that he was still fairly prosperous and hoped to see his way through. Another enterprise, which he discussed in this letter, was turning out a failure. The house had been purchased to help Winny in society, and perhaps he could write Parton in late March about giving her a chance in the world, because that week she had given her first party. Until then, her health had been very bad. He wrote to his father two days after the letter to Parton, "She has been out very little, this winter; but now she seems better, and has more spirit if not strength."[40]

With these failures, and especially this tormenting one concerning Winny, with his sense of compromise, with the strain of family expenses, Howells, now forty-seven, trapped into unsatisfactory work at a very fast pace, and suddenly aware of the plight of the poor and underpaid in America, stopped in the winter of 1884–85 and asked himself what it all added up to, what his life was worth, and where, if anywhere, he was going.

His interest in a talk with James Parton, a rather Bohemian friend, may have been for more reasons than meet the eye. In his August "open letter" for the *Century*, Howells had been fascinated by Ed Howe's John Westlock, who made *The Story of a Country Town* a "strong, hard-headed, clear-conscienced story." Westlock, who had made his country-town newspaper prosperous through a life of merciless industry and perfect morality, finally breaks under the strain of monotony and solitude "and abandons his wife for a woman whom he does not love." His circumstances and years of proved integrity do not excuse him, and he must suffer for his promiscuity. He goes "to ruin and disgrace." He "returns the night following the death of his wife, and, after looking on her dead face with his pitying and forgiving son, goes out into the snow-storm from which he has come, and is heard of no more." Howells, middle-aged, seeking a new lease, and engaged in an inner dialogue over his options, must have feared what some of his imaginings, if carried out, might do to his mental and social stability and to his family. His safe side was gratified by the fact that Westlock was punished; it was also hoping to see Grover Cleveland, father of an illegitimate son, go down in defeat.

Cleveland's victory was unsettling, and Howells by late November may well have been troubled by his propensity to rationalize his vote for Blaine, a man he did not respect, while men he greatly admired, formerly active and staunch Republicans, such as Curtis and Twain, had left the party. Had he, in fact, failed in integrity? Had he failed, through unthinking party loyalty, to be the "just citizen" and "honest & honorable" man Perry and Twain had referred to in their letters? The electorate, at any rate, had supported their decision and had for the first time rejected the Republicans. This suggested that the traditional Republican ideals no longer held meaning for the people — or for the Republicans. Howells felt that a "great cycle" had come to a close and that "the rule of the best in politics for a quarter of [a] century is ended."[41] But he must have seen that this had something to do with the party itself. He certainly had not been inclined to draw parallels between Blaine, Lincoln, and Grant. Nor could he have failed to notice that neither major party had shown any cognizance of the thousands of poor creatures stifling in the Boston slums.

In a letter to "Dearest Gossy," written shortly after Gosse's departure, Howells wrote, "The children are busy trimming their Christmas tree, and all our hearts go out in self-satisfied compassion towards you poor things." Though penned in fun, the words carry just an echo of the letters written from the Beacon Street house the previous August and suggest that the crisis derived at least partially from the social tension that had been bulding within Howells. A statement by Gosse years later supports this possibility:

I was walking with him once in the dingier part of Boston, when he stopped and looked up at a very ordinary house. "How happy I should be," he said, "if I could see everything that is done and hear everything that is said in such a house as that for a week!" I made a rude suggestion about what might possibly be going on behind those dull windows. Howells did not laugh: but he put up his hand as if to ward off a blow. "Oh! don't say that!" he cried. "I couldn't bear it; I couldn't write a line if I thought such things were happening."[42]

Howells's wish to know the lives in this section of the city was consistent with his police court visits and his "religious experience" at 302 Beacon. He sensed his distance from these people in his culture and prosperity and held an uncomfortable desire to know what they thought of their situation and of him.

This was all assimilated into the great dinner chapter that the writing of *The Rise of Silas Lapham* had reached or just passed at the time "the bottom dropped out."[43] Bromfield Corey, adopting phrasing from Howells's August 10 letter to his father, suggests that Clara Kingsbury undertake a charity that would enable the poor to inhabit "the beautiful, airy, wholesome houses that stand empty all summer long."

> "Yes, that is terrible," replied Miss Kingsbury, with quick earnestness, while her eyes grew moist. "I have often thought of our great, cool houses standing useless here, and the thousands of poor creatures stifling in their holes and dens, and the little children dying for wholesome shelter. How cruelly selfish we are!"

"Cruelly selfish" is a strong indictment for a Howellsian character. Corey replies, seriously but a bit playfully, that he can hardly restrain himself from "offering personal violence to those long rows of close-shuttered, handsome, brutally insensible houses." David Sewell marvels, as Howells had in August, at the patience of the poor: "The spectacle of the hopeless comfort the hard-working poor man sees must be hard to bear." At this point Lapham wishes to speak up, but finds himself unable: "He wanted to tell them that generally a poor man was satisfied if he could make both ends meet; that he didn't envy any one his good luck, if he had earned it, so long as he wasn't running under himself." Corey goes

on to say that in America we invite the poor man to think about his deprivation, and Charles Bellingham contributes to his brother-in-law's observation that it is the newcomers, the foreigners, who stir up labor trouble:
"The Americans . . . seem to understand that so long as we give unlimited
opportunity, nobody has a right to complain."

The viewpoints here are predominantly conservative and rationalized, and not only on the part of the characters. Lapham's thought may
be Howells's idea of what the underprivileged do think, and it is a consol-
ing idea, although it does imply, at least, that such people should be saved
from running under. Howells has not come much farther than he had on
August 10, although his concern is evident. His ambivalence is suggested
by the conversation's lack of resolution, by the stress of conscience in
Clara Kingsbury and David Sewell, and by the unavoidable fact that
these people are discussing the problem from a very comfortable position.
It would be no whim that would lead him in his next novel to take one of
these guests to the Wayfarer's Lodge and make him question some of his
"shabby motives."

VIII

A biographical approach to *The Rise of Silas Lapham* is not the best
one: Disparities between Lapham and Howells are many. Yet such an approach, if accompanied by a clear sense of both its limitations and its possibilities, can be very suggestive. The central issue in the novel is whether
Lapham, a man of financial and social ambition, will have the integrity
to resist exclusive commitment to property and "culture" and save his
soul. His unsung generosity toward Jim Millon's widow and daughter, his
troubled memory of crooked dealings with Rogers, and other characteristics make plausible his final resistance to temptation. Reading bio-
graphically, one might construe Lapham's conflict to parallel a crisis of
conscience for Howells: Did he himself have enough concern for the victims of society, enough personal integrity, a strong enough belief in the
equality of all men, or had he in fact become too committed to the house
on Beacon Street and the financial and social status it represented? That
he could decide the question favorably for Lapham need not mean that
he had finally so decided it for himself.

Kermit Vanderbilt, in fact, argues convincingly that the crisis derives in good part from Howells's ambivalence about his relation to Boston and Cambridge society. He stresses Howells's willingness to moderate passages in his novel that might be offensive to Bostonian friends and thus troubling to himself. For one thing, he deleted from the *Century* version a supposedly humorous reference to the newly filled-in Back Bay as the "Diphtheria District," presumably out of a reluctance to affront people like his nearly next-door neighbor and friend Oliver Wendell Holmes. Then Bromfield Corey's wry question as to what restraint had prevented the poor from blowing up the spacious mansions with dynamite was removed from the magazine text. "It may be well enough to joke about taking possession of the houses of the rich, &c.," *Century* publisher Roswell Smith writes, "but blowing open the structures with a charge of Dynamite, suggests nihilism, destructiveness, revenge, etc. ... Think of the recent events in London & elsewhere abroad & in New York." Vanderbilt suggests that Howells's own aspirations and social biases would not, as he thought about it, allow him easily to contemplate "the leveling power of dynamite" — although, one might add, its initial use in the passage does imply some latent, or not so latent, hostilities.

Howells also deleted, after magazine publication, some comments by Tom Corey and the Laphams on the rising status of the Jew in fashionable areas of Boston and at the resorts, including a reference to the effect on property values once they got in. Jewish readers objected that Howells was in fact encouraging anti-Semitism. Howells replied to the editor of the *American Hebrew*:

> I supposed that I was writing in reprobation of the prejudice of which you justly complain, but my irony seems to have fallen short of the mark — so far short that you are not the first Hebrew to accuse me of "pandering" to the stupid and cruel feeling against your race and religion.... In that passage I merely recognized to rebuke it, the existence of a feeling which civilized men should be ashamed of. But perhaps it is better not to recognize all the facts.

However, Vanderbilt points out, why delete the passage rather than strengthen it and make the irony more obvious? Probably he was reluctant to challenge the strong anti-Semitism of such people as Norton, Lowell, and Henry Adams, and probably his own feelings on the subject — Vanderbilt gives examples — were less than clear to himself.

During the dinner scene, finally, Howells must have been reliving the trauma of Twain's "boorish" speech at a Whittier birthday dinner, and Lapham's performance here and his final retirement to the country were for the old order an "oblique but unmistakable victory." One Lapham daughter, however, significantly absent from the grotesqueries of the dinner scene, does marry the enterprising son of Bromfield Corey, which implies the possibility of a revitalized Boston — an idea, Vanderbilt suggests, that is at least part of the pleasure that Norton and Lowell found in the novel. All of this — the deletions, the Lapham dinner, and marriage — implies that in late November Howells was troubled by his willingness to soft-pedal some of his remarks and was suffering an insight, through Lapham's career, into his own relation to Boston society.[44]

Uncertain that his own behavior would parallel Lapham's, it is possible that by December he also knew that in another way, he would be unable to tell the truth he had admired Hay and Howe for telling so frankly. It may be that he had recognized that there were limitations to his realism, that he could not become the American Zola, that as Gosse suggested, he could not face the ugly and unpleasant. He had failed to tell the truth about the underside of Boston, the side he wished to know and had not learned how to know; the dinner discussion touched the problem, then passed it off. Again, as Kenneth Lynn has suggested, it is possible that by now he knew he would not tell the truth about the American businessman, that Lapham's assertion of integrity was merely an ideal and did not represent contemporary reality. Early in the novel he had told the truth about men like Lapham:

> "I tell you Rogers hain't got anything to complain of, and that's what I told you from the start. It's a thing that's done every day. I was loaded up with a partner that didn't know anything, and couldn't do anything, and I unloaded; that's all."
>
> "You unloaded just at the time when you knew that your paint was going to be worth about twice what it ever had been; and you wanted all the advantage for yourself."

He could also tell the truth about Rogers and the English agents at the end, but he could only idealize his American hero from the country. It is not easy to decide whether he did this because of his personal identification with Lapham or because he could not admit the truth about American business integrity under such temptations. That his decision was important to him is indicated by an exchange of letters with Roswell Smith, who on March 21 had just read the June installment, which ran through Chapter 21. Smith did not know what Howells meant to do with Lapham, but in the entire course of his own business career he had known but one man "who took to speculative gambling in business, and especially when he was in business trouble who did not at the same time begin to drink," and this included the "best and brightest and truest, most honest, upright, and conscientious Christian men." Should Howells go on to the logical conclusion, Lapham will drink and go to the devil, never giving up his newfound passion for business gambling and pursuing the "ignus fatuous hope of recovering property." It seemed to Smith that if Lapham should "retrieve his character the story will fail in the truth of daily experience and that the opportunity for a splendid lesson will be lost if the story ends too precipitately." So far, Smith said, the story was full of moral lessons and had not a false note.

Howells immediately replied in defense of what he had already decided to do. We do not have his letter, but we have Smith's reply:

> Yes, there is a divine power which can reach down to us and which we can grasp, that can lift us out of ourselves. Here and there there is a man like Mr. Gough who escapes when the disease of drink has fast hold of him. I did not suppose that you proposed to teach that. I rejoice that you do. But this passion for gambling when it once takes hold of a man is more insidious than the passion for drink. . . . Lest the way of escape should be deemed too easy, I suppose you will take care to make the reader and Lapham realize that in his escape he is one of a thousand — and well nigh a miracle.[45]

Recognizing that he had represented something approaching a miracle, coupled with uncertainty as to whether anything short of a miracle could save him from the conservative mold into which he was sinking, may very well have contributed to Howells's disturbance in late 1884.

The strain of overwork, then, the drive to make money, the sense of compromise in his work, his daughter's ill health, his need to break free, Cleveland's election, and the vast gulf between Beacon Street and the Boston slums combined to put Howells into a severe state of depression. Such a state may merely crystallize for the moment certain painful elements of one's existence. It does not necessarily bring about profound change, or any change at all. Like most people, Howells was to weather his storm and go on much as before. The difference, an important one, was that he had a deepened perspective on himelf and his environment and was, accordingly, more likely to move in some directions than in others.

IX

In March 1885, Howells thought of taking the Old Manse for the summer, a house closely associated with the life, literature, and values of a certain segment of New Englanders in the pre-Civil War era. Whether this represented a reaction against the Republicans' defeat or against his growing doubts about America's economic structure and his place in it, or whether it was innocent of such conscious or subconscious motivations, the move did not go beyond the planning stage. The family spent part of the summer in western Massachusetts and part in the New Hampshire mountains. Winny's sickness continued to be a "great trial and a perpetual expense," and on their return to Boston, with the winter social season approaching, the Howellses realized that she had not profited by the vacation and was badly weakened. In late October, Howells wrote from the Woodland Park Hotel in Auburndale to Gosse that he had "let the pretty house on Beacon Street because poor Winny is too poorly to do any society in it, and without that her mother and I have no heart for it." He had burned Silas Lapham's house and all it symbolized, and perhaps, in addition to the reason given Gosse, something of the same impulse dictated his leaving 302 Beacon Street now. Assured by Dr. Putnam that there was no crisis in Winny's case, the Howellses were hoping the country freedom and quiet of Auburndale would do her some good, and in fact, by late December it looked as though she was improving.[46]

Winny was costing money, Howells's father and impecunious brother Sam were becoming expensive, and his own style of life was far from cheap. Partly to keep up with the financial strain, on October 6 he came to an agreement with Harper and Brothers, which he described as "incredibly advantageous to me." In what Edwin Cady has called a remarkable "literary bonanza" for the time, he was to receive $10,000 a year for serial publication of one novel and for three to five pages a month for the "Editor's Study" of *Harper's Monthly.* In addition, there was to be a 12½ percent royalty on the book publication and additional income for work done beyond that contracted for. To the casual observer, Howells was clearly an appropriate custodian of such money. A friend who visited him at 302 Beacon in early October described him in much the same words as other observers, noting his "enviable position in the literary and social circles of Boston" and concluding that someone "seeing him without knowing who he was would readily mistake him for a successful young banker" — an image that must have given Howells, if he saw the sketch, something of a jolt.

On October 20, the "young banker" wrote to S. Weir Mitchell, praising him for his perfect divination of Wendell's character in *In War Time*: "I felt all the time you might have studied him from me; for I am a coward, and all kinds of a tacit liar — not because I don't love the truth, heaven knows, but because I'm afraid to tell it very often."[47] He might at this point have been contemplating his own cowardice with additional seriousness, for the "Editor's Study" was to be a monthly column of literary opinion and theory, and he wanted his own fiction firmly to exemplify his assertions there as to methods and ethics in fiction. The letter to Mitchell intimates that with this pressure, he was again urging himself, as he had done in the *Century* for May and August 1884, to tell the truth frankly and boldly.

The Rise of Silas Lapham, leaving aside the ultimate idealization of its hero, was replete with arguments, both tacit and outspoken, for realism in fiction, and both its great success and the attacks that were mounted against it were stimulating to Howells. On April 28, 1885, reading with other authors at a gathering on behalf of the American Copyright League, he chose a chapter from the soon-to-appear *Indian Summer*. At a second reading the following day, he announced that he would read a selection from an uncompleted novel, *The Minister's Charge.* Howells had contemplated this novel perhaps as long ago as his first visit to the police court in the summer of 1880, and certainly by the time of his excursions with Edwin Mead in September 1883 — an account of which had found its way into the early pages of the novel. Chapters of it had been written probably as early as November 1883, and definitely by May 1884. That month, he had written to Osgood concerning his commitment to the book as he had conceived it, concluding, in defiance of Henry Mills Alden's desire for changes in its characterization and scheme, that "I

believe in this story and am not afraid of its effect before the public."
Now, free of *The Rise of Silas Lapham* and the Italian articles *(Tuscan Cities)*, which he had completed for the *Century* immediately after *Silas Lapham*, he was able to give himself entirely to its composition.

On June 6 he reported to Mark Twain that he was "far away from S. Lapham now, sailing on with the country boy I read a little about in N.Y., that day." Perhaps in his conception of *The Minister's Charge* and in some memories of *Silas Lapham*, he felt a temptation to italicize "far away." On July 1, accompanied by a "Doctor S.," Howells, on behalf of his novel, supplemented his 1883 visit to the police station with a visit to the station on Joy Street, and on the next day he visited the Hawkins Street City Lodging for tramps. In August, he expressed an enthusiasm for Daniel Defoe's *Roxana* that may have derived from its similarity in some aspects to the book he was working on: "Did you ever read Defoe's Roxana? If not, then read it, not merely for some of the deepest insights into the lying, suffering, sinning, well-meaning human soul, but the best and most natural English that a book was ever written in."[48]

X

"Let fiction cease to lie about life," Howells wrote in the "Editor's Study" in May 1887,

> let it portray men and women as they are, actuated by the motives and the passions in the measure we all know; let it leave off painting dolls and working them by spring and wires; let it show the different interests in their true proportions... let it not put on fine literary airs; let it speak the dialect, the language, that most Americans know — the language of unaffected people everywhere — and we believe that even its masterpieces will find a response in all readers.[49]

With Howells about to begin the "Editor's Study," it will be worth our while to pause a moment and supplement our Chapter 1 discussion with a more detailed statement of his notions of realism.

Looking back from 1897, he could see that his career had shown an increasing preference for the real as opposed to the factitious in fiction.[50]

His own criticism and fiction recorded this and were testimony to his modernity, for fiction was an evolving art, developing from its primitive stages in the eighteenth century to a highly refined form in the late nineteenth century. His best-known statement of this belief occurs in his provocative 1882 article on James:

> The art of fiction has, in fact, become a finer art in our day than it was with Dickens and Thackeray. We could not suffer the confidential attitude of the latter now, nor the mannerism of the former, any more than we could endure the prolixity of Richardson or the coarseness of Fielding. These great men are of the past — they and their methods and interests; even Trollope and Reade are not of the present. The new school derives from Hawthorne and George Eliot rather than any others; but it studies human nature much more in its wonted aspects, and finds its ethical and dramatic examples in the operation of lighter but not really less vital motives.

Not alone in its evolution, fiction shared the objective, realistic, scientific impulse with most other disciplines, whose serious purpose was "to make the race better and kinder."[51]

It was essential in this modern art to implicate the reader. Pérez Galdós's *Doña Perfecta* provided a substantial example:

> It is so far like life that it is full of significations which pass beyond the persons and actions involved, and envelop the reader, as if he too were a character of the book, or rather as if its persons were men and women of this thinking, feeling, and breathing world, and he must recognize their experiences as veritable facts. From the first moment to the last it is like some passage of actual events in which you cannot withhold your compassion, your abhorrence, your admiration, any more than if they took place within your personal knowledge.[52]

Galdós had reproduced life so closely that the reader of *Doña Perfecta* loses all consciousness of the medium.

To engage the reader so completely, the novelist must set a high premium on accuracy of observation. The great lesson, in fact, was that "you must not aim in art to be less than perfectly faithful; and you must not lie about the fact any more than you can help. Go to life; see what it is like, and then tell it as honestly as possible." Honest, accurate depiction, if inevitably qualified by the impressions of an individual mind, is to be gained by avoiding social, political, religious, and literary preconceptions. The novelist must avoid the romancer's realm of the merely possible; he must confine his vision to the natural and probable, to his own time and place, to life as it is lived by the majority of people. In all of this the universal must be revealed, for "one of the conditions of every art is that its created world must be a microcosm." Although opponents argued that the normal and average lacked interest, Howells replied again and again that they have an essential interest, being what most human beings constantly experience, and that attention to and understanding of them could make a substantial difference for one's life.[53]

The narrative form closest to life is the dramatic form. Authorial intrusion, sometimes insulting to the intelligence of the reader, always reduces the immediacy of the situation, and the modern novelist is both absent from the novel and impartial toward his characters. His endeavor is to "get the persons living before you," and his method is "to paint such facts of character and custom as he finds so strongly that their relative value in his picture will be at once apparent...without a word of comment." Such impartiality is not incompatible with "deep moral earnestness." Turgenev, for example, "is profoundly serious in behalf of what is just and good, even when he appears most impassive in respect to his characters; one feels the presence, not only of a great genius, but a clear conscience in his work."[54]

Plot — subordinate to character as in all realist theory — should have a clear beginning, middle, and end. It should have a standard of aesthetic formality whereby its time, space, and human relationships have a fundamental coherence. But it is also to reflect, as far as possible, life's formlessness and diverse natural sequences. It should be organic — not epic, dramatic, incessantly tragic, or thesis-ridden. It should, in other words, be like life.

Characters must not be caricatured or grotesqued or, with a few exceptions, one- or two-dimensional types. The realist must both maintain truth to human nature and enter as subtly as possible into the minute manners, motivations, and origins of a character. This process takes rare ability, for nothing is easier than to strike a false note and jar the reader's sense of actuality and thus his close connection with the work. By the same token, prose style and dialogue must avoid literosity and affectation. They must establish a plainness and directness, which is compatible with both refinement and complexity of character. The realist knows "we all have twenty different characters . . . and we put them on and take them off . . . for different occasions," knows "evil is a tendency and good is a tendency, but in each there are eddies and countercurrents," and knows that character evolves under the influence of conditions and relationships.[55]

Depending on the subject, portrayal of this real, evolving, average, complex human life may create critical comprehension of the reader's own social, political, and economic environment. It always creates, as the reader loses his awareness of the medium and becomes involved, a valuable kind of understanding: "In a little space these people's characters are shown in all their individual quaintness, their narrow life is hinted in its gloom and loneliness, and the reader is made to feel at once respect and compassion for them." The reader's reaction echoes the author's feeling toward his characters, for "it appears that we cannot learn to know others well without learning to pity and account for the defects in them which we must not excuse in ourselves."[56] With all his exactitude and justice, the realist also has understanding and mercy and refuses to condemn unqualifiedly, for in life one often is at a loss whom to blame and whom to praise, passions flame up and then die out, and all persons have strengths and all persons are inadequate. In realistic fiction, author, characters, and reader, bound by their common susceptibility to weakness, are humanized.

This goal, we have seen, developed early in Howells's career, and in 1879 he could write to Thomas Wentworth Higginson that "I should be ashamed and sorry if my work did not unmistakably teach a lenient, generous, and liberal life." His most pervasive method was a close rendering of the foibles and shortcomings of his characters. His awareness of how moods and circumstances cut us off from one another is omnipresent. One of the greatest virtues of *A Modern Instance*, for example, is its skillful portrayal of the gradual decline of the Hubbards' marriage through a number of small incidents, through little egotisms, misunderstandings, arguments and reconciliations, through the more and less serious weaknesses in two often well-intentioned human beings. Bartley races home with his money order for the lumbering-camp article, envisioning the ecstatic scene he will share with Marcia. He arrives, learns her father has been there, and lets fly a few brutal words. Marcia locks him out, and he wanders about until nightfall.

He went out shocked and frightened at what he had done, and ready for any reparation. But this mood wore away, and he came back sullenly determined to let her make the advances toward reconciliation, if there was to be one. Her love had already made his peace, and she met him in the dimly lighted little hall with a kiss of silent penitence and forgiveness... he took out the precious order and showed it to her. But its magic was gone; it was only an order for twenty-five dollars, now; and two hours ago it had been success, rapture, a common hope and a common joy. They scarcely spoke of it, but talked soberly of indifferent things.[57]

The result of Howells's realistic method, colored by the sympathetic understanding of his narrative voice, is a more penetrating insight into the barriers between us and thus a chance for us to become better.

XI

In discussions of *The Minister's Charge*, the tendency is to settle upon the career of Lemuel Barker, another Howellsian natural gentleman from the country who comes up to the city to confront the effete aristocrats. There is that side to the novel, but in stressing Lemuel Barker's parallel with Kitty Ellison and Silas Lapham, one tends to neglect the minister, who, after all, has a share of the title role. The first half of the book especially, while a study of Lemuel Barker's adventures in Boston, is also a study of David Sewell's attempts to cope with Lemuel Barker.

Sewell is basically a kindly man who has the best of intentions. It is his concern over the poverty-stricken farm that first brings him into Barker's sphere, and it is his mistaken kindliness in praising Barker's poetry that brings Barker to the city. Accompanying his goodness, however, are a number of weaknesses, habits, and circumstances that raise barriers between him and his charge. When Barker's letter arrives with its bad poetry and request for help in finding a publisher, Sewell realizes that a negative answer must be written "with the greatest sympathy." But the task being difficult and his diversions many, he manages to put it off until it is too late. He is then shocked to find Barker on his doorstep: "'Oh yes! How do you do?' he said; and then planting himself adventurously upon the commandment to love one's neighbour as one's self, he added: 'I'm very glad to see you!'"

Throughout the novel, the mingled attraction and repulsion Sewell feels toward Barker, as well as his failure to respond authentically and completely to him, are sympathetically studied. His relatively cloistered life unavoidably restricts his response. More avoidably he falls into preacher's rhetoric or into the language of his own background: When he shows his pictures to Barker, certain habitual phrases relating to them slip from his tongue, and he makes "no effort to adapt them to Barker's comprehension, because he could not see that the idea would be of any use to him." Or he is busy with a sermon at the moment Barker arrives with his troubled soul:

> ... and then Sewell said, with a cordiality which he did not keep from reluctance, "Oh — Mr. Barker! Come in! Come in . . . I'm here quite alone in the house, scrambling a sermon together. But I'm *so* glad to see you! You're well, I hope? You're looking a little thin, but that's no harm. . . ." He smiled more beamingly upon Lemuel, who felt that he wished him to go, and stood haplessly trying to get away.

Sometimes Sewell is so pleased with the way he says things that he makes mental notes of them for future use in sermons — a sign of his distance from Barker's immediate problems.[58]

The pattern repeats itself. The novel gradually, although not obviously and never entirely, shifts its focus from this inadequacy in Sewell to the growing social status and corresponding inadequacy of Barker. By the time he takes his position at Mrs. Harmon's, Barker has begun to see differences:

> His inner life became a turmoil of suspicions, that attached themselves to every word spoken to him by those who must think themselves above him. He could see how far behind in everything Willoughby Pastures was. . . . He esteemed the boarders at the St. Albans in the degree that he thought them enlightened enough to contemn him for his station.

His attitude toward Statira Dudley, the girl he had early "engaged" himself to, gradually becomes disdainful. This feeling becomes aggravated when he attains a position in the Corey household, where the "poison" works even more deeply. While, like Sewell, he maintains an underlying goodness, he finds it convenient to rationalize away Statira's just demands on him, just as Sewell does toward him.[59]

Economic factors play a larger part in this novel than in Howells's previous works. The American values challenged by men like Arbuton and Bromfield Corey were democratic values; their education made them aristocrats and made them sometimes scorn men who lacked their ties and sophistication. Sewell, much like Howells, desires to bridge the gap between himself and those of less advantageous background. The difficulties in so doing, if still expressed in terms of class and education, are more clearly based on differences of economic position. These difficulties can be traced in Barker's rise: His growing disdain for his own background, for his menial occupations, and for others like him corresponds to his growing awareness of economic categories. His early ignorance of city prejudices and sophistications prevents him from seeing anything inferior about the honest work of caring for Miss Vane's furnace, and Miss Vane's treatment of him at first sustains this deception, for she treats him "not like a servant, but like a young person" and shows respect for his independence and pride. But when Lemuel rejects Sibyl Vane's condescension and is scornfully told to befriend the cook, and when Miss Vane echoes her niece, ceasing "to be the kindly, generous soul she was, in asserting herself as a gentlewoman who had a contumacious servant to treat with," he becomes more conscious of differences. Later he asserts his pride by refusing to accept tips while suspecting that Miss Carver and Mr. Evans despise him for having waited table, as Mr. Evans, indeed, admits he did. "Why," asks Mr. Evans, "have all manner of domestics fallen under our scorn, and come to be stigmatised in a lump as servants?"

That some of the more painful barriers between men are derived from such differences is an indictment of American society, and it is the owner of 302 Beacon Street, the summer vacationer in the Massachusetts hills and New Hampshire mountains, the resident in the Woodland Park Hotel in Auburndale who laments with Sewell:

> "If I could only have got near the poor boy," said Sewell to his wife, as they returned withindoors. "If I could only have reached him where he lives, as our slang says! But do what I would, I couldn't find any common ground where we could stand together. We were as unlike as if we were of two different species. I saw that everything I said bewildered him more and more; he couldn't understand me!

Our education is unchristian, our civilization is pagan. They both ought to bring us in closer relations with our fellow-creatures, and they both only put us more widely apart! Every one of us dwells in an impenetrable solitude! We understand each other a little if our circumstances are similar, but if they are different all our words leave us dumb and unintelligible.[60]

That this passage concludes a chapter and that for once Mrs. Sewell does not contradict or undercut her husband give Sewell's lament a certain finality in the novel.

Howells, however, is not primarily trying to create social indignation, nor is he advocating specific political or economic measures. This is made clear at the end of *The Minister's Charge*, when Sewell preaches his culminating sermon on "Complicity," with its message of "the old Christ-humanity," a sermon of considerable challenge and appeal. No one, Sewell said, stood apart from his fellows, "but each was bound to the highest and the lowest by ties that centred in the hand of God."

If a community was corrupt, if an age was immoral, it was not because of the vicious, but the virtuous who fancied themselves indifferent spectators ... only those who had had the care of others laid upon them, lived usefully, fruitfully. Let no one shrink from such a burden or seek to rid himself of it.... The wretched, the foolish, the ignorant whom we found at every turn were something more; they were the messengers of God, sent to tell his secret to any that would hear it. Happy he in whose ears their cry for help was a perpetual voice, for that man, whatever his creed, knew God and could never forget him. In his responsibility for his weaker brethren he was Godlike, for God was but the impersonation of loving responsibility, of infinite and never-ceasing care for us all.

This sermon had the success Howells might wish for his novel; it was reprinted in pamphlet form, and it made Sewell "the topic of editorials in the Sunday editions of leading newspapers as far off as Chicago." A large class of underpaid and worthy workers had recently failed to win their right to a living wage against a powerful monopoly and had gained much popular sympathy, and many readers thought the sermon an indirect reference to their strike. Although Sewell-Howells might be pleased to have his work stimulate improvement in larger economic relations, Sewell's listeners who were aware of his "habit of seeking to produce a personal rather than a general effect, of his belief that you can have a righteous public only by the slow process of having righteous men and women, knew that he meant something much nearer home to each of his hearers."[61]

From the time Howells had prepared to pick up the book again he had his audience very much in mind. In February 1885, he had written to Holmes in praise of his latest *Portfolio* that the simple and homely things expressed in one passage would "let the poor average human soul come very near you and add to your lovers everywhere." He had also been intensely interested, he said, in Holmes's "thought about becoming part of the people that one ponders and writes about." In June he told an interviewer that he had "never written a book yet simply for the sake of writing something for somebody to read, but always with the purpose of giving his readers something to think about, that should be useful and profitable to them and to the world as well." Later, in his disappointment over genteel complaints about the low company in his novel, he remarked that his critics had entirely missed "the very simple purpose of the book."[62]

His simple purpose was to humanize the reader, and enunciation of it can be found in Howells's first columns for the "Editor's Study," written while he was hard at work on the novel. There he wrote that *In War Time* could hardly fail to stir the reader "with the wish to be a little truer," a statement echoed in Jesse Carver's attempt to express the character of David Sewell's sermons: "There's something about him — I don't know what — that doesn't leave you feeling how bad you are, but makes you want to be better.... And he shows that he's had all the mean and silly thoughts that you have."

Howells was also impressed with the anonymous *Autobiography of Mark Rutherford* for fixing the readers' minds "all the more intensely upon themselves." The author made no excuse for treating the psychological experience of a waiter, salesman, and porter, and he deals with the inner life of his characters, "that experience so sweet, so bitter, so precious, of almost any human soul, which we should always be better and wiser for knowing, but which we so often turn from in the stupid arrogance of our cultures and respectabilities." Rutherford, much like Sewell, was a man of "tremendous nerves, irresolute performance, vague aspiration, depression, frequent helplessness, faltering faith," who, nevertheless, found happiness in doing good to others as taught by Christ.[63] The focus is not primarily on his weaknesses and compromises but on his efforts to be true to the good that is in him, which, ultimately, is where the focus of *The Minister's Charge* lies.

Howells, then, in intention and in practice is the humanist described in Chapter 1, trying to engender self-knowledge in his readers and thereby increase understanding and sympathy between men in their everyday lives. We recognize ourselves in Sewell and in the ambitious Lemuel Barker and, ideally, are stirred with the wish to be a little better. Howells, speaking through Sewell's sermon, is also trying to touch those who merely *talk* a great deal of social concern and those "virtuous who fancied themselves indifferent spectators." He is trying to engage and sensitize them, then urge them to cross the divide between literary and actual experience. He is calling for *realization* of the reality experienced in the novel. He is attempting to engender in others, and in himself, an *active* response to the pain and evil in the world.

XII

Can a novelist in fact humanize a reader? The process, we have seen, depends on involvement of the reader in the lives of the characters, and it is worth asking a few of the thornier questions about this possibility. How many readers can respond to humane values in realistic fiction? How many allow themselves to become *personally* involved? How many do more than read the "stories" and enjoy the "style"? Who reads novels in the first place? How many bring to fiction insensitivity, inability to get out of themselves, the wrong kinds of expectations, desires, and need for thrills? Again, what really *is* the best way of implicating people in fiction? Reviews of Howells's books indicate that on the whole, critics were not intuiting his purpose: Why did a few of them respond and so many fail to do so? To carry the question further, just how implicated *can* we get in fictional lives? And what difference does any degree of implication make for the way we behave? Joan Bennett suggests both problems:

> When we read of the sufferings of fictitious ... characters, we can indulge in the natural human tendency to sympathize without any possibility of being required to act. In so far as an unimaginative

hardness of heart is normal, it is probably the result of unconscious self-protection against such a demand, and the satisfaction following upon reading a fiction ... suggests that, when there is no need to be on the defensive, we enjoy being made to understand our fellow-sufferers. The ultimate value of such aesthetic experience will depend upon how far the pleasurable exercise — playing at sympathy — can affect our workaday world.[64]

It is this core of self that is under attack by the humanist novelists, in their attempt both to create sympathy through involvement and to eliminate the defenses against action once the reader returns to actuality.

Some distance is inevitable, because we are always somewhat aware that we are not undergoing the experience ourselves. Beyond this, depth of involvement obviously depends greatly on the reader's susceptibility, and whether any degree of involvement will affect his behavior depends on his ability to integrate the fictional and actual worlds. How much fiction can create or stimulate such ability is a question central to the Howells theory. Can fiction, as he may have wished, directly teach us humane behavior, or is fiction in itself in no degree sufficient to bring about real change; are external shaping forces a must? For our souls to be bent and tempered, perhaps, it is necessary that we have living contact with the joys, struggles, and sorrows of others close to us:

> It is our habit to say that while the lower nature can never understand the higher, the higher nature commands a complete view of the lower. But I think the higher nature has to learn this comprehension, as we learn the art of vision, by a good deal of experience, often with bruises and gashes incurred in taking things up by the wrong end, and fancying our space wider than it is.[65]

The "higher nature" may indeed be necessary; it is certainly true that not all individuals gain a humanized outlook from close involvement in the joys and sorrows of particular relatives or friends.

If direct experience is necessary, and if fiction cannot provide that, then fiction can at best be a preparation for humanized behavior; while making no immediate difference in our lives, it may make a difference in our sensitivity to life. Through what we have been told, have seen, and to some extent have shared in the fictional world, we gain a new or enhanced sensitivity to others. This gives us at least some conception of possibilities, potent for actual human relations that parallel those in the fictional world. If we cannot undergo the actual experience of a dull, narrow life operating in a character's mind, still, when such a life confronts us, we may have learned to empathize, to treat that person with patience, charity, and even creativity. Howells possibly had this delayed effect in mind when he wrote that the best of realistic fiction would shame readers into at least wishing to be more helpful and wholesome and would stir them with the desire to be a little truer.[66]

Clearly, then, the fiction most fully involving readers of different backgrounds and susceptibilities is the most effective. If the reading experience comes home forcefully enough to become internalized, it has a chance of humanizing us in our own specific human relationships.

XIII

Howells attempted to engender in others and in himself an active response to the pain and evil in the world, and *The Minister's Charge*, of course, is itself such a response. Howells had worried in October 1885 about not telling the truth frequently enough. A year later he was attributing the critical animosity toward *The Minister's Charge* to his frankness about American civilization. Henry James had expressed his admiration for this frankness, and John William De Forest, while misinterpreting Howells's intention, praised his "honesty & courage" in building so much of a novel around low and commonplace people. That Howells *was* exercising courage, *was* striking out in a book that may seem to us comparatively mild, is suggested by the reviews he mentions, by Alden's reluctance to take the book, and by the frequent defensive protestations Howells felt he had to make in order to keep the idealist critics and romance readers at bay: An important segment of the reading public was fiercely opposed to this kind of work.

Howells had been candid about aspects of American civilization in *A Modern Instance*, *A Woman's Reason*, and *The Rise of Silas Lapham*, but never had he attacked the whole underlying structure of American society. He had finally confronted his readers with the underside of Boston, from which the cultured and rich found it so easy to turn away. And he had finally portrayed a newcomer to Boston who lacked most of the resources of Bartley Hubbard, Helen Harkness, and Silas Lapham. Lemuel Barker has his money stolen and spends his first night on a bench in the Common; worn out with famine the next morning, he nearly drops in a doorway to rest, but he finds "on an upper step a man folded forward like a limp bundle, snoring in a fetid, sodden sleep, and, shocked into new strength, he hurried on." He spends that night in jail, the next morning in police court, and a third night in the Wayfarer's Lodge for down-and-outs. It could have been worse; but as it was, the genteel critics did not like it.[67]

We can learn more from *The Minister's Charge* about Howells's uncertain stance at this time. He wrote for the February 1886 "Editor's Study" that "under our system the strong, rude native life will always be working to the top, especially in politics," but also now and then in society. At the same time, he could value the treatment of "plain, poverty-bound lives" in *The Autobiography of Mark Rutherford*. His experience, his hope and optimism, his need for respite from the unpleasant dictated that his own portrait would be on the positive side. He repeatedly shows Lemuel in his pride resisting any temptation to succumb to his circumstances. In his cell, for instance, Lemuel "was trembling with famine and weakness, but he could not lie down; it would be like accepting his fate, and every fibre of his body joined his soul in rebellion against that." At the same time, Howells is realistic enough to point out that not all of America is composed of this "strong, rude native life" and that not all country boys would be able to escape poverty and trampdom in coming to the city. Sewell at the Wayfarer's Lodge forebodingly imagines Barker as "entered upon the dire life of idleness and dependence, partial or entire, which he had known so many Americans even willing to lead since the first great hard times began."[68]

There is some ambivalence in Howells's treatment of these tramps and others like them, however. Abstractly he can take a significant look ahead: While some may say that the Lodge "is aiding and abetting the tramp-nuisance by giving vagrants food and shelter ... other philosophers will contend that it is — blindly perhaps — fulfilling the destiny of the future State, which will at once employ and support all its citizens." Yet, Sewell, who may or may not reflect Howells's thoughts here, is made to wonder if the Wayfarer's Lodge, with its coziness and cleanliness, does not really corrupt the poor, and Howells himself, as narrator, remarks that "the poor who housed themselves that night, and many well-to-do sojourners in hotels, had reason to envy the vagrants their free lodging." Howells's attitude toward the Irishwoman in the jail, for example, and more especially toward the hardened tramps, now and then tends to the satirical, the slightly scornful, the uncompassionate. Perhaps the critics who found him elitist and scornful in his treatment of the Hubbards and Laphams perceived, with all their lack of insight and with all Howells's efforts and intentions to the contrary, a subtle tendency in his makeup.[69]

It is true, at any rate, that Howells remained aware of his unfamiliarity and inadequacy with the new conditions he was describing. Howells had visited the Joy Street police station with a "Doctor S." In *The Minister's Charge*, two visitors are shown through the jail while Lemuel is being installed there, one of them a doctor, and Howells's treatment of them is not entirely flattering. One of the gentlemen speaks with "the bland respectfulness of people being shown about an institution"; both laugh at details that make Lemuel shudder; they make a "murmur of approbation" when the officer tells them that "we do the best we can for 'em"; and one of them says, "with both pity and amusement in his voice," that Lemuel does not look like a very abandoned ruffian. Howells also juxtaposes Barker carrying the empty broth bowls at the Wayfarer's Lodge with Sewell waking up for his leisurely quarter-to-eight breakfast and reading aloud the offensive police report. He also brings Sewell to the lodge, where he promises to buy firewood to "help the poor fellows to earn an honest bed and breakfast" but wonders if the vagrants should be treated so well.[70] As before, Howells here distances himself and the reader somewhat through the use of the two visitors, and he softens the effect of the Wayfarer's Lodge by introducing Lemuel to it through the droll commentary of one of the young tramps. This is very likely sugar-coating of what his readers would find distasteful, but it is also a result of Howells's own dislike of the sordid and of his sense of his distance from it.

It is also revealing that Howells sends Lemuel Barker back to the farm, as he had done with Silas Lapham, after allowing him to rise to a certain status in the city. Young Corey and his wife, not so incidentally, are reported to be doing very well. David Sewell is continually hoping that Barker will return to Willoughby Pastures, even after Barker has enlightened him as to the poverty and lack of opportunity there, and he argues that the result of encouraging people to rise is sometimes hideous: "I don't mind people taking themselves out of their places; but if the particles of this mighty cosmos have been adjusted by the divine wisdom, what are we to say of the temerity that disturbs the least of them?" The reader is meant to question this attitude,[71] even if Sewell himself never shifts very far from it, but in the end Howells does have Barker return home. This may represent a reasoned bias against the contemporary migration to the cities. It may also indicate an underlying commitment on Howells's part to the class structure he is indicting, a commitment we found in *The Rise of Silas Lapham*. It certainly implies a recognition that with all his personal desire for a sense of "complicity" with men of different and less comfortable circumstances, he has so far failed to achieve it.

Knowing that he had failed to reach a real rapport with Lemuel Barker, that he was a jail visitor and not an inmate, and that Sewell, for all his preaching, still had a long way to go in practice, Howells perhaps at this point had come to a decision important for his fiction. While continuing to strike out at American social and economic inequities, he would have to do so from the only standpoint open to him, that of an Atherton or, better, a Sewell. That he could not rest easy in such a position would add depth to his fiction. He would write not only out of social concern and desire to alter the lives of his readers but also with full awareness of the weaknesses, self-accusations, and tensions that must accompany his particular, representative standpoint.

3

Tolstoy,
the Anarchists,
and
Annie Kilburn

William Dean Howells was the leading literary influence in America when I was a boy in Central Illinois. His magazine writings guided and inspired us — the two or three who were striving. They helped to form our taste in a place where no personal influence was at hand to show us the way. I read his novels with profit moral and literary. He deepened my interest in Tolstoi. He introduced me to many new things. . . . They warred on him in those days for his realism. When he lifted his voice in brave protest against the strangling of the poor fellows in Chicago in 1887 I loved him for his humanity and his courage. . . . William Dean Howells, life is of more dignity, significance, trustworthiness, beauty, because of you. Can I, can any one say a better thing of another man?

— EDGAR LEE MASTERS, 1917[1]

I

AS WE HAVE SEEN, Howells, with considerable difficulty and tentativeness, was courageously attempting to extend his art into areas generally untouched by other writers. Yet at the same time, some of his contemporaries were growing increasingly critical of the limitations he seemed to be setting himself. Henry James — who in 1882 had written, "you have only to go on" — in an essay on Howells in 1886 reasserted some of his old concerns about Howells's fiction:

He is animated by a love of the common, the immediate, the familiar and vulgar elements of life, and holds that in proportion as we move into the rare and strange we become vague and arbitrary; that truth of representation, in a word, can be achieved only so long as it is in our power to test and measure it. He thinks scarcely anything too paltry to be interesting. . . . He adores the real, the natural, the colloquial, the moderate, the optimistic, the domestic, and the democratic; looking askance at exceptions and perversities and superiorities, at surprising and incongruous phenomena in general. One must have seen a great deal before one concludes; the world is very large, and life is a mixture of many things; she by no means eschews the strange, and often risks combinations and effects that make one rub one's eyes.

Others echoed and elaborated this opinion. Hamilton Wright Mabie in 1885 praised Howells for his growing seriousness of purpose, for the more complex problems of character he was setting himself, for his determination to see widely and deeply, and for the new substance and solidity in his work. He discerned limits to Howells's insight and imagination, however, and found nowhere in his work "a really decisive closing with life in a determined struggle to wring from it its secret." John Robertson in 1884, in a serious effort to appraise Howells's work, found his felicitous style an inadequate substitute for breadth and depth of thought; Howells had, "in short, deficient philosophic capacity." Horace Scudder, in concluding an 1883 review of Howells's *A Woman's Reason* and Bret Harte's *In the Carquinez Woods*, hoped that "the coming novelist, if he is heir to the grace and distinct naturalness of Mr. Howells, will have something of the large, vigorous, imaginative vividness which are the undeniable properties of Mr. Harte's fiction." Three years later he wrote of his "slowly hardening disappointment over the limitations which Mr. Howells chooses to set himself."

Hamlin Garland, who met Howells for the first time in 1887, wrote in a judicious defense of him in 1903 that the most pertinent criticism of his novels was "the apparent lack of large aim." Many younger novelists, he said, shared Zola's distrust of the "realism of the average" and failed "to depict in the realistic manner the life of some special locality, because of their fear of being dull." Many readers, he thought, did not recognize Howells's exquisite English, rare and delicate humor, and altruism, and found him "dull and slow." Many of his warm personal friends did not like his books, and Garland himself, as an author, had reservations: "I am willing to confess, even at the end of this paragraph of praise, that I cannot always follow him; but this is because my life is so much more active, not to say unreflective, than his. He sits above the tumult and his heart is sound and sweet."[2]

This case against Howells echoes through the twentieth century.

> William Dean Howells has never surprised anybody, thrilled anybody, shocked anybody. His career and his works alike seem devoid of inspired moments. He has never written a bad sentence, never struck a false note. To great numbers of people, he is simply "uninteresting.". . . His light is the light of common day. He has pictured nothing remote, fantastic, tragic.

Thus ran Van Wyck Brooks's commentary after a 1909 interview with Howells. Where earlier critics lamented that Howells's exquisite style lacked a corresponding depth of content, Vernon L. Parrington in 1930 argued, as did George Lukacs in other contexts, that an author's style results directly from his *Weltanschauung* and ideology. Howells's decision to locate himself in Boston, according to Parrington, created inhibitions in his outlook. These inhibitions caused the refined style that canceled the fuller, rougher narration that should have derived from his western origins:

> Subjected to such refinements his realism in the end became little more than technique — a meticulous transcription of New England conventions. . . . The fidelity of his observation, the refinement of his prose style, and the subtlety of his humor . . . do not compensate for the slightness of his materials. The record he has left is not that of a great soul brooding over the meaning of life. . . . He was restrained by too many inhibitions to deal frankly with natural human passions.

More recently Warner Berthoff, while acknowledging Howells's expertness in nearly every aspect of the art of fiction, asserted that Howells "saw what was in front of him, what presented itself to his leveling glance, but it was not in his nature to look deeper or to see matters through to an end."[3]

Not all the criticism is just; much of it occurs without close attention to Howells's better work. Yet there is some truth in what is said. If Howells is not without depth, if he does not merely cling to the surfaces of life, he does lack an overwhelming sense of the tragic in life and of the dramatic in human affairs. Why is this so? Why do his realistic theory and practice bar the strongest possible effects? Whereas, for example, George Eliot's goals were remarkably close to Howells's, her writing has a passion, depth, and resonance absent from his work. The cause may in part be constitutional, based in early experiences we have no access to: Howells may simply have lacked the ability or will to look at certain sides of life. Or an influence may be discovered in his early models as reader and writer and his later literary acquaintance.

One of the most difficult factors to assess, in fact, in Howells's life and writing is his early contact, through reading and then in person, with the older New England writers. Opinions range from Parrington's assertion that his genius was perverted by his worshipful contact with the genteel and effete Easterners to recent demonstrations of his critical attitude toward the Boston and Cambridge world he entered. The truth lies somewhere in between, and his mingled antagonism and worship are reflected in an anecdote he kept in his head as late as 1899: "I recall the awe with which Mr. Bret Harte, when he first visited Cambridge [1871], heard through my tale of authors in my own neighborhood, and then the hardihood with which he attempted to carry it off by saying, 'Why, a man couldn't fire a revolver from your front porch anywhere without bringing down a two-volumer.'"[4]

As a boy in Ohio, Howells eagerly imbibed the leading periodicals from the East and England. He shared the ambivalence of men like Charles Eliot Norton toward Walt Whitman, and in 1860, on his first trip east, preferred literary New England to Bohemian New York. In 1864, to justify his hesitation over returning to Ohio, Howells quoted to his father some recent praise from James Russell Lowell: "You have enough in you to do honor to our Literature. Keep on cultivating youself." In 1865, Lowell wrote Howells, "You are doing just what I should wish you to do," telling him of the "lawlessness & want of scholarly refinement" he feared in American literature. A year later, Lowell reviewed *Venetian Life*, lauding Howells for his matured poetic style, his refinement, and his conscious ideal of excellence. Lowell was well pleased on behalf of culture:

> This delicacy, it appeared, was a product of the rough-and-ready
> West, this finish the natural gift of a young man with no advantage
> of college-training. . . . A singular fruit, we thought, of our shaggy
> democracy. . . . Where is the rudeness of a new community, the
> pushing vulgarity of an imperfect civilization, the licentious con-

tempt of forms that marks our unchartered freedom, and all the other terrible things which have long been the bugaboos of European refinement? Here was a natural product, as perfectly natural as the deliberate attempt of "Walt Whitman" to answer the demand of native and foreign misconception was perfectly artificial. Our institutions do not, then, irretrievably doom us to coarseness and the impatience of that restraining precedent which alone makes true culture possible and true art attainable.

He went on to praise Howells for his charming tone, his "flexible and sweet" style, and his humor showing through the deep feeling like spots of sunshine.[5] Other reviews of this and all the books to follow would echo this praise for Howells's "exquisite" style, delicate touches, and light humor.

Howells's concern over this emphasis on genteel style seems clear in his juxtaposition of two clippings at the time *A Modern Instance* was appearing in the *Century*. One praised his refinement and delicacy and hoped he would not widen his field; the other complained of him and James: "Are our conditions such as that we must always have so much brilliancy, so much light without shadow, so much surface with such lightly-reflected depths?" The same concern turns up in an earlier letter to his father about *A Chance Acquaintance*:

> I am glad I have done it for one reason if for no other; it sets me forever outside of the rank of mere *culturists*, followers of an elegant literature, and proves that I have sympathy with the true spirit of Democracy. Sometimes I've doubted whether I had, but when I came to look the matter over in writing this story I doubted no longer.[6]

Yet, with his youthful literary propensities, with such early encouragement of his delicacy of style, with such literary friends and acquaintances, Howells, one might argue, despite his independence and resistance to criticism, despite his development toward a less charming vision of American life, was ultimately prevented from going far enough. The formal characteristics he never entirely abandoned enervated his vision. His attraction to culture, refinement, and pleasant people prevented him from speaking out as strongly and consistently as he might have. One might argue, as Kermit Vanderbilt does, that his friendship with men like Holmes, Norton, and Lowell made him reluctant to challenge some of their values, including their class and ethnic biases — biases from which he himself was not always entirely free. These are fair arguments, which do point to a taming factor in Howells's writing. This is one side to the picture.

On the other side is a Howells inspired and strengthened by the political integrity of many of these Easterners — of Lowell, Curtis, Longfellow, and Whittier. His own Swedenborgian and abolitionist upbringing prepared him to turn to this in them and to extol Boston, in an early review in the *Ohio State Journal*, for its uprightness, independence of mind, and humanity toward the slave.[7] To this side of the man we, like the young Edgar Lee Masters, are indebted for the humane insistences, the democratic balance, and the tough social concern that make up much of his fiction. We are indebted to him for his courage in taking steps, against some of his own preconceptions, to open his fiction beyond that of most of his contemporaries to the plight of the economically deprived in America.

II

Looking back, Howells felt that the "Editor's Study," which he wrote every month from 1886 to early 1892, had stolen time and quality from his fiction. The work often seemed mere drudgery and sometimes, through the vituperation of opponents, caused pain. On the other hand, it provided him with a long-desired forum for his critical opinions, and, as he wrote to Gosse, it was fun "having one's open say again, and banging the babes of Romance about. It does my soul lots of good; and how every number makes 'em dance! There hasn't been so much honest truth aired in this country since Columbus's second mate shouted 'Land, ho!' and Columbus retorted 'What a lie! It's clouds.'" He was pulling in, he continued, from his long fictitious voyage *The Minister's Charge* and expected to complete it by March 1; seven months before, he had written to Mark Twain that with Lemuel Barker he was sailing "far away from S. Lapham."[8] It was natural at this point that he would think of his fiction and criticism as needing to travel away from *The Rise of Silas Lapham* and as having something to do with discovery of America.

Discovery, at any rate, would soon be trumpeted in the "Study" and would sound on down through the years; it would be the most important discovery, perhaps, of Howells's life: Lev Tolstoy. *The Cossacks*, one of Tolstoy's early books, had lain unread for five or six years on Howells's shelf, and one autumn day in 1885 he took it down: "I did not know even Tolstoy's name when I opened it, and it was with a kind of amaze that I read it, and felt word by word, and line by line, the truth of a new art in it." By October 30 he had read Part I of *Anna Karenina* ("how good you feel the author's heart to be"); on January 17, 1886, he wrote his father that "one thing I discover is that pretty nearly every one is better than I am," adding "I want to send you a book soon that will interest you: it is called 'My Religion,' and is by the famous Russian writer, Tolstoi"; for the April "Study" he reviewed *Anna Karenina, My Religion*, and *A Confession*; and by July 13 he had read *War and Peace*, which he told Norton was a "great book."

The reading of Tolstoy in these months, he later wrote, was a revelation "somewhat comparable to the old-fashioned religious experience of people converted at revivals," and it was in some ways continuous with his "religious experience" of 1884 at 302 Beacon Street. He was struck by Tolstoy's unprecedented realistic rendering of life, yet the experience was not only in aesthetics, "but in ethics, too, so that I can never again see life in the way I saw it before I knew him." The compassion and understanding in the novels and, especially, the author's own practical living of the life of Christ, his giving up of wealth, society, and position to live and work among the peasants, touched the very soul of the American author who was questioning his own commitment to bettering the human condition. The experience was of such profundity that Howells eight years later would conclude *My Literary Passions* with a tribute to Tolstoy:

> I believe if I had not turned the corner of my fiftieth year, when I first knew Tolstoy, I should not have been able to know him as fully as I did. He has been to me that final consciousness, which he speaks of so wisely in his essay on Life. I came in it to the knowledge of myself in ways I had not dreamt of before, and began at least to discern my relations to the race, without which we are each nothing. The supreme art in literature had its highest effect in making me set art forever below humanity, and it is with the wish to offer the greatest homage to heart and mind, which any man can

pay another, that I close this record with the name of Lyof [*sic*] Tolstoy.[9]

Because of the fatiguing amount of work of these years, the increasing dependence of his father, and the costly illness of his daughter, and because of his age and sense of compromise in his art and life, Howells had recently felt an impulse to draw upon a simpler, more energetic childhood time for revitalization: In September 1885 he had completed his sketch "My Year in a Log Cabin." While rediscovering certain childhood fears, the grimness of death, and the unhappiness of his mother, he found he could put the emphasis upon a life undarkened by cares and burdened with few duties, upon a winter that was one long delight to himself and his siblings, and upon boyhood senses open to every intimation of beauty. He knew, however, that he would no longer take joy in the experience of stepping out of bed into a "snow-wreath," and he had, in all honesty, to conclude by telling of his return to the site thirty years later, in 1881, at the time he was also visiting the soldiers' hospital, the coal mines, and a divorce court. He found the road strange and his destination stranger, for everything, like himself, had aged; the timber was gone, leaving "a bald knob and a sterile tract of sand," the hill was no longer the mountain it once seemed, and the island no longer appeared the size of England.

> The grist-mill, whose gray bulk had kept so large a place in my memory, was sadly dwarfed, and in its decrepitude it had canted backwards, and seemed tottering to its fall. I explored it from wheel-pit to colling-floor; there was not an Indian in it, but, ah! what ghosts! ghosts of the living and the dead; my brothers', my playmates', my own! At last it was really haunted. I think no touch of repair had been put upon it, or upon the old saw-mill, either, on whose roof the shingles had all curled up like the feathers of a frizzly chicken in the rains and suns of those thirty summers past. The head-race, once a type of silent, sullen power, now crept feebly to its work; even the water seemed to have grown old, and anything might have battled successfully with the currents where the spool-pig was drowned and the miller's boy was carried so near his death.

The boy showing him about "could not make out why the gray-mustached, middle-aged man should care" about the disappearance of the sawmiller's cabin, and when Howells tried to tell him he too had once been a boy there, "the boy of whom I have here written so freely seemed so much less a part of me than the boy to whom I spoke, that, upon the whole, I had rather a sense of imposing upon my listener."[10] The return to the past would be of relatively little use in his search for revitalization.

Tolstoy, however, was something else, a man like himself, a novelist who at Howells's age had looked about him on the streets of Moscow, visited slums and police stations, attempted charitable work, and finally changed his entire manner of life. Tolstoy's example meant escape from the rut, and along lines in which Howells was already moving, and he provided a model of responsibility and courage. Howells was lucky. Not many people at his stage of life find a Tolstoy, nor are many prepared to respond when a Tolstoy appears.

III

After completing *The Minister's Charge* in February 1886, and after a month in Washington investigating a possible setting for a new novel, Howells, throwing out two hundred pages of false starts, in April slowly began work on another novel, which was to be called *April Hopes* and which he would finish sometime around the turn of the year. He later told Marrion Wilcox that this was the first novel he wrote "with the distinct consciousness that he was writing as a realist," the result of his having undertaken the "Editor's Study." But it is realism that does not probe the relations between classes and that for the most part lacks the kind of conflicts with which we have been concerned. Attempting to combat sentimental notions that love is all that matters in love affairs, Howells subtly reveals the problems that arise from a mutual passion unattended by common ideals, background, and temperament.[11] The situation, built around a young, relatively shallow, untroubled couple, Alice Pasmer and Dan Mavering, is commonplace, though with "pleasant people" rather than crude country boys, tramps, and streetcar conductors. As he had done so well in *A Modern Instance* and *The Minister's Charge*, Howells brings home to the reader the gaps that people open up between themselves through their little egotisms, selfishness, preconceptions, laxities, trite arguments, and failures in self-understanding and in sympathy toward others. It is a little curious that after *The Minister's Charge* Howells would write a book like this and not keep up his drive for socially and economically charged content. Similarly, he wrote *Indian Summer* close to the time of *The Rise of Silas Lapham* and while contemplating *The Minister's Charge, The Coast of Bohemia* at the time of the Altrurian works, and year by year, popular farces with little in the way of social concerns. Aside from the fact that he often enjoyed such writing, and aside from the fact that one can manage to trace similar concerns and techniques in all these works, one should realize that Howells had a clear sense of the kind of audience he had earned through his early writings. He knew that he needed to keep a sizable reading audience in order to convey his humane lessons, and he knew that the fight for realism in literature and social justice in life could be fought on many fronts.

There are no Sewell-Barker relationships in *April Hopes*, and for this reason the book will not be discussed at length; but it will be worth our while to glance at one suggestive passage. At a picnic outing of a group of Campobello vacationers, an amateur photographer, having taken a shot of Alice and several shots of the rest of the party, calls imperiously to a group of sailors to pose for a picture as they prepare to shove their boat into the water after gathering driftwood. They hold still, "with the helplessness of his victims," as he requests, but look around, causing the "artist" to groan, "Oh, idiots!" Mrs. Brinkley wonders what such people as the sailors think of such people as the picnickers, and in answer to Miss Cotton's speculation that "they envy us," she says that not all of them do. Those who do, furthermore, do so without respect: "They view us as the possessors of ill-gotten gains, who would be in a very different place if we had our deserts." Miss Cotton argues that only the city poor, misled by agitators, regard the well-to-do with suspicion.

> "It seems to have begun a great while ago," said Mrs. Brinkley, "and not exactly with agitators. It was considered very difficult for us to get into the kingdom of heaven, you know.... And there certainly are some things against us. Even when the chance was given us to sell all we had, and give it to the poor, we couldn't bring our minds to it, and went away exceeding sorrowful."

Miss Cotton wonders if such things were ever intended to be taken literally, but Alice comments that that story "always seems to me the most pitiful thing in the whole Bible . . . to see the right so clearly, and not to be strong enough to do it," to which Dan Mavering adds, "I always felt sorry for that poor fellow, too. . . . He seemed to be a good fellow, and it was pretty hard lines for him." The photographer concludes the scene, glancing at his hastily developed plate: "Confound those fellows! . . . They moved."[12]

Howells here is continuing to ponder the tensions recorded in Atherton, in the dinner party of *The Rise of Silas Lapham*, and in Sewell and Evans. He is also feeling the impact of Tolstoy on his own thinking. What right has the successful photographer of Pasmers, Maverings, Brinkleys, Cottons, Coreys, Hallecks, Hubbards, and Sewells, people of his own class, to take pictures of sailors and laborers, stepping briefly into their world from his own moneyed picnic and stepping as quickly back? How successfully, indeed, can he capture them with so little background for understanding them? To what extent does he even care to gain more of such background? *April Hopes*, if a serious book, represents also an uncertain and thoughtful biding of the author's time between *The Minister's Charge* and *Annie Kilburn*.

IV

Nearly the entire summer and fall of 1886 Howells spent at 302 Beacon Street working on his novel, reading, and keeping on top of the "Editor's Study" month by month. He wrote to Charles Eliot Norton in May, echoing Dan and Alice's concern for the sorrowful rich man, that "sometimes one is not *permitted* to be as good as he would like: in fact I think this accounts for all my sins." He would have liked to be as good as the great Russian novelist, whom he described in the April "Study" as "fully a believer in Christianity; too fully, perhaps, for those who believe it ought to be believed, but not that it ought to be practiced."

> He supposes that Jesus Christ, being divinely sent to make God known to man, was serious when He preached meekness, submission, poverty, forgiveness, charity, and self-denial . . . none of the sort who take Christ in the ironical way can help being startled by the attitude of this literalist, and suffering perhaps some pangs of disagreeable self-question.[13]

If disagreeable self-questioning was no new experience for Howells, Tolstoy proposed a philosophy and a principle of action, and Howells was now working out his position in a new light. If he had by this time realized that his standpoint as a novelist, because of his background and experience, must be that of an Atherton or Sewell, he also knew he was not comfortable with it.

He was pondering the relation between his writing and his own life and the lives of his readers. He continued to praise work that contained "thinking of a sort which is likely to invite the reader to do some thinking of his own," and in the "Study" for August 1886 he praised Grant's *Memoirs* as one of those books "of men whose lives have been passed in activities, who have been used to employing language as they would have employed any implement, to effect an object, who have regarded a thing to be said as in no wise different from a thing to be done." He felt that nothing could be forgiven to the genius of a man like Goethe, for the greater an author's power, "the greater his responsibility before the human conscience," and he concluded his Introduction to *Modern Italian Poets* with a long quotation from the novelist Francesco Domenico Guerrazzi, who said:

> In free and tranquil countries, men have the happiness and the right to be artists for art's sake: with us, this would be weakness and apathy. When I write it is because I have something *to do*; my books are not productions, but deeds. Before all, here in Italy we must be men. When we have not the sword, we must take the pen.... To write slowly, coldly, of our times and of our country, with the set purpose of creating a *chef-d'oeuvre*, would be almost an impiety.[14]

In March 1885, Roswell Smith had suggested to Howells a novel dealing with labor relations. He cited the great abuses of capitalism, the eager striving for wealth, which "is the one god that American society worships," and the opportunities for socialism to take root, there being so much for it to feed on and so little repression of ideas and parties. He drew a parallel that would come to have increasing significance for Howells: "Just as surely as the relations between labor and capital were all wrong in our Southern states under the system of slavery, just so surely are they wrong today throughout the entire country." Try to demonstrate this with facts, he said, and you will be ineffective and uninteresting, your articles will be subject to libel suits. America needed someone to tackle the problem in fiction: "As Dickens reformed the abuses in school life in England, and the Jewish quarter in London, so some writer of fiction may yet do a great service in this country, and help to postpone if not prevent the great impending struggle between labor and capital."

It is possible, although there is no direct evidence, that Howells, in response to this letter, was contemplating such a novel and that, therefore, he would have been especially attentive to the strikes on May 1, 1886, in agitation for the eight-hour day. The circumstances attending one of these strikes were to move directly and powerfully, though not immediately, into Howells's life. In Chicago, Cyrus H. McCormick, Jr., had resisted the strike by calling in scabs, but on May 3 he promised the eight-hour day, and a half-holiday was granted to celebrate the decision. A fight broke out between police and union men who were deriding the scabs as they left the factory, the police opened fire, and a number of workingmen were killed and wounded. On May 4, as an orderly protest at Haymarket Square was breaking up, a squad of police appeared, unnecessarily, to disperse the crowd. A bomb was thrown, killing one policeman and wounding many more. Shooting began, causing more dead among the police and the crowd, and many wounded.

Chicago and the nation were certain, and rightly so, that the bomb had come from an anarchist's hand. In a state of fear and desiring vengeance, the press, the police, and the public began a hunt that ended in the arrest and conviction, on August 20, of eight known anarchists: Albert Parsons, August Spies, Michael Schwab, Adolph Fischer, Samuel Fielden, George Engel, Oscar Neebe, and Louis Lingg. All except Neebe were sentenced to death, and he to fifteen years' imprisonment. A stay of execution was granted, and on November 25 the attorneys for the anarchists were given permission to appeal. The case was reargued before the Illinois Supreme Court beginning March 13, 1887, and a final decision was handed down on September 14 of that year.[15]

It was in the September 1886 "Editor's Study" that Howells defined the Russian novelists as "humanists," in a passage we discussed in Chapter 1. That "Study" also carried the well-known, often misused "smiling aspects" passage, which appears, especially out of context, to reveal a Howells terribly impercipient about the conditions of his own country. In context, the passage continues to present difficulties, but ones more easily resolvable. American fiction, Howells wrote, would be mistaken to strike a note so tragic as that in Dostoyevsky's *Crime and Punishment*. Few American novelists have been sentenced to execution or exiled to the rigors of a Duluth winter, and one might, said the man later to suffer on behalf of the anarchists, make Herr Most the hero of a labor-question romance with perfect impunity.

> ... in a land where journeymen carpenters and plumbers strike for four dollars a day the sum of hunger and cold is certainly very small, and the wrong from class to class is almost inappreciable. We invite our novelists, therefore, to concern themselves with the more smiling aspects of life, which are the more American, and to seek the universal in the individual rather than the social interests. It is worth while ... to be true to our well-to-do actualities; the very passions themselves seem to be softened and modified by conditions which cannot be said to wrong any one, to cramp endeavor, or to cross lawful desire. Sin and suffering and shame there must always be in the world, we suppose, but we believe that in this new world of ours it is mainly from one to another one, and oftener still from one to one's self. We have death too in America, and a great deal of disagreeable and painful disease ... but this is tragedy that comes in the very nature of things, and is not peculiarly American, as the large, cheerful average of health and success and happy life is. ... Apart from these purely moral troubles, the race here enjoys conditions in which most of the ills that have darkened its annals may be averted by honest work and unselfish behavior.

This passage has been much discussed, and recent critics have done well to return it to its context in the "Study" from its context in *Criticism and Fiction*. Several points should be made about it. It is true, first of all, as Cady realizes, that Howells's statement was a comparative one and more or less true: Comparatively speaking, America did enjoy a higher level of prosperity than Russia and had more communication and movement between the classes. Second, it is true, as both Carter and Cady note,[16] that this "Study" was written no later than sometime in July, before the results of the anarchist trial were known, and that Howells's later involvement in the anarchist affair was, with other causes, to darken his vision of America. Such an explanation, however, rests too much on the anarchist affair as a great turning point in Howells's career. It does not cover the seeming inconsistency between the Howells who in this passage can talk somewhat blithely about American possibilities and the Howells who wrote his father from Beacon Street in August 1884 about the wretched barracks of the poor, who possibly visited for Associated Charities, who knew what happened to some of the young men who came from the country to make their way in the city, and who was confronting the social and religious writings of Tolstoy.

It is possible that Howells at Beacon Street was writing from the side of him that was attracted to the life of privilege and to conservative politics and economics, that accepted the optimism of national rhetoric, that had celebrated the universally rising American in an 1882 article on Mark Twain. Very possibly he was also reverting to a defensive maneuver, a handling of "disagreeable self-question," a reply to Tolstoy, an answer to questions implicit in his portrayal of the photographer in *April Hopes*. American conditions are not those of Russia, says the author who composed Sewell's lament at the chasm between people of different socio-economic backgrounds in America. The disparities between our classes are minimal; we need concern ourselves with individual, not social problems; our life is mostly cheerful, healthful, successful, and happy, and therefore the kind of step Tolstoy took is unnecessary for an American author. The statement read this way is a rationalization, for Howells consulting his experience in any other mood would have hesitated to affirm the unqualified truth of all that he said here.

He certainly did not think America the free and tranquil country referred to by Guerrazzi, and, though not ready to change radically, he was interested in using his pen, at least, to fight injustice. The "smiling aspects" argument may even be seen as a battle maneuver. Probably he felt that what poverty and class disparity did exist might be overcome by inculcating an optimistic conviction about American possibilities. It might also be overcome by a fictional method like that of the Russians, which would bring Americans more closely together in humility, compassion, and self-awareness. The sin, suffering, and shame in this country being mainly between individuals or within oneself, self-realization, honest work, and unselfish behavior would go a long way toward clearing up social problems. With all the differences between America and Russia,

> . . . we may nevertheless read Dostoievsky, and especially our novelists may read him, to advantage, for in spite of his terrible picture of

a soul's agony he is hopeful and wholesome, and teaches in every page patience, merciful judgment, humble helpfulness, and that brotherly responsibility, that duty of man to man, from which not even the Americans are emancipated.[17]

The emphasis, in other words, should not be on what the critic or novelist actually *sees* but on his methods for *doing* something about it, and Howells's "optimistic" essay may have represented to him a positive deed.

The effect of the written word, too, could be far-reaching. Immediately after the last quoted passage, Howells goes on to assert his belief in the power of fiction. He refers to "undeniable" statements in Vernon Lee's *Baldwin* that claim for novels an "influence in deepening and refining human feeling" — statements like the following:

> Believing as I do in the power of directing human feeling into certain channels... believing especially in the power of reiteration of emotion in constituting our emotional selves... I must necessarily also believe that the modern human being has been largely fashioned in all his more delicate peculiarities by those who have written about him, and most of all, therefore, by the novelist.

Saying could be a very effective way of doing. Word and deed being different, furthermore, one might find reason, as Howells did in the June "Study," to choose pen over sword: "Men come and go, and what they do in their limited physical lives is of comparatively little moment; it is what they say that really survives to bless or to ban."[18]

V

On the night of February 12, 1887, Howells dreamed of his retarded brother, Henry, he wrote his father, "as I have several times, and he attacked me in that odious way; he does it in all my dreams of him. Poor, afflicted creature!" Perhaps with some dim awareness that this dream suggested irresponsibility toward those in need, he went on to invoke the religion of his youth: "In which of Swedenborg's works could I find the shortest and clearest statements of his philosophy?"

While a new novel was beginning to take shape in his mind, he and Elinor went for two days the next week to visit the Lowell mills. What they saw there made them "feel that civilization was all wrong in regard to the labor that suffers" in such mills, which were "as humanely managed as such things can be." Civilization was all wrong for a reason more striking than that Sewell had complained of in *The Minister's Charge:* It was not so much a question of socioeconomic barriers between men as a question of "slavery." In Lowell, Howells found conspicuous parallels to the world Tolstoy had discovered in his walks about Moscow not many years before. And he ran into a common stumbling block: The wrong was a large one, intricately woven into the habits and economics of a mammoth society. "I felt so helpless about it, too, realizing the misery it must cost to undo such a mistake." That he felt himself, personally, to be moving in the right direction in his visit to Lowell, in his reaction to it, and in his scheme for the new novel is recorded in his brother's change of heart a night or two before Howells returned home: "Last night I had a pleasanter dream of Henry; he forebore to 'jounce' me; and I can therefore freely rejoice with you that he's able to be out of bed."[19]

John Howells had decided the best training for his chosen profession of architecture could be had abroad. The family planned to accompany him at the end of July, and William did not wish to maintain the house while away for a year. So 302 Beacon, too expensive for them anyway, was sold in late March 1887, at a profit of several thousand dollars. The house did represent, however, a certain high plateau of success, and while he wrote to his father his reasons for the sale, a photographer circled, stopping him in mid-sentence to catch various poses: "I asked him to come because I want some record of myself in the place." In mid-April, during his last week in the house, he wrote his father that he would come visit after he had settled the family in Auburndale for May. He was by now well into Tolstoy's *Que Faire?*

> I have not seen the American Magazine, and so have escaped our picture. But I really don't care for these things any longer, and if *I* don't, who does? . . . I am just reading one of Tolstoi's books — on poverty, and prosperity's responsibility for it — and I confess it makes me very unhappy. His remedy is to go into the country, and share the labor of his peasants — to forego luxury and superfluity; but I don't exactly see how this helps, except that it makes all poor

alike, and saves one's self from remorse. It's a terrible question. How shall it ever be answered? Did you use to be troubled about it? When I think of it, my pleasure in possession is all spoiled.

Yet as to luxury and superfluity, the hotel in Auburndale was socially and economically no more humble than 302 Beacon, at least as seen through the eyes of one young visitor from the West coming to meet Howells for the first time, having been captivated by the vision and method of *A Minister's Charge:*

> As I came opposite the entrance of the hotel grounds, I entered a state of panic, for the towering portico of "The Elms" made it appear a palace for millionaires. . . . Entering the wide central hall, I advanced warily across the rugs on its polished floor to the desk behind which stood a highly ornate and haughty clerk. . . . For several minutes I waited, sitting on the edge of a fringed and gilded chair, with my eyes on the portières, vainly trying to swallow a frog in my throat.[20]

The visit to Ohio was pleasant, and Howells would look back often during the following year or so to the "moments of pure delight" when he reclined and talked with his father under trees on the property. It was on his return at the end of May that Edward Everett Hale met him in the station at Albany and reported to his wife:

> Tolstoi has really troubled him, because he does not know but he ought to be ploughing and reaping. But he is as sweet and good and eager to do right as he can be. I dare not begin to write down what he said, and I, I went nearer the depths than perhaps I have ever done to any one but you. . . . Really, if I did what was wise I should spend this morning in writing in short hand in my note book, all he said and all I said, about Tolstoi's theories and the Saviour's wishes. Howells is a loyal Christian, and hates to have anybody say that Jesus made plans or demanded things that are impossible.

By the middle of June, the family was rusticating in a long, low, rambling cottage at Lake George. In July a reporter for the *New York Tribune* discovered Howells there, sun-tanned and the picture of good health in a soft felt hat, white flannel shirt, and large easy pair of corduroy trousers. Only two days before, he said, he had written the first pages of a new, as yet untitled novel: "It will be a purely American story, its chief events centred in a New England country town, though it will relate to both city and country life." He thought it would be in good shape by October, when the family planned to leave Lake George. (By now John had decided to enter Harvard instead of seeking training in Europe, and so his parents had decided not to travel abroad that summer.) Asked for his opinion on contemporary novelists, he lauded Tolstoy and Turgenev. Their novels were "absolute truth," and they had "the ability and the courage to paint humanity and its affairs just as they are." This, Howells said, he regarded "as the highest art." Tolstoy was to fiction what Shakespeare was to drama.

> He has a very strong ethical side, and not only teaches it and portrays it, but lives it. He has given himself up to it. He believes that men should live precisely and literally as Christ lived, and abandoning literature, where he stood at the summit of fiction, he has adopted the daily life of a Russian peasant.

To the reporter's remark that this "seemed like simplicity itself," Howells replied, "Isn't that because our civilization is so sophisticated? We read, and say we believe that Christ is God, but sometimes our actions imply that we scarcely think He meant what He said about the conduct of life."[21] Howells, beginning a new novel, continued to be vitally concerned with the tale of the rich man who was "exceeding sorrowful."

In fact, on June 28 he had written twenty-two manuscript pages of a story or novel called "The Prisoner of Prosperity." In this fragment Mrs. Malden complains to Mrs. Tweddell about the mass of gifts and other items she and Mr. Malden have accumulated over the years, so much that they fill a room at the top of the house. "Mr. Malden thinks it's dreadful — to heap up uselessness as he calls it. He says that every one of these things represents the deprivation of some really necessitous person. He can't bear to look at them." Mrs. Tweddell advises a trip to Europe for Mr. Malden: As soon as the steamer leaves the dock, all care and anxiety should end. Mrs. Malden does not know if her husband is a good sailor, but she thinks "he's getting into a morbid state."[22] The fragment does not continue further, perhaps because the Howellses themselves had now de-

cided not to go abroad, but had it continued, and had the Howellses gone
to Europe, it is likely that in Mr. Malden, Howells would have made a
study very close to home. The denizen of 302 Beacon and "The Elms" was
certainly, to a large extent, a prisoner of prosperity.

Howells's review of Tolstoy's *Que Faire?* and his Introduction to an
English translation of *Sebastopol* both appeared in July. In the latter he
remarked that Tolstoy's lesson was one the comfortable rich and the literary romanticists and idealists might well heed:

> He teaches such of us as will hear him that the Right is the sum of
> each man's poor little personal effort to do right, and that the suc-
> cess of this effort means daily, hourly self-renunciation, self-
> abasement, the sinking of one's pride in absolute squalor before
> duty. This is not pleasant; the heroic ideal of righteousness is more
> picturesque, more attractive; but is this not the truth? Let any one
> try, and see!

He found *Que Faire?* a culmination of Tolstoy's arguments from *A Confession* and *My Religion* and recounted how Tolstoy tells, "with that
terrible, unsparing honesty of his," of his attempt to practice charity in
Moscow, his wishing "to live in idleness and ease, as he had always lived,
and to rid himself of the tormenting consciousness of the misery all
around him by feeding and clothing and sheltering it." Tolstoy found he
could not help the unindustrious poor while himself leading a life of ease
and luxury, "while a great social gulf, forbidding all brotherly contact, was fixed between them." He found his answer in his decision "to
leave the city, to forego his splendor in society and the sweets of his literary
renown, to simplify his life, to go into the country, and to become literally
a peasant and the companion of peasants." This greatest living writer
tells us

> ... that he finds this yoke easy and this burden light, that he is no
> longer weary or heavy laden with the sorrows of others or his share
> of their sins, but that he has been given rest by humble toil. It is a
> hard saying; but what if it should happen to be the truth? In that
> case, how many of us who have great possessions must go away ex-
> ceeding sorrowful! Come, star-eyed Political Economy! come Soci-
> ology, heavenly nymph! and soothe the ears tortured by this echo of

Nazareth. Save us, sweet Evolution! Help, O Nebular Hypothesis! Art, Civilization, Literature, Culture! is there no escape from our brothers but in becoming more and more truly their brothers?

Howells was taking this to heart. Tolstoy had "arraigned the present civil order as wrong, false, and unnatural," as Howells in February had felt that "civilization was all wrong." Tolstoy, in Howells's words, "sold all he had and gave it to the poor, and turned and followed Him," as the rich man in Luke had been unable to do: "From his work-bench he sends this voice back into the world, to search the hearts of those who will hear, and to invite them to go and do likewise." That Tolstoy is leading the life Christ taught "makes it impossible for one to regard it without grave question of the life that the rest of us are living."[23]

We can say only that Howells at this point was clearly troubled by the challenge. His perspective was more seriously shaken than even in the recent past, and he felt a strong need to reconcile his life in one way or another with Tolstoy's call. Although he had made no radical change in his behavior, he was at least urging himself to commitment along Christian lines when he argued for the viability — despite the invisibility of result — of "each man's poor little personal effort to do right."

VI

When the family arrived at Lake George, Winny, whose health in the last year and a half had been sometimes better, sometimes worse, was "not so well." Her digestion was very bad, and a local doctor speculated that there was some uterine trouble. Reports fluctuated painfully during the summer. In mid-July she seemed to be getting better as a result of the "remarkably fine and pure air of this region." On August 7 she was continuing "poorly, and we're almost at our wit's end about her.... You understand there's nothing dangerous in her case except the danger of life-long invalidism." A week later she seemed a little better, and Howells hoped the autumn air would be salutary. Two months beyond that, however, it was clear that she had had a "wretched summer," how wretched Howells would later recall. A poem of hers, "A Mood," was expressive, he said, of her despair at this time:

The wind exultant swept
Through the new leaves overhead,
Till at once my pulses leapt
With a life I thought long dead,
And I woke as one who has slept
To my childhood — that had not fled.

On the wind my spirit flew;
Its freedom was mine as well.
For a moment the world was new;
What came there to break the spell?
The wind still freshly blew;
My spirit it was that fell.

Ah! fancy so sweet and strange,
On whom shall I lay the blame
That a moment you made me change,
Then left me as when you came,
With my spirit's narrow range
And life before me the same?

By this summer, however, she had ceased to write at all; she was "too sick to complete anything":

> ... she had to give up her reading in great measure, and often she could not bear to talk or think. Life withdrew itself more and more to the inward sources in the long ebb, which had already begun, unknown to us but not unknown to her. One day at this period she gave way for the first time, and said, "Oh, papa, I'm afraid I shall never get well!" and she never recalled the expression of that fear. She was too true, too sincere, too wise to deceive us as we wished to deceive ourselves; but we succeeded only too well.

Midway through September, Winny was taken for new treatment to a sanatorium in Dansville, New York. There, on September 27, although it "seemed the place for Winny," she was still "so weak as not to be able to begin active treatment."[24] The entire family, except for John, who had entered Harvard, settled nearby until the middle of November.

VII

One may count the insects in the world, examine sunspots, and write novels and operas without suffering, according to Tolstoy, "but to teach men their welfare, which lies in denying oneself and serving others, and to express this teaching powerfully is impossible without suffering." One must not fear to differ from those about him. This call for courage in asserting political, social, economic, and not merely literary opinions, and for courage in acting publicly on such opinions, was not lost on Howells. On August 10 he wrote to George William Curtis, referring to a discussion the previous winter at Norton's when "we spoke in sympathy about the impolicy of hanging the Chicago 'Anarchists.'" He had recently read Nina Van Zandt's résumé of the trial, which he felt to be unfair both in the jury selection and the rulings of the judge: "The evidence showed that neither Parsons nor Spies was concerned in promoting riot or disorder, and their speeches show them to have been active friends of a peaceful solution of the labor troubles. They are condemned to death upon a principle that would have sent every ardent antislavery man to the gallows." He enclosed the résumé and suggested that Curtis speak out on behalf of the anarchists. Curtis, who in the previous November's "Editor's Easy Chair" in *Harper's Magazine* had stated that the anarchists were guilty and their sentence just, and who had been, since May 1886, controlling a *Harper's Weekly* editorial policy that condemned the anarchists, replied to Howells, inconsistently, that he had "not read the evidence at the trial nor the arguments before the Supreme Court" and thus was "not in a position to speak fairly." He urged Howells himself to make a statement, arguing that his name would give great weight to it.

On August 18, Howells sent Curtis another pamphlet, Dyer D. Lum's *A Concise History of the Great Trial of the Chicago Anarchists, Condensed from the Official Record*, which gave an account, from one point of view, of the original trial, with details about such matters as the packed jury. He marked certain passages to help Curtis read quickly, and an accompanying letter again urged his own feelings about the trial. Curtis wrote on September 1 to say he had not finished the pamphlet, noting that one should have the official record for an unbiased opinion. On September 14 the Illinois Supreme Court played its part in this American conspiracy trial by sustaining in almost every particular the rulings and verdict of the lower court; the execution was set for November 11. Curtis wrote again on September 23 that "I wish with all my heart that I could do what you wish," but "the men are morally responsible for the crime" and are being justly punished. Howells in the meantime, acting on Curtis's earlier suggestion, had composed a letter, which he enclosed with a note to Curtis on September 25 telling him that he might publish it without harming anyone, "and perhaps get a text from it for a few words of your own in behalf of those friendless men." Curtis replied on September 27:

> Your letter for Harper shows strong feelings of which I need no proof, and although your view of the case is not mine, I should very willingly publish your letter without comment, but I do not know how the Harpers might feel.... While I do not doubt that your name would give great weight to your plea for a pause, I think that the tone of the letter would tend to defeat its purpose. Yet I do not wonder that with your conviction you are impatient of what seems to you a terrible wrong and that in writing you speak with bitter sarcasm.

Howells meanwhile had received Curtis's letter of September 23 and had written on September 26 requesting his letter back: "If others like you feel as you do, it can't help the condemned men, and its spirit might only exasperate the public mind against them more and more." He was "disappointed" in Curtis's outlook and said he could not change his own opinion, but now he thought he would "make no public expression because it would be futile."[25]

He knew by now that others did share Curtis's feelings. John Greenleaf Whittier had replied on September 21 to Howells's appeal, explaining that he had never interfered with the law and could "see no reason for making the case of the anarchists an exception." Realizing that Curtis and Whittier would not speak out on their own, Howells penned for publication the letter he sent to Curtis September 25 and on that date also wrote to Roger A. Pryor, leading counsel for the anarchists. He wished Pryor success in his attempt to appeal to the U.S. Supreme Court: "I have never believed them guilty of murder, or of anything but their opinions, and I do not think they were justly convicted." He was to write to Whittier once more, on November 1, urging him to appeal to Illinois's Governor Oglesby for clemency:

A letter from you would have great weight with him. I beseech you to write it, and do what one great and blameless man may to avert the greatest wrong that ever threatened our fame as a nation.

Even if these men had done the crime which our barbarous laws punish with homicide, should a plea for mercy be wanting from *you?*

Whittier's second reply was no more positive. He thought Howells could write such a letter better than he, adding that although he opposed capital punishment, "he was not disposed to interfere with these criminals, because they were more dangerous than other murderers."[26] Why did Howells turn to Curtis and Whittier? An influential member of the Harper organization, Curtis in his "Easy Chair" column had encouraged Howells's polemics on behalf of realism and had recently expressed to Howells his great delight in Howells's "fight with the new form of Philisteria." He had also indicated in the discussion at Norton's that he thought "the excitement of feeling in Chicago made the fairness of the trial doubtful." Whittier had written Howells in March 1886 remarking that he painfully identified with Sewell in his kindly mistake of praising bad poetry and requesting Howells to serve as his biographer. Howells's commitment to Harper and Brothers would not permit this, and Whittier had to stay with Ticknor and Company, for "Ticknor and his father were my publishers at a time when I was unpopular and unprofitable, as an anti-slavery agitator." Here is Howells's central reason for turning to these men — literary men, like Tolstoy. In 1892, Howells wrote of his experience as a youth when Curtis, whom he then worshiped for the things he had done in literature, suddenly spoke out against slavery:

I do not remember any passage of the speech, or any word of it, but I remember the joy, the pride with which the soul of youth recognizes in the greatness it has honored the goodness it may love, and all the glow of that happy moment comes back to me, with the gratitude and the new hope that filled me. Mere politicians might be pro-slavery or antislavery without touching me very much, but here was the citizen of a world far greater than theirs, a light of the universal republic of letters, who was willing and eager to stand or fall with the just cause, and that was all in all to me.

Howells had been nurtured in the cause of abolition, had written a campaign biography of Abraham Lincoln, was still a liberal, if somewhat disillusioned, Republican, and all his life had admired the authors who had spoken out against slavery. It was natural that he would ask men like Curtis and Whittier to reassert the prewar spirit in the cause of a later time. He realized that behind the misguided theories of the anarchists was a passionate concern over the new "slavery" that Tolstoy wrote about and that he himself had recognized in the Lowell mills. Here, then, was a chance for a great continuity of American idealism through the example of abolitionists rising once again to protest misuse of power in America. That the old activists had lost their humanity and concern, in this important situation at least, that Curtis and Whittier had failed him, was discouraging. It added to his fear that the earlier American love of equality and justice was disappearing not only from the party that had once stood for it but also from the great men who had once been willing to stand independent of party and speak out for it.[27] This knowledge and this fear would temper with a tinge of pessimism and uncertainty his hopes for reform in America.

On September 24, Pryor wrote to Howells about the failure of the anarchists to receive a fair judgment, remarking that "it is in harmony with the spirit of justice and humanity pervading your writings, that you desire a fair and legal trial even for Anarchists." He made an analogy Howells could appreciate: The anarchists "are no more guilty of murder than was Wendell Phillips for his sympathy with John Brown's hatred of slavery and exhortations to its extermination." In a letter of October 3, Pryor suggested that Howells appeal publicly for a fair trial for the anarchists. Howells composed a letter of appeal and sent it to Pryor, who telegraphed Howells in Jefferson, Ohio, that it was "just the thing. May I publish?" and followed up the telegram with a letter the same day, October 12, explaining that he would have it published in the *New York Tribune* if Howells would quickly send permission by telegram. Howells, however, hesitated, as he had done with the original letter sent to Curtis, although here there was no hint of reluctant acceptance by the *Tribune*. In the end, he did not send Pryor permission.

The reasons for his hesitation may be guessed. A public protest would be a large step in view of the overwhelming sentiment against the anarchists, and Howells could easily estimate the sort of response he would elicit from the newspapers. He must have worried about the effect this would have on his family and income, should his large audience be angered. He needed a different kind of fearlessness than that he possessed as literary critic and novelist. No doubt, too, his distaste for the unpleasant made him reluctant to involve himself. Therefore, although his appeal to Curtis and Whittier came from a genuine belief in the greater efficacy of men whose names were connected with antislavery protest, at the back of his mind may have been a desire to escape responsibility. It would be wrong, however, to go too far in undercutting Howells's basically noble motivation. Caution, or reasoned conscience, was natural to him, and in this case appeared appropriate.

He does appear to have wished to act at the moment his gesture would be most significant and effective. On November 1, Pryor wrote again to Howells. He added the "now" to the first sentence in the following quotation as an afterthought, suggesting a different initial reaction to Howells's withdrawal of the letter:

> I think, now, you did well to suppress the publication; because I am satisfied that, while your chivalry might have somewhat compromised you, it could do no good to the condemned. In the ardor of my zeal for my clients, the possible detriment to yourself, escaped my consideration; but that fact, as well as the no effect of the publication, are obvious on cool reflection. No man should challenge public obloquy without a commensurate object.

But, he added, at this point an appeal for executive clemency might do some good. Although the Supreme Court did not deny the writ until the next day, Pryor suspected it would do so and thought that such an appeal would be the final resource for the anarchists.[28]

On the same day, Howells had written to Whittier, vainly asking that he appeal for clemency. A day or two later, a note came from Francis Fisher Browne in Chicago, enclosing a poem by Browne that pleaded for Christian justice for the anarchists. At this time, Howells also sent a letter to the *New York Tribune*, where, despite the fact that Whitelaw Reid did not "sympathize one bit with it," it would appear on November 6. In this letter, Howells told of the petition he had sent Governor Oglesby asking commutation of the anarchists' sentences. He urged others to do the same, pointing out that the Supreme Court had

... simply affirmed the legality of the forms under which the Chicago court proceeded.... it did not affirm the propriety of trying for murder men fairly indictable for conspiracy alone; and it by no means approved the principle of punishing them because of their frantic opinions, for a crime which they were not shown to have committed. The justice or injustice of their sentence was not before the highest tribunal of our law, and unhappily could not be got there. That question must remain for history, which judges the judgment of courts, to deal with; and I, for one, cannot doubt what the decision of history will be.

On November 4, Howells replied to Browne, telling how the impending tragedy had blackened his life for months: "I do not dread the consequences so far as those who believe in anarchy is [*sic*] concerned, but I feel the horror and the shame of the crime which the law is about to commit against justice." On November 8, Browne and Henry Demarest Lloyd had this letter published in the *Chicago Tribune*. Howells also wrote his friend Edward Clement of the *Boston Transcript* on November 5 or 6, trying to enlist the help of that paper, but Clement, who would reprint the *New York Tribune* letter on November 7, replied that his colleagues and assistants were all, to a man, for hanging, and he could do nothing with them.[29]

On November 10, Lingg committed suicide, and Governor Oglesby commuted the sentences of Fielden and Schwab to life imprisonment; next day, Spies, Parsons, Fischer, and Engel were hanged. Howells had done what he could, and the result was disheartening. He was called a coward, a mere sentimentalist, a friend of the condemned, and was threatened with loss of his audience. A paper in Maine, for example, said that Howells's words in the *New York Tribune* letter "embody the sentiments of the greatest of American novelists."

What — after they have been judged guilty of murder; after the Supreme court has affirmed the legality of the lower court proceedings which convicted them, and dynamite bombs are found concealed in the cells where they are now confined? They are murderers, bomb throwers, enemies of our civilization, destroyers of homes, villains and cut-throats. Why should they not suffer for their wrong doing like other convicted murderers? This position which you have taken, Mr. Howells, must sever you from the loyal friendship of thousands of your readers and admirers.

Life, noting the petition to Oglesby, queried, with questionable intelligence and humor, "Has our Boston friend followed Tolstoi so far as to have become a non-resistant? If so, how long may we expect him to keep personally clean and wear boiled shirts?"

On the other hand, he received a good number of sympathetic letters, including one from Edwin Mead, who had also written to Oglesby, one from Courtlandt Palmer, who reported that Andrew Carnegie had unsuccessfully tried to humiliate him at New York's Nineteenth Century Club for his stand on the trial, and one from Orlando Jay Smith, president of the American Press Association. And the following communications must have given him great pleasure, reminding him of his own response to Curtis during the antislavery crusade. Edmund Noble of the *Boston Herald* wrote that it was "more than gratifying to find the profession of letters, in the person of one of its foremost representatives, faithful to those humanising influences which have given it a true mission among men." Harriet Prescott Spofford, a novelist and poet, stated that, "great as your work is, you never wrote more immortal words than those in behalf of these men, who are dying for free speech." And Karl Marx's daughter, Eleanor Marx Aveling, a noted political thinker in her own right, informed him, later, that "ever since you had the courage to sign the appeal demanding a new trial for the Anarchists, I have known you were not only a true artist & a great writer, but that even rarer thing, a brave & just man."[30]

Howells contemplated a strong reply to the vituperation. He composed several drafts of a long letter, entitled "A Word for the Dead," addressed to the editor of the *Tribune*. To guarantee it a chance at publication, he requested that the managing editor open the envelope in Reid's absence. The letter began:

> I have borne with what patience I must, during the past fortnight, to be called by the *Tribune*, day after day imbecile and bad citizen, with the others who desired mercy for the men killed yesterday at Chicago, in conformity with our still barbarous law. I now ask you to have a little patience with me.

Like the opening, the entire letter is vehement and almost savagely ironic.[31] It reviews the details of the trial and sets in relief the unfair course of "justice" that was followed. It was a trial that realism, with its concern for truth, its humanistic compassion and merciful judgment, could scarcely conceive. State's Attorney Grinnell had shown "gifts of imagination that would perhaps fit him better for the functions of a romantic novelist than for the duties of official advocate in a free commonwealth."

> It was apparently inconceivable to him that it was the civic duty as well as the sacred privilege of such an officer to seek the truth concerning the accused rather than to seek their destruction. He brought into court the blood-curdling banners of the Anarchists, and unfurled them before the eyes of a jury on which eight or nine men had owned themselves prejudicial against Anarchists before the law delivered the lives of these Anarchists into their hands. He appealed to the already heated passions of the jury; he said the seven were no more guilty than a thousand other men in Chicago, but he told them that if they would hang the seven men before them the other nine hundred and ninety-three equally guilty contrivers of bombs would not explode them in the bosom of the impartial jurymen's families and Society would be saved.

Throughout the trial, Grinnell was the "expression of the worst passions of the better classes" that Howells was coming more and more to distrust, of "their fear, their hate, their resentment, which I do not find so much better than the worst passions of the worst classes that I can altogether respect them."

The perversion of law that doomed the anarchists would also have doomed William Lloyd Garrison, Emerson, Parker, Howe, Giddings and Wade, Sumner and Greeley, Wendell Phillips, Thoreau, and "the other literary men whose sympathies influenced Brown to homicidal insurrection at Harper's Ferry." The parallel is potent, but kept in limits: Howells does not go on to spell out for the reader the connections he had made between two kinds of slavery.

The letter to Reid was dated November 12, 1887, placed in an addressed envelope, but most likely never sent. Howells, as with the letters to Curtis and Pryor, hesitated and withdrew. Another person might not have done so, and we can wish Howells had not, but we must acknowledge that he had already done much more than nearly all other prominent figures in the nation had been willing to do. And one must acquiesce to Cady's belief that Howells knew the letter, with its potentially libelous statements on Grinnell and Judge Gary, probably would not be published, and knew that if it were, he would have laid himself open to even fiercer attacks from the press. Although such a letter might give spirit to some other people, there was no tangible object to be gained.[32]

For more than a month after the executions, Howells communicated with several other men about the possibility of publishing, with various commentaries and statements, a record of the trial and the clemency movement, but in the end, possibly owing to discouragement by Harper and Brothers, nothing came of it.[33] The "Studies" that Howells wrote during the crucial months and in the immediate aftermath, however, reveal some of his bitterness. The "Study" for March 1888 carries his strongest statement. Reviewing H. C. Lea's *History of the Inquisition of the Middle Ages*, Howells reflects that the primitive passions that once stirred the cave dweller's heart still animate civilization.

> We need not go far afield for exemplifications; if we cannot find them in our own hearts, we may see them in the lives of our neighbors all round us. . . . The Inquisition flourished up from the roots of greed and hate and fear that take hold on hell in every Protestant and Anglo-Saxon heart to-day as firmly as in the dark ages and the Latin races. Wherever one man hates another for his opinions, there the spirit of the Inquisition is as rife as ever.

Lea's book showed "how natural it was that the faithful should attack the heretics rather than the corruptions, the effects rather than the causes." This is still intolerance's way: "Its highest wisdom is to suppress the symptoms and to destroy the obnoxious theory in the person of the theorist."

For the February "Study" he had seized upon J. E. Cabot's *Memoir of Ralph Waldo Emerson* and discovered much significance in a man he had, personally, little sympathy with. Emerson too had hesitated: "His sympathies perhaps lagged a little. He was not a man who *felt* his way; he had to *see* it; though when once he saw it, lions might be in it, but he went forward" with complete indifference to consequences. He spoke out in those prewar days when "good men thought that their sense of justice was preeminently binding upon their consciences, and brought all laws and decisions that conflicted with this sense into lasting discredit with those whom their teachings schooled." And Emerson, like Howells, had opposed the real anarchy: "The man in whom conscience and intellect were angelically one perceived that the law and order which defied justice and humanity were merely organized anarchy, and that as a good citizen he could have no part in them." Emerson was a humanist, and for him "to be just was to be generous." "In humanity, as in his theories of what literature should be to us, Emerson is still the foremost of all our seers, and will be so a hundred years hence."[34] Here, whether his readers recognized it or not, was Howells's published reply to his critics.

Those critics did not know what they were doing, he implied in a letter written to *Harper's Weekly* on Christmas Day; they did not realize the cruelty of their harsh and ready condemnation of human beings to *death*. The letter, written at the season "when every influence and association reminds us of One who died that mercy might live forever in the wills of men," questioned a proposed substitution of electrocution for hanging. Trying to bring his readers closer to the meaning and experience of death for the condemned, he imagines how under the proposed system the governor might invite distinguished persons to his office and ask some lady, or even a small child, to touch the little "annunciation-button" with which a murderer could be dismissed "with the lightest pressure of the finger." ("Or," he wrote in manuscript, "if an Anarchist it is not perhaps necessary that the criminal should be a murderer.") Should the New York legislature hold out for hanging, however, he had a parallel proposal:

> ...that the executioner should be drawn from society at large, as jurors are, and that no excuse should avail, except the oath of the person drawn that he is conscientiously opposed to capital punishment. This system, which is perfectly practicable, would give, from time to time, men of every profession and station the opportunity to attest their devotion to the great principle that if it is wrong to take life, a second wrong of the kind dresses the balance and makes it right.[35]

Howells recalled, on the day of the execution, that the last time he and Francis Browne had met, "we disagreed about a man named Blaine and a man named Cleveland. How trivial the difference between them seems in this lurid light." The murders would not disappear from the memory, for humanity would now begin to judge the law, and people everywhere would wonder, "What cause is this really, for which men die so gladly, so inexorably? So the evil will grow from violence to violence!" Cartoonist and illustrator F. H. Temple Bellew, in a letter that arrived a few days later, agreed: "I fear these executions are but the bugle note formally announcing war between two classes of society." These were not isolated opinions: Laurence Gronlund had recently announced that most reflective minds agreed that America was on the "brink of an extraordinary change; that a crisis of *some sort*," possibly with "horrors ten-fold worse than those of the French Revolution," was "impending, no matter if it is likely to burst out now or in ten or fifty years from now."[36]

Feeding these fears were newspaper reports of demonstrations with red flags and incendiary slogans on behalf of the anarchists, reports of planned work stoppages and trouble at the jail on November 11, and anxiety-provoking news of the Chicago funeral procession of four thousand participants, with more than twice that number still on the trains coming for the funeral, a procession composed of well-dressed men and women flaunting the symbol of revolution and singing the "Marseillaise" and "Annie Laurie," the song Parsons had sung in his cell the night before his execution.

Whether Howells, Bellew, and Gronlund were correct or not, it was clear that hope for mediation and communication had suffered a serious setback from a savage, paranoid reaction of the American people to an era of financial instability, community breakup, labor violence, increased immigration, and a general sense of loss of control.

VIII

On November 18, Howells wrote his sister Annie that "the last two months have been full of heartache and horror for me, on account of the civic murder committed last Friday... it's all been an atrocious piece of frenzy and cruelty, for which we must stand ashamed forever before history." He could not write about it then but hoped someday "to do justice to these irreparably wronged men." He was busy at the moment with another novel, "which will deal rather with humanity than with love," and which, he thought, would be entitled *The Upper and the Nether Millstone* — its hero a minister "who preaches the life rather than the doctrine of Christ. Have you read," he added relevantly, "Tolstoi's heart-searching books? They're worth all the other novels ever written."

The anarchist experience had joined the example of Tolstoy as another uncomfortable bedfellow in Howells's present mode of living, but they had not quite dislodged the last. The letter to Annie was written from Buffalo, where the Howellses had come because the doctors judged it best they should be away from Winny because her cure "must be moral quite as much as physical," and where they were lodging in a new hotel, the Niagara, "the most exquisite place of the sort that I ever was in." The only objection they had to the Niagara was a "queer one," and he was afraid, he said, suggesting his own doubts, that Annie would not think it sincere: "Elinor and I both no longer care for the world's life, and would like to be settled somewhere very humbly and simply, where we could be socially identified with the principles of progress and sympathy for the struggling mass. I can only excuse our present movement as temporary."[37] Tolstoy had left the world's life, and the hero and heroine of *Annie Kilburn* (the eventual title of his novel) would at least wish to do the same.

He continued to ponder the relation of his work to the social condition. Men could not thank "the novelist who teaches us not to know, but to unknow, our kind...let us make [men] know one another better, that they may be all humbled and strengthened with a sense of their fraternity." No discipline was serious unless it tended somehow to make the race better and kinder. He praised a story by Octave Thanet that might be read "with equal pathos and instruction in these days of labor troubles, when Society is tempted to forget, in the duty of 'saving itself,' that the poor are also Society." He spoke of

> ...the humanity which seems never absent from sincere work — which is indeed as much a part of realism as the truth itself; for it appears that we cannot learn to know others well without learning to pity and account for the defects in them which we must not excuse in ourselves.

He praised Tolstoy's sympathy and rectitude, but for the first time — in the February 1888 "Study" — he wrote that he did not commend Tolstoy as a whole: "The Russian's devotion to the truth is so single that he is apparently unconscious of the existence of limitations."[38] It is possible that Howells had by now begun writing the dinner scene in his new novel and with it had made some decisions about his own frame of reference.

This is not to suggest that Howells was tempering his social thought — quite the contrary. In fact, his ability to downplay Tolstoy may mean that he was feeling his weight as an active liberal, it may mean he had hope that his novel would be a vital contribution to reform, it may mean he was catching a glimpse of some potent possibilities short of Tolstoyism. Economics, he wrote Edmund Clarence Stedman, now seemed very important to him, and it was during the two and a half winter months in Buffalo that he first came into contact with socialism. Hearing Laurence Gronlund lecture one evening at the Fortnightly Club, he was inspired to read his *Cooperative Commonwealth* and would go on to read the *Fabian Essays* and the tracts of William Morris.

He had written his father on January 22 that he was greatly inclined toward socialism, "though as yet the Socialists offer us nothing definite or practical to take hold of. They mostly show us a general theory, with no immediate steps leading to it." A letter to Garland reveals the distance this kind of reading and thinking was carrying him. "You'll easily believe," he wrote, "that I did not bring myself to the point" — his choice of words reflects the struggle it took — "of openly befriending those men who were civically murdered in Chicago for their opinions without thinking and feeling much, and my horizons have been indefinitely widened by the process." He did not agree with Garland that Henry George's single-tax theory represented the first step, because he could not yet look upon confiscation as a good thing. He did favor nationalization of the telegraph system, railways, and mines, a national labor bureau, and other such schemes, which would "insure to every man the food and shelter which the gift of life implies the right to." He did not yet know what was best, but he was "reading and thinking about questions that carry me beyond myself and my miserable literary idolatries of the past; perhaps," he added, "you'll find that I've been writing about them." In the same letter, however, he remarked that a "name" sometimes hindered full use of one's strength. It was hard to break from the mold he had set himself, and he knew that disappointing his readers' expectations might affect his income. Composing this letter at the exquisite new hotel in Buffalo, he wrote that he was "still the slave of selfishness," but was "no longer content to be so . . . that's as far as I can honestly say I've got."

In the April "Study," he reviewed Gronlund's *Cooperative Common-wealth* and *Ça Ira* and Richard T. Ely's tract *Land, Labor, and Taxation*, and the June "Study" carried his review of Edward Bellamy's utopian novel *Looking Backward*, one of the three best books he had read in some time. He noted its immense popularity and marveled at how, "in the sugar-coated form of a dream," it had administered a dose of undiluted socialism that had "been gulped by some of the most vigilant opponents of that theory without a suspicion of the poison they were taking into their systems." However much Bellamy might really believe in his utopian socialism, he was certainly "keenly alive to the defects of our present civilization." In a letter of June 17, 1888, to Howells, Bellamy would write, "What you say about 'nationalist' having occurred to yourself as a good designation for a party aiming at a national control of industry with the resulting social changes, strongly corroborates my belief that the name is a good one and will take," being much superior to "socialist," a label suspect in the United States. The length of his letter, he would conclude somewhat farther on, would show Howells how much he would prize a few hours' talk with him "on the practical aspects of this big business which we have in hand."[39] With more than the potential of a movement afoot and with visions of a third party dancing in their heads, these men were eager to talk, and Bellamy would receive an invitation to visit the Howellses at their summer place at Little Nahant on Massachusetts Bay.

In February, while Winny had stayed on at the sanatorium, the Howellses had moved to New York City, and late in the month, for all the old reasons, but with a wider background of experience and a broader understanding of economic forces, Howells once again had made excursions into the dingier parts of a city: "Foreign faces and tongues everywhere . . . loathsome . . . gutters . . . ash barrels with kitchen offal. . . . The poor have to stand all wrong finally." In his mind he saw a relationship between the squalor of these New York streets and the gas boom he had witnessed (and been tempted to invest in) in Findlay, Ohio, nine months before: *A Hazard of New Fortunes* was germinating. He was also prepared to speak out again. Early in 1888, the Brotherhood of Locomotive Engineers had called a strike against the Chicago, Burlington and Quincy Railroad. When the strikers failed to bring the railroad to the negotiating table and engineers belonging to the Knights of Labor took their jobs, the strike ended on April 4. On April 5, Howells wrote to Mark Twain praising two papers he had written, one attacking industrialism's exploitation of labor:

> It is about the best thing yet said on the subject; but it is strange that you can't get a single newspaper to face the facts of the situation. Here the fools are now all shouting because the Knights of Labor have revenged themselves on the Engineers, and the C. B. & Q. strike is a failure. No one notices how labor has educated itself; no one perceives that *next* time there won't be any revenge or any failure! If ever a public was betrayed by its press, it's ours. No man could safely make himself heard in behalf of the strikers any more than for the anarchists.

Howells was anticipating the possible reaction to an article of his own, to be published in *Harper's Weekly* on April 21. The press, he said there, had told the public that the fault was the employees' and had read many lectures to the engineers for their misbehavior. His own purpose was to give a little lecture to the railroad, which "has, strictly speaking, *no* private affairs. It is a corporation which in return for certain franchises has assumed certain obligations, and before all corporate rights it has these public duties," including the duty of submitting to arbitration so that public commerce and travel will not be impeded. Unions would become so perfectly organized in the future that nothing would defeat them, which raised an essential question: "Shall the railroads fulfil their public obligations by agreement with their employes, or shall the government take possession of them and operate them?" The latter course, if Howells did not entirely advocate it, had some precedent: "The country belongs to the people, and they are not going to let it be ruined. Their possession of the railroads would involve much trouble and anxiety, but the Railroad Receiver, who is an agent of theirs, is not unknown, and his management of roads is good; so that the public may take heart of hope, if the worst ever comes to the worst."

This was defiance of the newspapers, and yet, as Howells himself well realized, his own motivation was mixed. This he admitted in his opening sentence: "With grief that I think must be shared by a good many other holders of Chicago, Burlington, & Quincy stock, I saw that stock go down from 129 to 112 under the effect of the private war waged between the railroad and its engineers and switchmen." "When the strike began," he added further on, "I suppose that nearly every humane person said to himself, 'Well, between men who want to make a better living and a corporation that wants to make more money I can have no choice.' I said something like this myself, not remembering my C. B. & Q. stock in my magnanimity." He was writing "in quality of timid capitalist" and wished his readers to know that he had "no particular affection for the Brotherhood of Engineers," which in the past had shown itself shortsighted and selfish.

These statements show a cautious awareness of his audience and publishers and can be read to some extent as a humorous attempt to disarm them by seeming to be by one of their number. If there is no agony here, there is an uncomfortable consciousness of the tension between his different sympathies, which might be thought significant in the writer approaching the final stages of *Annie Kilburn*. Although he was writing with much less antipathy for strikers than had appeared in his 1884 review of Hay's *The Bread-Winners*[40] and with more extensive and committed arguments in their behalf, in some respects his position had not changed.

IX

Although the reports from the Dansville sanatorium had often been encouraging during the winter, by March 25 Howells had to acknowledge that Winny "seems to be much the same," and he and Elinor determined to bring their "sad problem" home, where they could care for her themselves. In her first two weeks at home she did "very poorly," suffering "a good deal of pain always after eating; but her mind exaggerates all her experiences." Her new doctor seemed to have made a good beginning with her, and they were hoping now — they were forever grasping at these straws — for "good results." In early May she was "much the same" and her case was one "requiring all our patience." The family stayed on in New York through most of May to give her new treatment a chance.[41]

In early June the Howellses took a "wide-verandahed villa in forty acres of seclusion" at Little Nahant, where they hoped the sea air and quiet would have a curative effect upon Winny. Hamlin Garland came to visit during the summer and spent with Howells

. . . several hours lying on the sunny slope of a hill which fronted the sea, dreaming out an ideal world in which poverty would be unknown. He said to me that day many of the things which he afterward recorded in "The Traveller from Altruria." I remember wondering at the moment how poverty and sickness and crime could exist in a world so beautiful as that upon which we looked, as the dusk began to fall, and the lamps burst into bloom along the beach across the bay, and yet at the moment the illness of his eldest daughter was filling his heart with almost intolerable anxiety.

The same day, "in the shaded, exquisitely cool and odorous dining room," Garland met Winny, a "frail and lovely girl." When he left, Howells walked with him a short way and confided his fears. "'I must take her to a specialist,' he said." In mid-June, Winny was "getting slowly, very slowly better; she now sometimes eats without being forced to do so." On the last day of the month there was "a very decided change for the better . . . she was up most of the time, and out on the hay for an hour." July 8, she was out driving for an hour and a half: "We have got her to eating fairly well, but she's still addicted to keeping indoors, and this we have to fight." She had been allowed to form every bad habit of invalidism at the sanatorium, and the Howellses were having "to break them up by force." In a letter refusing an invitation, Howells explained that his time was taken up in "trying what the most constant devotion can do" for Winny and that it was a "terrible drain."

In retrospect, Howells told more of the sorrow, Winny's and theirs, that they were going through that summer. It was then that, "faltering down to the Valley of the Shadow, in such pain and despair as we never realized, she wrote these broken lines":

> She had been used to write these rhymes like this;
> First from description, Nature in her eyes;
> Then part she felt when she had writ of Nature,
> Commenting on her own. . . .
> Then pondering rhymed she of her introspection,
> Till like a spider lost in her own web,
> She suddenly stopped, and ceased to rhyme at all.

Her last distinct pleasure in life, he recalled, was in the music Frank Boott had written for her "The Wind Exultant."

> She was already very sick when it first came to her; but it gave her life, and she rose from her bed and played it over. She liked people to know of it, and in her last, sad summer, when our love was tormenting her with its futile endeavors to keep her interested in the things of this world and so strengthen her hold upon an existence that was a mere dream of pain to her, this song was one of her greatest joys. I can see now how she drifted to the piano one day with the sheet in her hand, a frail, weak phantom of her beautiful youth, and feebly struck the keys. She faded away from the instrument before she had played her song half through, and let the sea-wind come in and blow the leaves to the floor unheeded.[42]

Painfully involved in this personal sorrow, Howells also told Garland during their talk on the hill that he had been "deeply moved by Bellamy's eloquent pages," and he entered into a "sadly accusing description" of those empty Back Bay mansions and packed, sweltering South End tenements: "This was a subject on which he felt deeply and to which he returned again and again in the years which followed. He could not reconcile himself to the waste of the idler and the hunger of the poor." Garland found Howells "passionately alive" to Tolstoy and other authors voicing the "'noble discontent' of the time." Howells was then, in Garland's opinion, "doing his part in the task of quickening the social conscience of his neighbors" by including in the "Study" "criticism and comment of the most vital and stimulating sort. With all the power of his pen he emphasized the value of Americanism in fiction and the unrighteousness of the current exploitation of labor."

It was at Little Nahant that Howells completed the novel whose title was meant to call to mind *Anna Karenina*, the novel he had been working at since his reading of Tolstoy had opened new questions about his own life, the novel that was so far "the most difficult of all my stories," as he confided to his father in early July. It was a novel he found in 1913, upon rereading it, a "grim story," and which, Henry Van Dyke speculated, "had such a place in his affection that he sent it to me with his own portrait, as if to say, 'Here I am, and thus I believe.'" The final installment was in Alden's hands by early August.[43]

X

When the citizens of Hatboro', Massachusetts, write to Annie Kilburn in Rome, asking her aid in procuring something fit and economical in the way of a Civil War monument, "she overruled their simple notion of an American volunteer at rest...as intolerably hackneyed and common-place," deciding instead to give them something "ideal." The result is a "winged Victory, poising on the summit of a white marble shaft, and clasping its hands under its chin, in expression of the grief that mingled with the popular exultation." As Mr. Bolton drives her home from the station after her eleven years' absence from Hatboro', her eyes come to rest on the Victory, and she prays, "Oh, may I be very humble; may I be helped to be very humble!"

Annie is returning home a rebel against the comfortable life she had shared with her late father, and is returning to Hatboro' because she believes she will know how to do good to the unfortunate and underprivileged there. Mr. Bolton rambles on about Mr. Peck, the liberal chosen to replace the deceased minister of the Orthodox church, while Annie follows her own train of thought, imagining her offer to replace the Victory with a Volunteer. She "instantaneously closed her transaction with the committee, removed the Victory, and had the Volunteer unveiled with appropriate ceremonies, opened with prayer by the Rev. Mr. Peck." She emerges from her reverie to ask Bolton to repeat Mr. Peck's name, and in disliking the name she allows her mind momentarily to leave the monument, whereupon the Victory seizes the opportunity to recapture its place. This identification of Mr. Peck with the commonplace Volunteer — the real spirit behind the Civil War — in opposition to the suspect Victory and Annie's uncertain attitude toward Volunteer, Victory, and Peck sets the tone at the opening of the novel.[44]

Annie's problem is precisely how to go about doing good. From her parlor window on the right side of the tracks, everyone going by seems occupied, self-sufficient, and prosperous, and she shrinks from a more thorough investigation of Hatboro'. "She found she had fancied necessity coming to her and taking away her good works, as it were, in a basket." Howells's practice of exposing the egoism that separates people is here more economically oriented than ever before. Annie, with her "obtuseness about those she fancied below her which is one of the consequences of being brought up in a superior station," tries to be gay about shaking hands with a grocer, wondering "if this were meeting the lower classes on common ground," and forces herself to face the unpleasant misery of the tramps when they come to beg for food.[45]

The America of *Annie Kilburn* is only now and then the America of "smiling aspects." That all Americans of conscience abroad feel a duty to come home and do something for their country "is the impulse of no common patriotism; it is perhaps a sense of the opportunity which America supremely affords for the race to help itself, and for each member of it to help all the rest." This is the America of possibility, but the America of actuality is grim, and Howells in so describing it reflects all his disturbing experience of the preceding few years. Going about among the middle and upper classes of Hatboro', Annie discovers "what must always astonish the inquirer below the pretentious surface of our democracy — an indifference and an incredulity concerning the feelings of people of lower station which could not be surpassed in another civilization." She learns the lesson taught in Lea's book on the Inquisition, "that she was a moral Cave-Dweller, and that she was living in a Stone Age of social brutalities." At Mr. Wilmington's hosiery mill an inner door swings ajar, and Annie hears a "roar mingled of the hum and whirl and clash of machinery and fragments of voice, borne to them on a whiff of warm, greasy air." As Howells must have done at Lowell, she finds her mind wandering to the men and women operating the machinery, "who seemed no more a voluntary part of it than all the rest, except when Jack Wilmington curtly ordered them to do this or that in illustration of some point he was explaining."

This was an America in which "the conditions are all wrong," an America where the newspapers opposed the workingman, where manufacturing trusts could combine to deprive workingmen with impunity but labor unions were defeated in the courts, where employers could pay unfair wages, demand unfair hours, and refuse to submit to arbitration. And the author who had cried out mockingly to Evolution and Political Economy to save us from having to become true brothers to our fellow men allows sharp-tongued Ralph Putney to uncover the corrupt use of both theories.[46]

Annie, in her Howellsian desire to make contact and get on common ground with the lower classes, is confronted with another, if somewhat new, Howellsian figure, the Tolstoyan minister Mr. Peck. While some

Tolstoyan lessons are gleaned by Annie from other sources, it is Peck who most consistently and potently challenges her preconceptions and principles. He tells her, for instance, that he will not participate in the theatricals if the South Hatborians plan to follow them with an exclusive supper and dance. Money given in charity, he argues, is a palliative, but it cannot bring love between rich and poor, "because sympathy — common feeling — the sense of fraternity — can spring only from like experiences, like hopes, like fears. And money cannot buy these." To attain to such sympathy, a rich man would have to make a sacrifice he would really feel. He would have to give all he has and follow Christ; and Peck in his sermons, like Tolstoy in his tracts, stands for the practical life of Christ in this world.[47]

Peck's challenge is not limited to Annie, and his influence is like that of David Sewell in *The Minister's Charge*. According to Putney, Peck refuses to make one feel comfortable, and, like Sewell, "he has a sneaking style of being no better than you are, and of being rather stumped by some of the truths he finds out." One of his sermons, at least, Putney knew, "was a private conversation that he was publicly holding with me." Peck is even a kind of realist: He refuses to project his own personality into his sermons or conversations. While perhaps feeling intensely, he dispassionately presents the truth and in so doing puts others "in a fever," making them see "the stupidity and cruelty of things that always seemed right and proper before."[48] Peck, in his provocative statements and in his challenging stand, clearly represents Howells's effort to make words a kind of deed, to make his fiction reverberate in the behavior of his readers, and this is a main thrust of the novel.

It is possible, as juxtapositions at the beginning of the novel suggest, that Howells, with his Tolstoyan sympathies and after a recent reading of *Que Faire?* at the time he began work on *Annie Kilburn*, was intending a marriage between his heroine and the minister, who would go off to live and work among the factory hands at Fall River. It is possible, also, that this was his intention up until the time he wrote his sister about his and Elinor's own wish to leave the worldly life. However, at some point a change of mind occurred, possibly at the time he first wrote of Tolstoy's limitations, at the end of 1887. It may be that he discovered better solutions, that he thought his art could be a sufficient and effective effort. It may also be that in his identification with Annie he recognized his own inability to make such a move. At any rate, Annie and one other guest have been invited to dinner by the Putneys: "We expected Brother Peck here this evening," Ralph tells Dr. Morrell; "you're our sober second thought."

During dinner, Ralph tells of meeting in Boston one of the deacons of Peck's last parish, and Howells, whether he knew it at this point in the writing or not, foreshadows his novel's dire conclusion. "The way Brother Peck behaved toward the needy in that last parish of his," Ralph reports, "made it simply uninhabitable to the standard Christian. They had to get rid of him somehow — send him away or kill him." During the ensuing conversation, Howells's own ambivalent feelings toward Tolstoy emerge. The irascible, middle-class, nouveau-riche department store owner Billy Gerrish, says Ralph, thinks that Peck walks too much with the poor, that the pew owners in his church have some rights to his company. Dr. Morrell asks whether there is not something to be said on that side.

> "Oh yes, a good deal. There's always something to say on both sides, even when one's a wrong side. That's what makes it all so tire-some — makes you wish you were dead." He looked up, and caught his boy's eye fixed with melancholy intensity upon him. "I hope you'll never look at both sides when you grow up, Win. It's mighty uncomfortable. You take the right side, and stick to that."

Peck's old suit of clothes, his neglect of his daughter, his coldness and seeming lack of emotion are also brought up for discussion. These sides of Peck were evident earlier, but they are here stressed by his sympathizers at the moment his substitute in the marriage scheme has been fully intro-duced.[49]

Dr. Morrell, whose "amused voice" is the first aspect of him intro-duced, is, unfortunately for this novel, the Howellsian humorist, the droll man who deflates pretentions in others. He is not a simple man, is often sincere and serious, but his function is to diminish and alleviate, by tak-ing them lightly, both Annie's emotional concern with social conditions and her efforts to do something about them. If this helps Howells to back off from the Tolstoyan character about whom he now has reservations, it also undercuts some of the force of the novel. The effect for readers who take Annie's concerns seriously is annoyance, and Mabie's comment on Howellsian humor cited in Chapter 2 is especially telling here: "When-ever the reader begins to warm a little, a slight turn of satire, a cool phrase or two of analysis, a faint suggestion that the writer doubts whether it is worth while, clears the air again." That Howells himself felt some of the reader's annoyance is evident from his allowing Annie to express it, and he does not hesitate to undercut Dr. Morrell's arguments against the theories of Peck.[50] In the end, however, it is Dr. Morrell, the man who smiles at Annie's concerns and belittles their importance, and not Mr. Peck, whom Annie is to marry.

In a frustrated and probably guilt-ridden reply to Hamlin Garland's letter wishing a stronger statement than he thought *Annie Kilburn* gave, Howells, although he knew it was far from the total message of the novel, told him to read Mr. Peck's sermon: "It could hardly have been expected that he should preach the single tax, but short of that, what more could you have?" Once again Howells uses a sermon as a realistic means of preaching the social theories and lessons at which he himself has arrived. A frightening conflict between labor and capital is developing in America; yet Peck can see some good in both the unions and the monopolies, which he, like Gronlund and Bellamy, believes will spell the end of competition. The sermon builds to an indictment of economic injustice in the United States. Peck pleads against the sort of social and legal justice that hanged the anarchists and for a real, compassionate justice toward the underprivileged. He appeals for recognition of the forces making for fraternity in his country and asks each member of the congregation to examine his own impulses and motivations and his own relation to the destitution of others. Howells is right; it is strong, and it is no wonder that before the sermon is finished, Billy Gerrish rises noisily, stomps out of the church with his family, and sets in motion the denouement of the novel.[51]

When Putney, at the church-society meeting that follows, forces the issue to a question of approval or disapproval of the practical Christianity preached by Peck, the church society votes unanimously in favor of Peck. Peck, however, who had made no pulpit address in his defense, now announces his intention to resign from his work in the Hatboro' church for reasons he will "give at length should I be spared to preach in this place next Sabbath."[52] Peck's next sermon, then, was to be a justification of his Tolstoyan decision to leave his elevated position in order to live and work among the poor, and such a sermon would have to carry Howells farther than any previous fictional statement.

Peck is leaving for Fall River to teach in a public school there, or, if it is necessary to establishing rapport with the workers, to work in a mill. His decision is an implicit challenge to Annie, and as we know, to Howells, and his words reflect the dark converse to Howells's hope for the written word, especially as he was utilizing it in this book:

> I am less and less confident that I have become anything useful to others in turning aside from the life of toil and presuming to attempt the guidance of those who remained in it.... I have done with preaching for the present. Later I may have something to say. Now I feel sure of nothing, not even of what I've been saying here.

Annie, wishing to keep Peck's daughter, who has been staying with her, volunteers to give her money away and live and work in the cooperative house Peck is planning to set up with Mr. and Mrs. Savor. Peck's reply is kindly, knowing, and sorrowful: "I know you cannot do it. Even for me it is hard to go back to those associations, and for you they would be impossible.... You might come, but you couldn't stay. You don't know what it is; you can't imagine it, and you couldn't bear it." Annie, however, even when she realizes her mistake, continues to plan to go.

   On Saturday evening Peck returns from Fall River to preach his final sermon in Hatboro'. As he crosses the track from his train to the station, he is caught by an onrushing express and fatally injured. Annie is released from her pledge to follow Peck to the factory town; Howells is released from the necessity of preaching the ultimate Tolstoyan sermon. He has also vividly demonstrated just how far he will go with the Russian master — vividly, because it is the railroad in which he has stock and against which he had protested in his April article. Peck's manner of death thus indicates the fear and self-interest mingled in Howells's choice to do away with him. Howells is expressing a wish to be released from the necessity of coming to a decision. Peck, he says,

> ... had not lived to offer that full exposition of his theory and justification of his purpose which he had been expected to give on the Sunday after he was killed; and his death was in no wise exegetic. It said no more to his people than it had said to Annie; it was a mere casualty; and his past life, broken and unfulfilled, with only its intimations and intentions of performance, alone remained.[53]

To kill off Peck and to choose Morrell were to choose the status quo. The very ground chosen for the story, a rural community, and the restriction of point of view to that of Annie and people mainly of her social and economic level reveal that Howells did not want or was unable to commit himself further. It was to this limitation, probably, that Garland was reacting.

Of course, it would be wrong to stop there. For one thing, Ralph Putney — scion of the old responsible, elite, aristocratic Putney stock — for all his weakness, is outspoken in his criticism and defends striking and boycotting laborers in court. One might lose some faith in a Curtis or Whittier, but the New England tradition, the antebellum idealism, if crippled and diminished, was still potent — perhaps, Howells might be suggesting, through its critical spirit infused into his own novels.

Again, the novel does not end with the death of Peck but goes on to consider the results of Annie's experience with him. She has gained a mature perspective on her past attempts to do good and sees her failure, frustration, and folly as limited in importance and even good in their "effect of humbling her to patience with all imperfection and shortcoming, even her own." She can see that her elitist propensities are not necessarily evil but can even be made to produce good when "mixed and interwoven" with her better inclinations. When the money from the theatricals is entrusted to her by the departing South Hatborians, she is not even tempted by their suggestion that it be used to garnish the setting of the Victory monument but resolves to put it to use in the contemporary American battle. When Dr. Morrell suggests that she use the money for a cooperative boardinghouse like the one Peck intended to start in Fall River, she balks at first, and because of Peck's teachings, she refuses to meet working people "in the odious character of a patron." She knows she has no desire to join in "scullionwork" and knows she hasn't the need "to forego my comforts and luxuries in a make-believe that I haven't them."

A compromise is possible, however. In the cooperative housing project that does evolve, Annie is "as cordially welcomed to the charge of its funds and accounts as if she had been a hat-shop hand or a shoe-binder," and she learns of the mutual kindness possible when people of different backgrounds share an interest. The cooperative, then, known as the Peck Social Union, is a viable middle ground between the falsely conceived South Hatborian Social Union and the kind of ultimate step that Peck thought necessary. While not a brilliant success, Howells reports, it is by no means a failure: "The people of Hatboro' are rather proud of it, and strangers visit it as one of the possible solutions of one of the social problems." Ralph Putney compares its survival to his own and "argues that if they can only last long enough they will finally be established in a virtue and prosperity as great as those of Mr. Gerrish and his store."

This does not mean that Annie is finally certain of where she stands. She is uncomfortable taking work from someone who needs it and accepting a small salary that only adds unnecessarily to her wealth. She knows she cannot give the pay to another, because that would pauperize and degrade him. And so, Howells concludes, "she dwells in a vicious circle, and waits, and mostly forgets, and is mostly happy." The happiness, however, is neither shallow nor static, for although in the end Annie outwardly maintains her former life, her life "was inwardly all changed" through her confrontation with Peck and his ideas. Howells in the Hotel Niagara, similarly, had no longer cared "for the world's life." Annie recognizes her likeness to Dr. Morrell, who admits the force of her reasons but is "content to rest in a comfortable inconclusion as to his conduct" and realizes that her only difference from him lies "in the openness with which she proclaimed her opinions."[54]

Howells has once more struggled with the problems of establishing contact between classes, and the treatment of his heroine indicates that under greater stress than before, he has reaffirmed that his point of view must necessarily remain that of his David Sewells. That Peck's social and economic thought has profoundly changed Annie's inner life, and that she, unlike Dr. Morrell, is not content to keep her opinions to herself, represents an advocation of conscientious effort within one's own limitations. There is pressure too to escape such limitations, for neither Annie nor her creator are content with their mere verbal affirmation of Christian social ethics. Howells wrote to Hale on August 30, 1888, that if he will read *Annie Kilburn* "to the end you'll see that I solve nothing, except what was solved eighteen centuries ago. The most that I can do is perhaps to set a few people thinking; for as yet I haven't got to *doing* anything myself." But so far as the kind of appeal Sewell and Peck made from their pulpits is concerned, the kind of appeal he wished to make from his books to the individual consciences of his readers, Howells would have been pleased to read Norton's remark to Curtis on *Annie Kilburn*: "There is more power in the book than in anything he has done before. A reader must either be very good or very unfeeling who is not made better by reading it."[55]

If there is a lack of final, forceful conviction in the book, still the very act of writing such a book, Howells's willingness to state his opinions openly, his attack upon American evils, his effort to stress social union as one solution to them, and his honesty, through the study of Annie and Mr. Peck, about the human struggle for a way to be better and to make others better are at the very heart of a book that is not a brilliant success.

The emphasis throughout the novel on Peck's lack of care for his daughter amidst all his care for others is puzzling. Although Howells has literary precedents, neglect of one's responsibilities does not seem a necessary adjunct to philanthropy, and it seems an unfair stacking of the cards against Peck. However, when in the end Annie is given possession of the child, retains possession of her own money and position, and is about to marry a kindly, talented, and capable doctor, who had advised her to request the child from Peck earlier and who had argued strenuously against her following Peck to Fall River, Howells's personal stock in so contriving the novel suddenly becomes evident. On October 10, he wrote to Henry James from Little Nahant:

> I'm not in a very good humor with "America" myself . . . I should hardly like to trust pen and ink with all the audacity of my social ideas; but after fifty years of optimistic content with "civilization" and its ability to come out all right in the end, I now abhor it, and feel that it is coming out all wrong in the end, unless it bases itself anew on a real equality. Meantime, I wear a fur-lined overcoat, and live in all the luxury my money can buy.

And yet, he added, "this non-ended summer it bought us the use of a wide-verandahed villa in forty acres of seclusion where poor Winny might get a little better possibly." Given the terrible strain of Winny's situation, Howells could come to no other conclusion, and, clearly, to follow Tolstoy would be to deprive his daughter of proper medical attention at a crucial time.[56] Dr. Morrell is a close friend of the parents of crippled little Winthrop (read, Winny?) Putney, and Putney's activity suggests that as compromised as he might sometimes feel, there were valid forms of commitment short of Tolstoyism.

Howells was unable to follow Tolstoy into the life of a common laborer, through some combination of simple common sense, inability to break from firmly structured habits and conditions, attachment to luxury and comfort, and commitment to the physical well-being of his family. But he was eminently prepared to speak out on behalf of anarchists denied common justice and to castigate the American social and economic structure through his criticism and fiction. Because of this position, he found it easier to identify with another novelist whose "success as a humanist," like Tolstoy's, "is without flaw," as he wrote of Zola after his death and several years after the Dreyfus affair:

> ...the ethics of his work, like Tolstoy's, were always carrying over into his life. He did not try to live in poverty and privation and hard labor, as Tolstoy does; he surrounded himself with the graces and the luxuries which his honestly earned money enabled him to buy; but when an act of public and official atrocity disturbed the working of his mind and revolted his nature, he could not rest again till he had done his best to right it.[57]

Howells's choice of a title heroine with the initials and first name of the title heroine of Tolstoy's *Anna Karenina* may have been intended (although no one appears to have noticed it) to call attention to the Tolstoyan principles his novel would propagate. It may also have been intended, with all the differences between the two novels, to suggest that both an American novel and the social outlook and behavior of a nineteenth-century American novelist would of necessity differ from their Russian counterparts.

4

The Mission of
the Novelist and
A Hazard of
New Fortunes

Is that not also an American habit — that quaint blending of private conformity and public protest? The American atmosphere of
prosperity has made even fairly high-minded people desperately
afraid of the loss of public repute, of position, of money. No one
has the courage to be poor; no one dares to be an outcast. Yet a
handful of flaming, voluntary outcasts might serve as a sterner
monition to the young whom alone one could hope to affect than
tons of liberal and radical printed matter.

— LUDWIG LEWISOHN[1]

I belong to the generation whose youth was profoundly influenced by Mr. Howell's [*sic*] books. They not only gave us keen
pleasure as works of literature, but they helped us towards a spirit
of kindliness and justice in dealing with our fellows, and they
stirred our souls to the strife for national ideals.

—THEODORE ROOSEVELT, 1917[2]

I

Annie Kilburn, like Howells's previous novels, no more than touched on
the lives and conditions of the poor and underprivileged. "One might have
expected," wrote Robert Underwood Johnson,

that the man who pleaded for the lives of the Chicago anarchists
would have done more in fiction to present the claims of the workingmen and the proletariat. The fact of it is, perhaps, that his sympathy came from the kindness of his heart and from his conclusions
in his study, rather than from close contact with the laboring classes
in their everyday life. He was not a slumming novelist.

This more than half truth has been a frequent charge against Howells. Because of it, he has seemed to compare poorly with later writers if not with his contemporaries of the 1880s. In 1900, he told Theodore Dreiser, then well into the writing of *Sister Carrie*, that the struggle in the cities was growing more bitter, with millions crowding into regions of bare subsistence, where they sometimes died of starvation. Dreiser remarked, "You have had no direct experience of this great misery." Howells's reply did not really bridge the gap between their backgrounds: "No, but I have observed it. All my experiences have been literary, yet in this field I have seen enough."[3]

In the looser sense of the term, Howells was, of course, now and then a slumming novelist. But, as we have seen, when he did venture into lower-class purlieus, he did so as a very self-conscious outsider, a man of culture, an investor in railroads, a middle-aged man with family responsibilities seeking means for a fresh start, a man who wished to avoid the unpleasant and painful. And this man's point of view controls the fiction. The realist, he believed, could not tell the truth about the poor unless he somehow shared their lives, and, like Annie Kilburn, he could not bring himself to do so.

Making it increasingly difficult was the fact that he was not getting any younger. Asked by Senator Ingalls several months before his fiftieth birthday in 1887 why he did not come to Washington and write the great American novel, he replied, "I am too old now...I could not stand the going into society to catch the spirit of things. There will come a young man who will yet write it." Looking ahead to the same birthday, he wrote Henry James that he had heard people say they were not conscious of growing older: "But I am. I'm perfectly aware of the shrinking bounds. I don't plan so largely as I used, and without having lost hope I don't have so much use for it as once. I feel my half century fully. Lord, how it's skipped away!" This was not a new note — in 1885 and 1886 he had worried about being written out — but one that had alternated and would continue to alternate with more buoyant statements of energy and enthusiasm for new material. He would, indeed, go on in 1888 and 1889 to attempt a great novel centering in an American city relatively new to him. In doing so, however, he would feel the restrictions imposed by his age,[4] his central figure would be a middle-aged man, and his book would suffer from the same limitations in its treatment of poverty as his previous novels.

In October 1888, Howells was not a terribly self-satisfied or happy man. We have already glanced at his letter of October 10 telling James of the audacity of his social ideas but acknowledging that he himself continued to wear a fur-lined overcoat "and live in all the luxury my money can buy." This recognition of his material needs reinforced a wish for peaceful, orderly evolution. He wrote Edward Everett Hale the same day that Hale was right in teaching patience with social wrongs "that must be borne, with all the possible alleviations, till they can be very gradually changed. I do not think there is any fixed hope of justice under them," he added, "but then I know from myself — my own prejudices, passions, follies — that they cannot be bettered except through the unselfishness you enjoin, the immediate altruism dealing with what now is."

This sort of solution suited Howells's humanistic goals, but he knew it was not enough. Reviewing Alice Rollins's *Uncle Tom's Tenement*, he thought the abuses, extortions, abominations, and indecencies she described were undeniably sickening, atrocious, and unspeakable. He took issue, however, with her somewhat Howellsian solution that the landlords should have more conscience. It was the entire American economic system that was at fault:

> Is there any hope of permanent cure while the conditions invite one human creature to exploit another's necessity for his profit, or a bad man, under the same laws, may at any moment undo the work of a good one? This is the poignant question which the book seems to leave unanswered. It is so poignant that we are fain to turn from it to more strictly literary interests again, and try to forget it.

This final twist turned outward toward his readers, but it also turned inward, for it was written by the man who slew Mr. Peck, the man who wrote Hale at the end of August that he had not "got to *doing* anything" himself, the man whose rather autobiographical central figure in *A Hazard of New Fortunes* would remark to his wife that the person searching the garbage represented "things possible everywhere in our conditions," and then reply to her assertion that "we must change the conditions" by saying with some ironical self-awareness, "Oh no; we must go to the theatre and forget them."

Although he had determined that he could not follow him into poverty, he still felt the potent and troubling influence of Tolstoy's testimony "against the system by which a few men win wealth and miserably waste it in idleness and luxury, and the vast mass of men are overworked and underfed." As he wrote to Hale in October, he knew that the best in men "cannot come out till they all have a fair chance," and he no longer believed that America gave that chance. And accordingly, he now wondered whether his fiction could have any effect either in bringing out the best in people or in changing the underlying conditions:

> I am neither an example nor an incentive, meanwhile, in my own way of living; I am a creature of the past; only I do believe that I see the light of the future, and that it is this which shows me my ugliness and fatuity and feebleness. — Words, words, words! How to make them things, deeds, — you have the secret of that; with me they only breed more words. At present they are running into another novel, in which I'm going to deal with some mere actualities; but on new ground — New York, namely...[5]

By October 12, the Howellses had negotiated their way into a two-story flat at 330 East Seventeenth Street in New York, where they would spend the winter. In a letter to his father, Howells explained that they were difficult to suit because Winny's need for a nurse meant a large house. They were well into the "sad story of her last year." Back from a September trip to Ohio, Howells had consulted with two New York doctors but remained unsure what to do. Winny, he wrote to his sister on October 12, was holding her own, "but it's very little to hold, poor girl." Family life had become a life of harassing worry. Added to Winny's illness and the continuous presence of the nurse was the extreme fatigue of Elinor, resulting from the care of Winny and her own low health. A large house would be expensive, and, Howells wearily reflected in a letter to his father:

> It's wearing, sickening business; and I watch my money flow as a stuck pig its life-stream. It's horrible to me to spend so much, but I seem bound to it hand and foot. How I envy your simple, quiet, righteous life! Some day I should like to write the tragedy of a man trying to escape from his circumstances. It would be funny.[6]

II

If his religious experiences at 302 Beacon Street, his confrontation with Tolstoy's life and work, and his further disillusionment with America on account of the anarchist affair did not make Howells an authentic slumming novelist, still it could not be said of him, as James said of Zola after the Dreyfus affair, that they came too late to have an effect on his creative intelligence. His fiction had become increasingly concerned with the inequities in the economic and social system and the human culpability for them. It would seem, then, that if he wished to do so, he could argue that he was indeed doing something to rectify American conditions. But the October letter to Hale shows characteristic honesty and doubt over the value of his words. For the November "Study" he wrote that "there is no very deep, no very wide, interest in even the greatest of authors" and that writers should recognize the truth of this matter "concerning which it is easy and sweet to gammon ourselves." Readers are not entirely to blame for this, for only rarely has literature "come home to their business and bosoms." Usually, instead, it is an "amusement, a distraction, a decoration, taken up for a moment, an hour, a day, and then wholly dropped out of sight, out of mind, out of life." And yet, Howells laments,

> . . . it sometimes seems as if it ought to be unlike the other arts, since if it would it could speak so frankly, so brotherly, so helpfully to the mass of men. Heaven knows how it gets bewitched between the warm thought in the brain, the heart, and the cold word on the page; but some evil spell seems to befall it and annul it, to make it merely appreciable to the taste, the aesthetic pride, the intellectuality, of the reader.

Such doubt was excruciating because the implications of Mr. Peck's destruction placed Howells in a position where he needed to believe that the written word was an effective instrument for reform. This need began to affect his critical work, and the "Editor's Study" in late 1888 and thereafter became increasingly outspoken about American conditions and about the social role of the American realist. A single example will suffice. Howells wrote in the December "Study" that in the 1880s a new

Christmas literature was appearing, different from the old soothing literature of coal and turkeys for the poor. It did not mock gifts and alms but warned that they are merely provisional and that the "practice of charity in this form is not inconsistent with the hardest selfishness." This literature

> ...appeals to no sentimental impulse, but confronts its readers with themselves, and with the problems which it grows less and less easy to shirk. Turkeys to the turkeyless...yes, these are well, and very well; but ineffably better it is to take thought somehow in our social, our political, system to prevent some future year, decade, century, the destitution which we now relieve.

All good literature, now, is Christmas literature, "and the best art... tends to be art for humanity's sake." Art is now learning that it must perish if "it does not make friends with Need.... It perceives that to take itself from the many and leave them no joy in their work, and to give itself to the few whom it can bring no joy in their idleness, is an error that kills." Such literature is represented not only by modern masterworks, but by "all expressions, the crudest and hastiest, which have tended at any time during the year to make one think less of one's self and more of others." This includes articles dealing with the treatment of women servants in hotels, the hardships of sewing-girls in Chicago, and the lives of miners in the Pennsylvania coal pits. Let us think of these things, Howells pleads in conclusion:

> Let us light the pretty tapers, and as many of them as possible, and let us do all the good deeds we can; but let us not forget the lesson of the new Christmas literature; let us realize that they are merely palliative, and that infinitely deeper than their soothing can reach festers the plague that luxury and poverty, that waste and want, have bred together in the life-blood of society. Let us remember this, and take thought for its healing.[7]

When he wrote this last "Study," *A Hazard of New Fortunes* was well under way — he would have 500 manuscript pages (the equivalent of about 140 book pages) done by December 23. Needless to say, he was determined that more than ever, his fiction would be the kind of Christmas literature he was describing in the "Study," the kind of literature that challenged the lives of those readers who, like himself, had a tendency to rest contented, or at least rest, in their comfortable lives and forget the problems of their society. Hale, when he read the completed novel, recalled this determination:

> The Hazard of New Fortunes is more than masterly. It is good. It is good in all ways — chiefly because it will make people better. It will make them think and it will make them think right. In other words it is going to do — what before you began it, you swore by the Living God it should do.

Howells's intention might also be read in his assertion in the December "Study" that "the literature that shows human nature as human wilfulness and error have made it is fulfilling a 'mission' to men's souls, in spite of all theories and professions to the contrary."[8]

III

Because of his frequent moves, Howells had no place where he was eligible to vote in 1888, and accordingly, he sat out the November elections. The previous April, when he was protesting the position of the railroads in the C. B. & Q. strike, he wrote to Perry that "if there were a labor party, embodying any practical ideas I would vote with it." In July he told his father he expected to vote the Republican ticket, although he might not, should candidates appear who embodied his hopes of "nationalizing the industries, resources and distributions of the country."[9] With the key issue between Cleveland and Harrison the tariff, an issue only indirectly concerned with the problems of labor and poverty, he was not likely to have cared much about the outcome. His letters, in fact, show relatively little interest in either the campaign or the result. His political leanings led him to endorse certain socialist ideas and led him, for instance, on December 1, to the organizational meeting of Boston's first Nationalist Club, which with other such clubs throughout the country, had evolved from the great popularity of Bellamy's *Looking Backward.*

On November 3, Howells sent a short note to Victor Yarrows, declining an invitation to speak at the November 11 memorial meeting for the anarchists. The *New York Tribune* the next day described Howells's letter, read at the meeting, as a "letter of sympathy." Henry Mills Alden of Harper and Brothers found this a serious matter, and he arranged to have printed in *Harper's Weekly*, as it had already been printed in the *Boston Transcript*, the actual letter written by Howells, which was clearly only a polite refusal. But some damage had been done, for it was probably the *Tribune*'s linking of him with the anarchists that touched off in a newspaper two articles on Howells's "socialism," one of which identified his petition on behalf of the anarchists as an example of "sentimentalism." On November 23, Howells penned a reply, another unsent letter, as strong and bitter as his "Word for the Dead." He wondered whether men like Henry Demarest Lloyd, Ingolf Boyesen, and ex-Senator Lyman Trumbull of Illinois requested mercy for the anarchists "because they were sentimentalists" or whether "they become sentimentalists by virtue of that act." If neither, he continued, then from which of his books did the editor infer that *he* was a sentimentalist:

> You are so good as to say that you hold me in affection and esteem; you add even stronger expressions of regard: at the same time you call me a novelist of the watering-place piazza, and you say that I hold sentimentally the theories you attribute to me. You must see that all this is a little confusing. I am used by this time to being called hard names by those who hate my way of writing novels; but if *you* like me and respect me, why do you treat me with contempt?

Novelists of the present are not sentimentalists, not even himself, "for if my trade has taught me anything it has taught me to abhor sentimentality: the sentimentality which lusts for blood, and cries out for an 'example,' as well as the other kinds."

Was the editor, Howells continued, sure of his facts on Howells's socialism? Were there any facts beyond Howells's admiration for Tolstoy and his respect for Gronlund's books? To put the record straight, Howells then gave as good a rendition of his position as one could hope to find. Socialism is not a positive but a comparative thing, "a question of more or less in what we have already."

> Every citizen of a civilized state is a socialist. You are yourself a socialist, if you believe that the postal department, the public

schools, the insane asylums, the slumhouses are good things, and that when a railroad management has muddled away in hapless ruin the money of all who trusted it, a Railroad Receiver is a good thing. If I believe that the postal savings-banks as they have them in England; and national Life-insurance as they have it in Germany, are good things, I differ from you in degree, not in kind; and even the socialist who wishes to see the whole of commerce and production in the hands of the state (with us, the people) differs from you in degree and not in kind. The Treasury Department now does its own printing. If the War Department employed poor women to make the army uniforms at a living wage instead of giving the job for contractors to fatten on, it would be exactly the same thing in kind; and why should you think it so very bad?

Howells decided to close his letter with a little story. He had been out in the streets again, taking some notes for *A Hazard of New Fortunes.* On Third Avenue,

I saw a decently dressed man stoop and pick up from the pavement a dirty bit of cake or biscuit, which he crammed into his mouth. . . . Then I saw this man go along the curbstone, and search the garbage of the gutter like a famished dog for some thing more to eat. Being a sentimentalist, a promoter of bloody riots, a wateringplace piazza novelist and what else you like, the sight made me sick, sick at heart; and after I had got by a little I went back, and made shift between the poverty of the man's English and my French, to know his need, and ~~corruptly~~ [crossed out in original] gave him some money. It was not much, it was very little; but he caught my hand between his work-hardened palms, and clung to it, and broke down, and cried there on the street in the most indecent manner.

"For me," Howells continued, showing how relevant to him that passage from Luke had become, "I went away sorrowful, not because there were not places enough for that hapless wretch to go to for charity, if he could find them, but because the conditions in which he came to such a strait seemed to me Christless, after eighteen hundred years of Christ." A truly Christian society, he wrote, would have had a labor bureau where the man could go for work.

This was a piece of my "socialism," I suppose. Even then I had read your first article, and I knew that there must be some occult connection between my "sentimentalism" and the throwing of dynamite bombs; and that I, who deplore all violence and think that every drop of human blood shed in a good cause helps to make a bad one, must somehow be playing into the hands of the most murderous minded criminals.

Howells here is responding to an attack from the right, potentially backed by the American public Bellamy feared when he chose "national-ist" over "socialist," because the latter word "smells to the average Ameri-can of petroleum, suggests the red flag with all manner of sexual novel-ties, and an abusive tone about God and religion." But Howells was not so much hurt by the damage this misuse of a word, this name-calling, might do to his reputation and readership. What hurt him more, what really enraged him, as he was now turning to literature as his principal, perhaps single instrument of reform, was that his methods and aims were not being felt, that he lacked sensitive and responsive readers. He had not humanized the editor. He concluded the letter, continuing from the passage just cited, by remarking that except for the editor's reasoning on the subject, "I should have supposed that the whole tenor of my literature and my life was counter to disorder of all kinds, and especially to disorder that in a free country applies the theories and methods of those who strug-gle against a despotism." He hoped there would be some "who will think it superfluous for me to have said this even in reply to your reasoning."[10]

Howells's socialism, then, combines the following: (1) an assault upon contemporary inequalities and other wrongs; (2) a belief in national-ization, or, better, governmentalization, under which states and local authorities were to be given responsibility too; and (3) Christian altruism. His assault on inequities, he hoped, would be sufficiently revealing and troubling to call up enough altruism for men to legislate new conditions. The new conditions would engender universal and continuous altruism.

Howells was not a tough-minded socialist, not a militant, not a Marx-ist by any means, not an entirely practical critic, not an organizer or fighter among the ranks. He was, perhaps, not even a socialist in the stricter sense of the term, as Abraham Cahan argued in a lecture before the New York Labor Lyceum in the spring of 1889. Yet, Cahan said, "un-consciously ... merely at the bidding of his realistic instinct" his works brought into high relief "a fact in American life which lays bare the ficti-tiousness of American equality." He was a potent force, because the "same public-spirited American citizen who sets down critical socialism for the cranky babble of foreigners 'unacquainted with our institutions' takes pride in the great American novelist, whose pen makes a more dangerous assault on the present system than the most eloquent speeches of the most rabid 'foreign socialist.'" This was an affirmation of the power of his pen, which, if Howells learned of it, must have been very stimulating to him.

It is, of course, encouraging to those working for reform that major artists verify their insights and second their concern. It means that simple representation of the facts of injustice, together with analysis of those who are accountable, *is* effective in the cause of justice, whatever doubts Howells may sometimes have had and whatever George N. Bennett may argue.[11] Tolstoy's writing and example troubled the souls and sometimes changed the lives of his contemporaries. Howells's honest agony over American economic conditions also played its part.

IV

Something more of Howells's social and political position can be ascertained by a look at the action groups to which he was attracted. The Nationalists, whose Boston organizational meeting on December 1, 1888, has already been mentioned, and the Society of Christian Socialists, which held its initial meeting at Tremont Temple in Boston on February 18, 1889, had a number of members in common and a shared goal — the nationalization of all industry in the United States. The chief distinction between them, according to one observer, "is that the Nationalists pro-ceed directly upon the economic line of reform, while the Christian So-cialists proceed more upon the theory that it is first necessary to change the moral side of man before he can be brought to sympathize with their principles." The latter group had a more specific program than the former: Having learned to treat all mankind as brothers, its members were to stimulate public interest through speaking, writing, and organiz-ing. They were to move into the political caucuses and prevent them from being run "in the interest of the capitalist or the saloonkeeper." And they were to make informed efforts to help pass specific socialist legislation.

The makeup of these groups was fairly uniform. The "names" among them were people like Edward Everett Hale, Thomas Wentworth Higginson, Frances Willard, the Reverend Dr. Heber Newton, Richard T. Ely, and Edward Bellamy, their affiliation varying in degree. The writers for their publications, *The Nationalist* and *The Dawn*, *The Nation* reported, were, almost without exception, "Americans, with the best of Puritan blood. Quite without exception, they belong to what they themselves would call 'the privileged classes.'" One hostile critic let it be known that the Nationalist Club in Boston consisted principally of women and clergymen, and Cahan, looking back from 1920, recalled:

> In the aristocratic American city of Boston, there was a time (a very short time) when representatives of the highest society were converted to the socialistic idea (also in a mild rosy-glassed fashion). . . . At that time so-called nationalist clubs were founded. In Boston alone there were three such clubs, and representatives of the highest Bostonian aristocracy belonged to the first two of these. To the meetings of these clubs, people came in "full dress" — men in tuxedoes, and the women in décolleté dress, as if to a ball.

Like some of the all-white, upper-middle-class groups that formed during the 1968 presidential campaign of Senator Eugene McCarthy and in the aftermath of the Martin Luther King slaying, these groups were obviously limited in their experience, perspective, staying power, and from some points of view, political respectability. Some recognition of this, in fact, derived from self-observation, may have been one factor preventing Howells from actually joining either organization. Neither group — particularly the Christian Socialists — acquired a large following, and neither endured a long time. Yet they were symptomatic, by their very formation, of unusually disturbed times and of a widespread recognition of blatant injustice. They were sincere, in their limited way, and had a decided effect. They gave some minimal respectability to unpopular and forward-looking ideas. They expressed the basic need for more centralized control in a splintering society, an issue the "new middle class" progressives would carry into the new century. They were sometimes successful pressure groups for legislation, and they provided incentive for social action on the part of the churches. Many of the Nationalists joined the Populist movement in the early 1890s and, in that way, had their effect on the programs of the major parties. The Progressive movement, in all its complexity of motivation and effect, had some of its roots in these organizations.[12]

With all his sympathy and interest in the Nationalists and, especially, the Christian Socialists, Howells was to commit himself finally neither to them nor to any other socialist group. His reluctance probably derived in part from a recognition of his limitations vis-à-vis the membership of the two groups named. Again, such a step might seem to demand compromise of certain comforts and impulses. His innate caution, too, would keep him from joining, as might the kind of motivation he attributed to Emerson in the August 1889 "Study," where one might read "Nationalists" or "Christian Socialists" for "abolitionists":

> In fine, freedom in all things was his ideal, and this meant with him freedom to seek the good, the only real. Yet because Emerson supremely loved the untrammelled use of his own being he never would bind himself even to the cause of the abolitionists, though sometimes he asked leave to sit on the platform with their speakers, when there seemed unusual danger of violence to them. He held that the scheme of his life included their work, and undoubtedly he was right, just as undoubtedly he must have seemed deficient to some true and noble friends of the slave in refusing their label.[13]

This statement may be a rationalization of the complicated forces that kept Howells from acting with the force of a Tolstoy. But it is true that he felt the themes of his writing paralleled the work of the Christian Socialists and that he could play an active role through the outspoken use of his pen in the "Study" and in his fiction.

As he worked at his new novel and thought about its mission, he attended discourses by social thinkers with whose views he was sympathetic. He attended at least one socialist lecture that "dealt patiently with hard facts." He went to hear Edward McGlynn, who had been excommunicated by the Catholic Church for making political speeches in support of Henry George's economic theories and whose followers had been threatened with denial of the Church's rites were they seen at meetings of his antipoverty society. And on January 27, 1889, he attended a sermon by the Episcopal minister and Christian Socialist R. Heber Newton at All Souls' Church in New York, after which he wrote to Newton of his "unspeakable satisfaction" and of "such unflagging interest as I have never before bro't to any public discourse." The effect on him was like that he hoped to have on his own audience, and he wondered how extensive Newton's influence was.

> Surely such words as yours must have weight at last with those who hear you; I found myself wishing I knew how many they put to shame (as they did me) for the comfort we dare to take while there is a hopeless want in the world. I thank you for my share of the humiliation. Some time I should like to "tell my experience" — my religious, my economic experience; for it is that, rather. It seems a strange thing that I should once have been wholly deaf and blind to such truth as you preached today, such gospel.[14]

V

The winter was a bleak, painful one for Howells, and he probably had little mind, anyhow, for active affiliation with the Nationalists or Christian Socialists. While he was attending meetings, writing the "Editor's Study," and completing *A Hazard of New Fortunes*, he was at the lowest point in his life. In late November 1888, he took Winny, who now weighed fifty-eight pounds, to Philadelphia, where he put her in the hands of Dr. S. Weir Mitchell. It was a last effort, "for if he cannot help her, I don't know who can." Their own experiment in caring for her had failed: "She has fairly baffled us, and has almost worn her mother out." They had reason to believe, Howells said, that she actually suffered little or no pain, but she worked so on their sympathy that they were unable to carry out their plans for her. The new experiment was to be "fearfully costly... perhaps $2000 in all — but we *must* make it, or else let her slide into dementia and death." Home was lonely enough without the poor child, Howells wrote his father, but with such a prospect otherwise ahead, "this temporary bereavement is better." Her treatment was to consist of "rubbing, heavy doses of iron, and milk in great quantities; that is, she will be fattened, and roasted by that means out of her mania for heat."

Mitchell thought it a very difficult case, one badly complicated by "her hypochondriacal illusions and obstinacy in her physiological theories." He told Howells that his hope lay in her condition changing when her body and brain had become nourished: "His feeding is for this end, and he will of course keep it up, whether she consents or not. It has already come to a tussle of wills, and he believes that as soon as she finds that he is absolutely unyielding, she will give in." The family is "rejoicing in a short thanksgiving visit from John, who is always such a comfort, and is doubly so at this time of trouble. Elinor is very much run down with the care of Winny, and is extremely nervous, and John interests and occupies her."

The story, in the letters to Ohio, now became one of Winny's gradual gain in weight, of her continuing stubbornness and "hypochondriacal fancies," and of the moderate hope to which the Howellses clung. The strain was great, and it was not mitigated by other news. Howells's father wrote about his concern over Sam's financial troubles and the sickness of Joe, another son, and Howells responded on February 3 by enlarging the monthly check:

> I wish you to keep the $25 for Sam's use, and send it to him from time to time, or to his family, in such sums as you think best. — I myself am heavily loaded down. I've lost about $4,000 by shrinkage of R.R. stocks. I've a most expensive flat, which I got extra large and comfortable for Winny, and now she's away at the cost of nearly $100 a week. I tell you these things partly to explain why I oughtn't now to do much for Sam, and why I don't come forward and offer to free Joe from debt. I *must* put by something for Winny.

He went to visit Winny in Philadelphia on February 10 and found her looking "extremely well"; a week later Dr. Mitchell called to report that she was up to seventy-eight pounds and that he was going to send her into the country for better air and exercise. The most the family was hoping for was a lengthy invalidism leading to a final return to health. Howells wrote Gosse on February 28 that "black care has not left so much laugh in me as there used to be.... Our poor Winny is a wreck of health and youth — sick for years yet to come, I'm afraid." Two days later even that hope ceased, and Howells telegraphed his father on March 3:

> Our poor suffering girl had ceased to suffer. It was Saturday evening, at Merchantville, near Philadelphia, from a sudden failure of

the heart. The funeral will be from Dr. Mackenzie's church in Cambridge, tomorrow at 2 o'clock.

Some time I will try to tell you more.

"Her Angel doth always behold the Face of our Father."

With love to all from our broken hearts,

Your aff'te son,
WILL.

She loved you dearly, and Aurelia [Howells's sister].

The funeral service in the Cambridge chapel was attended by Lowell, the Norton family, Thomas Bailey Aldrich, Horace Scudder, who had made most of the arrangements, Mrs. Child, and others — by "those who had loved her in her innocent and joyous childhood" — and "Lowell followed her dust to where it shall return to the dust of the common death, the common life." This was the greatest sorrow Howells was ever to experience. When Garland saw him for the first time after the visit at Little Nahant, "Winifred was dead, and he was older and sadder. Never again did he seem the perfectly happy man I had thought him when first we met in Lee's Hotel in Auburndale."[15]

The months following Winny's death were very painful, with all the indescribable experiences of those who have lost a child: the self-blame, the gradual but never final dulling of the grief, the living over and over of events of the past, all ending in the ineradicable fact. In the memoir of Winny that Howells wrote in the following fall, after he had completed his novel, he told in various direct and indirect ways of "that hopeless and helpless striving with which we go back and reconstruct the history of those we have lost, from this point and from that, as if we might so keep them with us." He thought that Henry James, Sr., "may have had his misgivings about my fitness to be her keeper . . . it is one of the great mysteries that creatures so precious should be trusted to the care of ignorance and inexperience and presumption."

> We knew how precious she was, how rare; but there were many stresses in which our knowledge was not expressed in our behavior. Throughout her whole little day, and to the very end, we made many mistakes concerning her. These are bitter to remember; they are wounds that bleed and burn; nothing can ever heal them, nothing can soothe them, but the thought of the love that overflowed even the error with its abundance.

Two facts that tormented especially were that of Winny's homesickness at the time she died and the possibility, as he wrote Dr. Mitchell on March 7, that "the poor child's pain was all along as great as she said, if she was so diseased, as apparently she was."[16]

Winny's death of a misdiagnosed organic but otherwise unidentified disease made him, quite naturally, reflect on his behavior toward her. Had he understood her? Had he lived up to her? Had he been worthy of her? If he could live his life over, he wrote his father at the end of March, "it would be to love more, to be gentler and kinder with all. Nothing else is worth while; and it is sad to realize this too late." He could not say anything fitting about Winny, he told Alice James a month later. "Only this I say, that she now seems not only the best and gentlest, but one of the wisest souls that ever lived. It is hard to explain; but she was *wise*, and of such a truth that I wonder she could have been my child." This was significant to a man who valued truth above all else, who sometimes found it difficult to get it into his own writings, and who sometimes was unable to be true to himself. Winny had been, he wrote in the memoir,

> ... an unconscious conscience. Every impulse in her was wise and good; she seemed no more to think or to feel evil than to do evil. She had the will to yield, not to withstand; she could not comprehend unkindness, it puzzled and dismayed her. She had an angelic dignity that never failed her in any squalor or sickness; she was on the earth, but she went through the world aloof in spirit, with a kind of surprise. She was of so divine a truthfulness that in her presence I felt the shame of insincerity as in no other.

He had in the past expressed a need to be worthy of his family, and Winny now, as he worked on his novel, served as a goad to his social conscience.[17]

His close acquaintance with mortality was another such stimulus. Winny's sickness and death at age twenty-five, the day after his birthday, made Howells feel his own frailty. He was nearly fifty-two, he wrote to Gosse on February 28, recalling that "when we lived in Cambridge, an old gentleman came 80, and a lady sent him 80 English violets. These graceful acts console us for the loss of youth." He would like life in New York, were he not "old and sore and sad." One night in the middle of June he felt "so anxious" about himself that he resolved to write his son and inform him as to what funds he would leave the family upon his death. He enumerated his life-insurance policies, the rent from the Concord Avenue house in Cambridge, the $11,000 in the New England Trust Company, the $11,000 in the C. B. & Q. and Atchison, Topeka and Santa Fe stocks, and the income from his books as assets which would yield the family an annual income of approximately $4,500. Again in November 1890, then approximately every other year, he would draw up statements of his effects, the total figure ascending from $60,000 in 1890 to $68,809 in 1892, $83,961 in 1894, and $93,999 in 1897.[18]

VI

Although Howells, with some rationalizations and some misgivings, had done well as a capitalist, he continued to take a strong line against the abuses of capitalism, and the "Studies" of 1889 reflect his deepening displeasure. Attacking America's "fat optimism," he pointed out that our splendor and opulence, like that of any country, owe their existence "largely to the hopeless poverty of those that dig in fields and delve in mines and toil in mills, that hew the wood and draw the water." Men had never been tempted by a "wilder rush of interests and ambitions," and "even here," as in Europe, "vast masses of men are sunk in misery that must grow every day more hopeless, or embroiled in a struggle for mere life that must end in enslaving and imbruting them." Competition everywhere had reduced pay to the level of mere subsistence, and large commerce had devoured the small: "There is absolutely no hope of better things, not even the hope of exile; for greed has seized even the waste places." Carlyle had once looked to America for relief for the millions of suffering laborers in England, but America was now no longer labor's city on a hill.[19]

The optimism and hope implicit in Howells's fictional theory were much at odds with such a view of things. Still, he was able, here and there, to refer to such underlying American qualities as "our faith in humanity, our love of equality," and our ability to lift ourselves above the war of interests "when there is supreme need." Because of these qualities and because of the increasing visibility of misery and waste, by early summer he thought he could recognize a significant "movement." Men at last were longing to embody the Word as a rule of life in their social and political ideals and were doing so "with an impulse that animates every humane thinker, whether he calls himself Christian or not." One might refuse to recognize this impulse or might deny that it was shaping life more than before, "but no one who has the current of literature under his eye can fail to note it there." People "are thinking and feeling generously, *if not living justly*, in our time; it is a day of anxiety to be saved from the curse that is on selfishness, of eager question how others shall be helped, of bold denial that the conditions in which we would fain have rested are sacred or immutable." "This is the age of hopeful striving," he wrote, in an attack on William Sharp's prediction of a romantic revival in literature.

> ... when we have really a glimpse of what the earth may be when Christianity becomes a life in the equality and fraternity of the race, and when the recognition of all the facts in the honest daylight about us is the service which humanity demands of the humanities, in order that what is crooked may be made straight, and that what is wrong may be set right.

And instinctively, not consciously, the humanities were working through realism to this end.[20]

The novelist, therefore, might painfully acknowledge limitations to his own capacity for real action and commitment, but by mirroring for Americans their own complacency and revealing the nature of the society for which they were ultimately responsible, he could still fulfill a mission to men's souls, and thus a mission to civilization.

Toward the end of September 1889, Howells completed *A Hazard of New Fortunes*, which in its early stages had been slowed as he worried about Winny and then struggled with his grief. The sorrow, he wrote nearly two decades later, "took away everything but work, and it so palsied the hand and brain that it seemed as if the work added to the anguish. But doubtless the work helped the bereft to bear his loss; it was something that must be done; and after a manner it was done through the leaden hours and days." Eventually, the book was composed at an unusually fast pace, but without the control of his earlier novels. As he admitted in a letter to John Hay, it "seemed to flounder along on a way of its own as I wrote it, [adding] interests, incidents, individualities which I had not known lay near." The result was an often haphazard and stylistically imperfect novel, which was, nevertheless, the work most acclaimed by his contemporaries and, he later thought, "the most vital of my fictions."[21]

VII

For Basil March there is no question of giving up his riches and position and following Tolstoy into poverty. He cannot easily comprehend those who aspire to do so, and when his wife asks what good it would do if they shared all they had with the poor of New York and settled down among them, he replies, as Tolstoy's critics had replied:

> Not the least in the world. It might help us for the moment, but it wouldn't keep the wolf from their doors for a week; and then they would go on just as before, only they wouldn't be on such good terms with the wolf. The only way for them is to keep up an unbroken intimacy with the wolf; then they can manage him somehow. I don't know how, and I'm afraid I don't want to.

March elsewhere realizes that at his age he must follow the path he had chosen long ago: "He was not master of himself, as he once seemed, but the servant of those he loved ... he could not do what he liked, that was very clear." He is not here contemplating Tolstoyan action, but his mind does wander ironically to Lindau, the Civil War veteran who late in life had chosen to live among the poor. Lindau, however, as he himself points out, has no children, and in *A Hazard of New Fortunes* the same dilemmas are at the back of Howells's mind that were more to the fore during the writing of *Annie Kilburn*. When March makes an independent stand reminiscent of Howells's behavior during the anarchist affair and puts his job on the line by refusing to fire Lindau for his opinions, his thoughts immediately turn in agony to the possible consequences for his wife and two children.[22] One has a double, sometimes conflicting, responsibility toward one's family: One must both support it and be worthy of the best in it. Either too much compromise of one's income for the sake of ideals or too much compromise of one's ideals for the sake of income can spell disaster for one's dependents.

With all its diversity of characters, it is evident that *A Hazard of New Fortunes* centers on Basil March and his confrontations with New York, with Lindau, and with the Dryfooses. Like Howells, March is quiet-looking, rather stout, and a little above middle height, and like Howells he moves, somewhat more definitely, from Boston to New York. He is also middle-aged, although probably a little younger than Howells when he wrote the book — March's children are a few years younger than the Howells children — and his surname is that of the month of Howells's birth. It is true that through most of the novel, if not at the end, March has not come so far as Howells in social outlook. Still, the negative characteristics studied in March are not merely mirrors for negligent Americans; they are also characteristics that continued to operate in Howells himself. For Howells, like his painter Alma Leighton, either saw "all the hidden weakness that's in men's natures" and brought "it to the surface in their figures" or put his own weakness into them. "Either way, it's a drawback to their presenting a truly manly appearance."[23]

Before bringing the Marches to New York, Howells lightly and sympathetically delineates the limitations and preconceptions that tend to separate them from their kind. They consider themselves, and are considered, very cultivated, and their taste and their beautified house give them a feeling of special distinction. March is proud of being up to date in literary matters and

> ... could not help contrasting his life and its inner elegance with that of other men who had no such resources. He thought that he was not arrogant about it, because he did full justice to the good qualities of those other people; he congratulated himself upon the democratic instincts which enabled him to do this; and neither he nor his wife supposed that they were selfish persons.

They are, like David Sewell and Annie Kilburn, good people and as such serve well to implicate the reader in their lives. They are "very sympathetic," wish well to all good causes, scorn narrow-heartedness, teach "their children to loathe all manner of social cruelty," and think they would sacrifice themselves for others if the opportunity ever came their way, but they never ask why it had not done so.

These gentle but serious indictments of the Marches are multiplied throughout the novel. Confronted with destitution, they turn and go off to the theater, or they rationalize: "I don't believe there's any *real* suffering — not real *suffering* — among those people; that is, it would be suffering from our point of view, but they've been used to it all their lives, and they don't feel their discomfort so much." When March's "life of comfortable reverie" is confronted with Lindau's violence, indignation, and anger, he attempts to cheer Lindau up by explaining that the world is really not so bad. Any American, he adds, would wish to lend Lindau a hand for the one he gave in the Civil War. March — and here one recalls David Sewell — "felt this to be a fine turn, and his voice trembled slightly in saying it," and he is hardly prepared for the vehement outburst of Lindau's reply. He had once accidentally come across such language in a blatant labor newspaper, "and once at a strikers' meeting he had heard rich people denounced with the same frenzy. He had made his own reflections upon the tastelessness of the rhetoric, and the obvious buncombe of the motive, and he had not taken the matter seriously."

This kind of superior nonresponse to underlying realities is typical of the Marches' tendency to see experience from an aesthetic point of view. When Conrad Dryfoos remarks to March that he thinks some good can be done with *Every Other Week*, the new magazine March has come to New York to write for and edit, March asks whether he means improving the public taste, elevating the standard of literature, or giving young authors and artists a chance. No other good had ever been in his mind, "except the good that was to come in a material way from his success, to himself and to his family." Conrad means, however, that "we might help along." When he mentions March's proposed sketches of New York life and March's authorial vanity tickles him into acknowledging that he could make something "attractive" out of them, Conrad counters, underlining one of Howells's intentions in the novel: "If you can make the comfortable people understand how the uncomfortable people live, it will be a very good thing, Mr. March. Sometimes it seems to me that the only trouble is that we don't know one another well enough; and that the first thing is to do this." "'That's true,' said March, from the surface only. 'And then, those phases of low life are immensely picturesque. Of course, we must try to get the contrasts of luxury for the sake of the full effect.'" He laughs and causes the Christ-like Conrad to turn his head away.[24] It is not coincidental that as Margaret Vance grows closer to Conrad and becomes more authentically dedicated to her social work, she gradually drops the aesthetic side of her life.

March has an "American ease of mind about everything" and the kind of light, evasive humor that tends to appear in Howells's writing. He jokes at Lindau's seriousness, finds it a "droll irony" that Lindau should unknowingly be working for the millionaire Dryfoos, is amused when Fulkerson tries to use Conrad's humanitarian tendencies for advertising purposes, is affected comically when Lindau reacts violently to the story of Dryfoos's union-breaking, and turns off the urgings of his conscience with a joke. The result for the reader, however, is not that caused by Dr. Morrell in *Annie Kilburn*. If Howells is reflecting his own continuing need to distance the unpleasant, it is also even more clear in his treatment of March than in his treatment of Morrell that he disapproves of such a tactic, for March is undercut at every point, mostly by the self-evident gap between what is before him and his response to it. The portrait of the Marches is a subtly devastating one. At one point, when with some effort they finally get a laugh out of their increasingly troubled sense of the disturbing aspects of New York, they laugh "with some sadness at heart, and with a dim consciousness that they had got their laugh out of too many things in life."[25]

While undercutting the average, privileged reader through March and other characters, Howells gives the reader credit too, for the Marches are capable of self-realization and development. March, early in the novel, is seriously aware of the misery "in the really squalid tenement-house streets," and it is this that allows him to improve in the course of the novel. This development is carefully depicted. It is undramatic, and in the end, it represents no final and complete conversion; it represents a beginning of new growth.[26] Howells intends the reader through identification with March to begin new growth as well.

New York forces upon March certain "pensive questions" and a "vague discomfort," which bring "nothing definite" at first but gradually deepen his insight until he recognizes his complicity in the suffering he sees. In the *Every Other Week* dinner that comes at this point, Howells contrives a new mixture of characters in order to create a disaster different from that of the dinner scene in *The Rise of Silas Lapham*. The discussion also touches on literature, the Civil War, and the American poor, but the proper Bostonian Bromfield Corey has become the nouveau-riche millionaire businessman Jacob Dryfoos, and for the comfortably troubled humanitarians Clara Kingsbury and David Sewell are substituted Lindau and Colonel Woodburn. Thus the sense of economic injustice that underlay the former dinner bursts to the surface. When Dryfoos, as a result, tries to fire Lindau, and Fulkerson, manager of the periodical, wavers in his support of March, March asserts his integrity first by resisting Dryfoos's efforts and then by tendering his resignation. But when Lindau returns the capitalist money he had taken for his previous translations, March begins to feel shabby. He himself will continue to take Dryfoos's money, he is released from pushing the issue to its end, and he has no desire to push it so. The issue remains the same — Dryfoos is still willing to punish Lindau for his opinions, so far as March knows — but the Marches acquiesce and go once again to the theater.[27]

If March has not played the role of hero, his outlook has been affected. During the streetcar strike soon after, the reader finds March repeating Howells's opinions from "Was There Nothing to Arbitrate?" And when Lindau lies dying in the hospital, his influence speaks through March, who wonders if God intended "our civilization, the battle we fight in, the game we trick in," our grim world of chance where "some one always has you by the throat, unless you have some one else in *your* grip." He argues that every man has a right to rest and to eat if he will work, and a right not to have that work taken from him, a right to feel that "he shall not suffer in himself or in those who are dear to him, except through natural causes."

> But no man can feel this as things are now; and so we go on, pushing and pulling, climbing and crawling, thrusting aside and trampling underfoot; lying, cheating, stealing; and when we get to the end, covered with blood and dirt and sin and shame, and look back over the way we've come to a palace of our own, or the poor-house, which is about the only possession we can claim in common with our brother-men, I don't think the retrospect can be pleasing.

Some of the blame, he admits, can be put on the greedy and foolish character of individual men, but still "conditions *make* character," and our values make men greedy and foolish. Yet we dare not behave otherwise, or dare to teach our children otherwise, for fear of the results.

March has come a long way from Boston, but no farther than Howells's own troubled conscience and strikingly grim vision of America, tempered here and there by a mild look toward a future utopia. Without a specific plan for political or economic change, March's natural goodness and generosity leave him with Howellsian altruism, and he lectures to his children on kindness and thinks of an "order of loving kindness" as basic and ideal in the universe.[28] This is admirable in itself and potent to some degree, but hardly a tough, vital posture toward social restructuring.

The characterization as a whole is a study of the attitude and motivations that cause social evils and prevent their alleviation. There is no need here to sketch the character of Beaton, whose selfishness and lack of moral fiber lie at the base of the novel and are reflected in lesser degrees in the majority of the other characters. Nor need we dwell on Fulkerson, whose low business standards and amorality and whose blinking of the conditions of American labor and paying homage to millionaires are all too American. Dryfoos, who as a rare if somewhat thin study of one of America's new millionaires probably sold the novel to so many of Howells's contemporaries, is ultimately pitiable as he learns that money cannot buy happiness. Yet Howells is now telling the truth about American business, and Dryfoos is no Silas Lapham: He continues to show his old hardness at the very end, in the details of making over the ownership of *Every Other Week* to Fulkerson and March. By having Dryfoos mistreat his son, scorn his values, and deny him his wish to be a preacher, Howells states that the self-interest bred by American money-centered values cuts off one's humane, Christian side and turns Christ away to His death.

Lindau and Conrad are for the most part exceptions to this generalization about characterization. They stand in the place of Tolstoy and Mr. Peck in this novel, and both, like those two, are called "cranks" by the less committed characters. They are juxtaposed toward the end, during the strike of the streetcar operators. Conrad finds himself standing on a corner looking at a streetcar surrounded by a crowd of "shouting, cursing, struggling men."

> The driver was lashing his horses forward, and a policeman was at their heads, with the conductor, pulling them; stones, clubs, brickbats hailed upon the car, the horses, the men trying to move them. The mob closed upon them in a body, and then a patrol-wagon whirled up from the other side, and a squad of policemen leaped out, and began to club the rioters. Conrad could see how they struck them under the rims of their hats; the blows on their skulls sounded as if they had fallen on stone; the rioters ran in all directions.

Lindau is suddenly at Conrad's side, shouting at an approaching officer, who lifts his club; a shot rings out from the turmoil around the streetcar, and Conrad is struck in the chest. He tries to tell the policeman not to strike the old soldier, but he cannot move his tongue. He sees the policeman's face, "not bad, not cruel; it was like the face of a statue, fixed, perdurable; a mere image of irresponsible and involuntary authority." March, seeing Lindau clubbed to the ground, rushes up to find Conrad "dead beside the old man."[29]

Much can be said against Lindau. By making Victor Hugo his favorite author, Howells possibly meant to suggest that Lindau sentimentalized the poor and tended to think in terms of black and white; Howells had said this of Hugo in the December 1888 "Study." That Lindau chooses Dostoyevsky for his first translation may be meant, as Kermit Vanderbilt suggests, to associate him with behavior and an outlook inappropriate for the United States, where conditions are scarcely so grim as in Russia — a point made twice in the "Study." That Beaton paints Lindau as Judas may mean that Lindau betrays the effective, peaceful side of the labor movement and the efforts of Christian Socialist types such as Conrad. The reader is probably expected to recognize Lindau's language as overviolent, to equate his "paternalism" with Woodburn's "feudalism," to reject, with March, his failure to recur to the American means of the vote, and to decide that he dies in the cause of disorder.

At the same time, he is, as March says, the best, the kindest, the most high-minded and generous man March had ever known. He has many of the qualities of those great Russian realists Howells described as humanists in his review of *Crime and Punishment*. His refusal to forget the poor and his decision to live among them, helping them as he can, are Tolstoyan, as is his indictment of economic values that allow such vast disparities of human existence. He is painted not only as Judas, but as a variety of figures of the Old and New Testaments. Howells created him from his memory of an old German revolutionist in exile he knew in Jefferson, Ohio, who recognized "the face of freedom in the cause of the Union, and . . . willingly gave up for it what was left of his generous life." Lindau is not only associated with the idealism that fought the Civil War; he also represents the disillusionment with society that had grown from that war. He has rejected his pension:

> Besides, they owe me nothing. Do you think I knowingly gave my hand to save this oligarchy of traders and tricksters, this aristocracy of railroad wreckers and stock gamblers and mine-slave drivers and

mill-serf owners? No; I gave it to the slave; the slave — ha! ha! ha! — whom I helped to unshackle to the common liberty of hunger and cold. And you think I would be the beneficiary of such a state of things?

He stands also for the continuing fight against slavery: The arm that must be amputated at the shoulder, when clubbed during the strike, is the same that lost a hand in the Civil War. He, and eventually March, knows that democracy is a shuffling evasion, that rich and poor are not equal before the law, that in America there is no equality of opportunity, and that at least half the American people live in hopeless, self-propagating conditions. And these things hurt him deeply as, in their various forms, they have always hurt Americans who have seen them after having been educated to believe otherwise. With all its suggested limitations, his attack on American society has the weight of justifiable outrage and of truth. For his character Howells later confessed "a tenderness . . . which I feel for no other in the book, and a reverence for an inherent nobleness in it which I know derives not from me, but from my old German revolutionist."[30]

His desire to join the ministry having been defeated by his father,[31] Conrad Dryfoos struggles to fulfill himself "in acts of devotion to others." He aspires to become a brother in the Episcopal priesthood and work among the poor in the East Side tenements. Although he lacks a pulpit, his behavior and oft-voiced convictions make him "a preacher all his life just the same." When March argues that Lindau has only a partial truth, Conrad interrupts him with recourse to Luke: "Partial truth! Didn't the Saviour himself say, 'How hardly shall they that have riches enter into the kingdom of God'!" When March replies, "Do *you* agree with Lindau?" Conrad's answer is "I agree with the Lord Jesus Christ, and I believe he meant the kingdom of heaven upon this earth, as well as in the skies." A light of exaltation *and* fanaticism enters his eyes, and he, if admirable, like Lindau seems somewhat extreme. Although March and his wife realize that Conrad has, like Christ, taken upon himself the sins of others and suffered for them in his death, it is only Margaret Vance who wishes to follow in his path. The sympathetic Marches are still fundamentally committed to their lives of distinction and gain and to the perhaps selfish but certainly justifiable care of their family.

There was no question for Howells of taking the Tolstoyan step in this novel, and he felt strong in his determination to work March's position for all it was worth to evoke painful self-recognition in his readers and to make his words take hold in their minds as Lindau's and Conrad's took hold in the minds of March and Margaret Vance. Yet there was still, necessarily, unhappiness about not doing more, and there was the same need as in *Annie Kilburn* to kill off his Tolstoyan heroes with violence. They were close to his heart, however, models in many ways he wished he could emulate, and at their deaths, he later wrote, "I suffered more things than I commonly allow myself to suffer in the adverse fate of my characters."[32]

VIII

"The book is so d——d humane!" William James wrote to Howells. Hale thought it "good" because "it will make people better." Bellamy expressed his enthusiasm for the book and said, "You are writing of what everybody is thinking and all the rest will have to follow your example or lose their readers." Twain preferred in the novel the "high art by which it is made to preach its great sermon without seeming to take sides or preach at all." Lowell's reaction was one Howells wanted for the book and one Conrad Dryfoos had wanted for *Every Other Week*: He wrote to a friend that a noble sentiment pervades the book, "and it made my inherited comforts here at Elmwood discomforting to me in a very salutary way. I felt in reading some parts of it as I used when the slave would not let me sleep." Robertson James wrote that he could always find the Gospel in Howells's books: "The reading of *Annie Kilburn* and *A Hazard of New Fortunes* has lifted and purged me and made me feel for awhile anyhow how deep and vast is the circle of the human love and suffering in which we all are knit."

James Parton wrote thanking Howells "for this holy and august work"; he was thanking him not for himself and his family alone "but for our country and the whole English-speaking race." He warned Howells not to write too much. "Don't think of these works as mere alleviations of idleness. They have a profound importance. They are the highest and soundest moral influence now active in the United States. Write only what you alone can write." When Howells replied with gratitude, mentioning that he had been thinking of doing some charity work in Boston that winter, Parton returned, "What an idea.... You, who do nothing else!"

And when Howells wrote to George William Curtis to thank him for his review in the "Editor's Easy Chair," Curtis replied that his voice was only one of a chorus and perhaps recalling Howells's "Study" on the new Christmas literature, that all the notices he had read recognized the book to be what it is, a "strain of the music that murmured in Bethlehem on this Christmas eve, and despite everything has never ceased to murmur." The "Easy Chair" review praised the vitality of the novel, the "sweet and open and generous mind" of the author, and the "picture firm with clear insight and glowing with human sympathy." Here was "such a piece of realism as holds the mirror up to nature, and at once illustrates and vindicates every principle which the Study has maintained and applied in its judgments of contemporary story."[33]

A Hazard of New Fortunes, then, with this kind of response, justified its author in his critical beliefs, in his humanistic purpose, and in the increasingly serious vision of American civilization he was allowing to enter his fiction. He had every encouragement to go on. He had left the rural community of *Annie Kilburn*, he had done somewhat more "slumming" than before, and he had confronted his readers "with themselves, and with the problem which it grows less and less easy to shirk." He was fulfilling a "'mission' to men's souls," thus proving that the novelist could play an effective social role. His emphasis remained humanistic, stressing self-knowledge, kindliness, and a sense of brotherhood with other human beings as the keys to a better world. But his acknowledgment that "conditions *make* character" and his grim indictments of American civilization revealed an uneasiness about the viability of such a remedy. The facts of American life were an imposing enemy for an appeal to altruism to combat, and he hoped for some peaceful political means of drastically changing the conditions. The novel itself, of course, represents an effort to stimulate sensitive, responsible people to take that step toward achieving a just society.

As for the conflict within himself, the novel reveals that it had by no means disappeared. It is likely, however, that in working it out once more, through Basil March, he had reached a resolution with which he could live. He would never be a man of action, but his tendency to explore and express his position as its implications radiated out into American behavior and attitudes at large had met with success, and he would be sure to repeat the approach in the future.

5

The Early 1890s:
Anguish and the
Ongoing Effort

I think I could deal with the present, bad and bothering as it is, if
it were not for visions of the past in which I appear to be mostly
running about, full of sound and fury signifying nothing. Once I
thought that I meant something by everything I did; but now I
don't know.
— HOWELLS to Thomas Bailey Aldrich, July 3, 1902[1]

... in the night ... I wake to the sense of what a toad I am and always have been. Your letter, so fully, so beautifully kind, will help
to take away some of those dreadful moments of self-blame, and I
can think, "Well, there must have been something in it; James
would not abuse my dotage with flattery; I was probably not always such a worm of the earth as I feel myself at present."
— HOWELLS to Henry James, March 17, 1912[2]

Perhaps the greatest service of his pen has been his criticism of civilization and the projection of his social vision into the darkness of
the human struggle. For this all honor!
— EDWIN MARKHAM, 1917[3]

I

A Hazard of New Fortunes was the last work by Howells to appear in the
1880s and is frequently considered the high point in his career as a
novelist. The 1890s, it is generally acknowledged, brought a falling-off in
the quality of his work. Descriptions of this decline, however, are often
too negative. They ignore the high quality of a number of novels
published immediately after *A Hazard of New Fortunes* and during the
next twenty-odd years and fail to consider the other directions in which
Howells was moving with his pen. Such a description is even less useful

when it faults Howells for failing to develop his fiction toward, say, a *Sister Carrie* or *The Jungle* and accuses him of a loss of social concern. In *The Realism of William Dean Howells*, George Bennett argues cogently that socially puposeful humanism continued to inform all of Howells's fiction, but it should be clear also that he continued to lend voice and pen to protests against specific evils and that outspoken indictments of America remained for many years at the center of his criticism and fiction.

When the "Editor's Study" ceased after March 1892, his accusing voice still spoke out through the novels, through *An Imperative Duty*, *The Quality of Mercy*, and *The World of Chance*, through the Altrurian studies, which began to appear in November 1892 and ran monthly for almost two years; through the poems he was beginning to write again; and through the social and critical essays that proliferated from 1893 onward. His attacks in these years on capitalist society and his Tolstoyan advocacy of brotherhood and socioeconomic equality gained him considerable reputation in America and abroad as a "socialist." By 1891, he himself was beginning to draw parallels between the attacks against the early abolitionists (attacks for the most part repented) and those against the socialism he and others were advocating, a clear indication that he thought himself in the mainstream of American reform.[4]

Although this is true, and it is true that he continued to explore his own representative inadequacies, he did not, as he was very much aware, go much farther toward a treatment of working-class experience. This is so for reasons we already know: his background, his personal habits and inclinations, his advancing years. It has been argued by such scholars as Everett Carter and Edwin Cady that his years were now slackening his creative impulses, although his literary capital and ability made possible in the 1890s an immense productivity. This productivity, in fact, hindered him from developing new experiences, approaches, and techniques that would have enabled him to probe more fully and at closer range the social problems that disturbed him. Probably he had this in mind when he wrote in 1892 that "like all of us who work at all, the country printer had to work too hard; and he had little time to think or to tell how to make life better and truer in any sort." His own overwork, he said, was a result of his expenses, but it may also have derived from fear of sustained confrontation with the more demanding implications of his

material, method, and insights. It is not easy to say. Certainly, given his
established readership and his desire for steady income, and given the unnerving resurgence of romantic fiction in the 1890s, he would be reluctant
to leave, even in his most direct and telling works, the successful,
polished, well-written prose that requires the habitats of the middle and
upper classes for its best expression.[5]

II

But more than all this underlies the quality and character of Howells's
work in this period. The Howells of the early 1890s, mainly owing to his
daughter's death, was emotionally an altered man. Outwardly his personality was much the same, and he had every reason to proceed hope-
fully and forcefully after *A Hazard of New Fortunes*. Inwardly, however,
he was living in a different world: His personal dimensions and horizons
had shifted. He was weary of moving, he wished to avoid the city, wished,
sometimes, to stop writing and retire, a wish reflected in an autobiographical urge to sit back and reflect at leisure on the past, to sum up. In
November 1889 he found himself "in the strange mood of wishing to live
only from moment to moment: to write, to read, to eat, above all to sleep
and forget." Beyond this he had no objects or incentives: "The finality
seems forever gone out of earthly things. It may come back, but I doubt
it." He told Parton at the beginning of 1890 that with Winny had gone
"most of the meaning and all the dignity of life. And where is she, and
shall I ever see her again? The world has largely resolved itself into this
question, for me." In June he woke one morning with a severe headache,
which gave him some sharp thoughts,

> ...and I confess I look forward with terror to the pain that must
> come probably before my life is let out of this gross bulk of mine,
> when it is time. I suppose it is right, so, and no doubt I shall be
> helped to bear it. But think what mother suffered! And Johnny, and
> Sissy and Winny! And why? — That Why is so much in my mind
> that I wonder it doesn't show phosphorescently on my forehead,
> and still more on my bulging stomach.

When a young couple he knew became engaged, he felt bitter that

Winny "should have been blotted out of life in her blossom." This feeling found form in a short, terse play, "Bride Roses," that he was to write in 1893. An older woman and a young man in love come at the same time, though separately, to a florist's to buy for a young girl some flowers that resemble her, "the most ethereal creature in the world . . . very, very fragile looking; a sort of moonlight blonde, with those remote, starry-looking eyes [Winny's eyes, Howells wrote in the memoir, had "a strange, starry, wondering purity"] . . . and just the faintest, faintest tinge of color in her face." A second woman enters the shop to buy flowers for a girl who has died suddenly — it turns out to be the same girl — and she also chooses the bride roses, picking those with "very long stems, and slender, with the flowers fully open, and fragile-looking — something like her." So close were the possibilities of joyful life and of death. "'To be young and gentle and do no harm, and to pay for it as if it were a crime,'" Howells wrote in the memoir, quoting James's words that seemed to him the most perfect expression of Winny's life and death, "that was her part 'in the great play of destiny,' as she called this phantasmagory."

At the end of 1890, he asked Howard Pyle whether the Winny he saw in his dreams was a true visitation, and when Pyle read the first of the poems Howells's troubled heart was pouring out, a poem in which Howells struggles with his metaphysical doubt, he wrote that it made him feel again the ache of sympathy Howells's letter had aroused in him: "What a dreadful valley of shadows it must be through which you are passing!" On March 1, 1891, Howells asked his father to say little about his fifty-fourth birthday: "It will be two years tomorrow since Winny died. I must pass from my birthday into this shadow as long as I live." Whenever he thought of Winny, he wrote S. Weir Mitchell in April, "I fall lame within, as it were, and so not know what to do or say."

Some of the poems now appearing in *Harper's Monthly* give an idea of what his daily existence sometimes became for him. One is entitled "Mortality":

> How many times have I lain down at night,
> And longed to fall into that gulf of sleep,
> Whose dreamless deep
> Is haunted by no memory of
> The weary world above;
> And thought myself most miserable that I

Must impotently lie
So long upon the brink
Without the power to sink
Into that nothingness, and neither feel nor think!

How many times, when day brought back the light
After the merciful oblivion
Of such unbroken slumber,
And once again began to cumber
My soul with her forgotten cares and sorrows,
And show in long perspective the gray morrows,
Stretching monotonously on,
Forever narrowing but never done,
Have I not loathed to live again and said,
It would have been far better to be dead,
And yet somehow, I know not why
Remained afraid to die!

In "Life" he contrasted the beauties and possibilities of youth to now, "a blind alley, lurking by the shore / Of stagnant ditches, walled with reeking crags, / Where one old heavy-hearted vagrant lags / Footsore, at nightfall limping to Death's door." Considering Elinor's serious illness during the 1890-91 winter and his father's many afflictions during the same period, Howells wondered: "If we were offered our choice of life or not-life before birth, who would choose life?" Elinor's continuing ill health, his own vertigo, and the "dreadful shocks" of many calls to the bedside of his father during the next three and a half years would not much ease this outlook, an outlook that tempered the enthusiasm and energy behind his literary undertakings.[6]

So far as there was ever any resolution to all his questioning, it may be found, perhaps, in his story "A Circle in the Water," which, he later recalled, was an "effect from a smouldering rage of mine against the cruel injustice of things." As the story, written in 1894, opens, Basil March, in a "sort of impersonal melancholy," drags himself to a pool, where, in harmony with a dreary November sunset, he ponders the transience of life and the power of evil. The story's specific question, whether an ex-convict has a right to see his daughter, is answered in the belief that central to existence are love and compassion between human beings, feelings that should not be intruded upon by sophisticated, insensitive theories. Time often resolves the evil and suffering in the world, and "in certain luminous moments it seemed to us that we had glimpsed, in our witness of this experience, an infinite compassion encompassing our whole being like a sea, where every trouble of our sins and sorrows must cease at last like a circle in the water."[7] Whether this view provided Howells with a final or merely momentary satisfaction, it is hard to say. It is where, at any rate, he was sometimes able to rest.

III

He continued to live with his old dichotomies. He visited among the well-to-do classes and visited for the Associated Charities. He advocated nationalization of the railroads and gained substantial income from his railroad stock. When his stock, $5,000 worth, in the Atchison and Topeka fell from $1.13 to $0.24 as a result of Jay Gould's rascality, he began again to think about nationalization, as he had done in his 1888 article "Was There Nothing to Arbitrate?" when his stock had fallen because of a private war between the C. B. & Q. and its employees. The money he lost, he wrote, was "honest money, that I had earned, not made; but perhaps I had no right to have money in stocks."

In composing *A Boy's Town* in 1890, he discovered in himself as a boy an inner hero and outer conformist. Or, as he phrased it in a letter to his father: Mark Twain "and his wife and Elinor and I are all of accord in our way of thinking: that is, we are theoretical socialists, and practical aristocrats. But it is a comfort to be right theoretically, and to be ashamed of one's self practically." The tone is light but ironic, and Howells knew, sometimes excruciatingly, of the fallible, inadequate human being beneath the successful writer. He wrote to Hale that he did not deserve praise: "I am all the time stumbling to my feet from the dirt of such falls through vanity and evil will, and hate, that I can hardly believe in that self that seems to write books which help people." He was struck by a statement in William James's *The Principles of Psychology* and quoted it in the "Study," the passage from Luke still very much with him: "The consciousness of inward hollowness that accrues from habitually seeing the better only to do worse, is one of the saddest feelings one can bear with him through this vale of tears." "One knows what is selfishly best," Howells wrote to Norton in 1892, "and acts upon inspiration — mostly from the Pit, I dare say."[8]

His recurrent dreams troubled him. Anxiety over financial security is suggested in his frequent dream of burglars breaking into his house, especially his house on Concord Avenue in Cambridge, one of his sources of steady income. Dreams of running away in battle or not knowing his part when the curtain went up touched his doubts about his courage in art and life. When he had some part in creating and controlling his dreams, he would fight tendencies toward evasive historical romances by having "bands and groups of people scurrying, in mediaeval hose of divers colors, and mediaeval leathern jerkins, hugging themselves against the frost, and very miserable," affecting him with a "profound compassion" and representing the "vast mass of humanity, the mass that does the work, and earns the bread, and goes cold and hungry through all the ages" — the mass, clearly, for which his modern, humanistic realism was to do something. He was appalled at dreams that revealed his fears of being slighted or snubbed in society, especially in the homes of American gentry where, in his dreams, he would try to appear a man of fashion; this made him ask himself "if I am really such a snob when I am waking, and this in itself is very unpleasant."

It was perhaps that disparity between his convictions and his practice, between what he tried to be and what he suspected he was, that in 1902 brought him "visions of the past in which I appear to be mostly running about, full of sound and fury signifying nothing," and in 1912 was keeping him awake in his "dreadful moments of self-blame," after he woke "to the sense of what a toad I am and always have been." It was the irrevocability of this disparity that seemed to trouble him most, and led him to write in "Peonage" in 1891:

How tired the Recording Angel must begin
To be of setting down the same old sin,
The same old folly, year out and year in,
Since I knew how to err, against my name!
It makes me sick at heart and sore with shame
To think of that monotony of blame
For things I fancied once that I should be
Quits with in doing; but at last I see
All that I did became a part of me,
And cannot be put from me, but must still

Remain a potent will within my will,
Holding me debtor, while I live, to ill.

His repeated follies and sins, the death and illness about him, and his
metaphysical doubts made these years for Howells years of anguish.

IV

Henry James took him to task for such "deplorable talk": "How can
you take any view of your long career of virtue and devotion and self-
sacrifice, of labour and courage and admirable and distinguished production, *but* the friendly and understanding and acceptingly 'philosophic' view, I decline even to lift an eye to comprehending.... We all fall
short of our dreams."[9] James is right in restoring the balance, for although Howells may have been an unhappy sinner, his idealism was far
from confined to the internal and theoretical. If he had reason to be
dissatisfied and frustrated with himself for doing too little, he had nevertheless done a great deal. His contradictions had not vanished, but he
went on from *A Hazard of New Fortunes* — and attempted to go on with a
difference.

This difference did not lie in activism. Howells's one substantial en-
gagement in this period, aside from his work for the Associated Charities,
appears to have been his participation in the effort to defeat the treaty
with Russia that was to allow extradition of any Russian who had plotted
against the life of the czar. He served as vice-president, along with Edward Bellamy, George Kennan, and Samuel Gompers, of an antitreaty
meeting on March 7, 1893, at Carnegie Hall. Their work also involved
efforts to keep "respectable" Americans active in the movement. In the
midst of this project he vowed to avoid such engagements in the future,
for he found them very time-consuming.[10] And because of this resolve, his
principal reform endeavors during the early 1890s remained literary.

The difference in these literary endeavors was that he increasingly
adopted the essay as his instrument of reform. In late 1890, for instance,
he and the publisher and writer Charles Wolcott Balestier discussed the
possibility of collaborating on a periodical that would propagate socialist
ideas, a possibility aborted Balestier's early death in 1891. This same
goal attracted him to the coeditorship of *The Cosmopolitan*. Howells

wrote in 1891 to John Brisben Walker, a millionaire "with socialistic tendencies," a note in praise of a lecture on "The Church and Poverty," and Walker replied, asking Howells for a series of social essays for the magazine, which Walker published. When Howells declined, Walker offered him $15,000 a year to work in "the interests of The Cosmopolitan," as co-editor with himself. Howells would have his mornings free for his writing and would have complete control over literary contributions. He found Walker compatible "in many other matters," had hopes of doing "something for humanity as well as the humanities" with the periodical, and by March 1892, was in fact writing the requested essays — in the guise of a romance called *A Traveler from Altruria.*

Elsewhere, in published letters, in articles, and in an essay for *The Niagara Book* (1893), Howells pointed out the benefits of socialist programs. On his earlier visits to the falls, "stupid and squalid contrivances" defaced the landscape "at every point, and extorted a coin from the insulted traveler at every turn." Now, under state control, "the whole redeemed and disenthralled vicinity of Niagara is an object-lesson in what public ownership, whenever it comes, does for beauty."[11]

Probably because he felt that a label, especially one suspect to a large number of readers, would be damaging to the kind of communication he was trying to effect, Howells avoided affiliation with the Christian Socialists, the Nationalists, or the Society for the American Friends of Russian Freedom. He had not seen the newspaper reports that he was writing a socialistic novel, he replied to Howard Pyle in late October 1893, "and I do not believe it is true, except so far as every conscientious and enlightened fiction is of some such import; and that is the kind of fiction I try to produce." A year later he told Stephen Crane that the novel "in its real meaning, adjusts the proportions. It preserves the balances. It is in this way that lessons are to be taught and reforms to be won. When people are introduced to each other they will see the resemblances, and won't want to fight so badly."[12]

How central this humanistic purpose remained to his work is seen in the two newspaper reports on J. Milton Northwick's embezzlement in *The Quality of Mercy* (1891). Lorenzo Pinney's report, written for Bartley Hubbard's old paper, is "loathsome": It is "flashy and vulgar and unscrupulous," calculated to suit the corrupt expectations of a large body of newspaper readers. Brice Maxwell's report, on the other hand, treats Northwick with humane temperance, describing him as the victim of conditions and placing the burden of his crime on American society. Maxwell's realistic approach, his refusal to blink the facts or distort in any fashion, and his calm and understanding consideration lead the reader to sympathy and appropriate indignation. Even Eben Hillary, president of Northwick's company, who normally would take offense at the "social-istic" implications of the report, is favorably moved by its forbearing and enlightened temper. Although he himself experiences difficulty in always paralleling its tone, the report succeeds in tempering his later behavior toward Northwick.[13]

In his effort to get his socialistic fiction to a wider public, Howells arranged with Harper and Brothers to have *Annie Kilburn* and *A Hazard of New Fortunes* reissued simultaneously in cheap editions and "adver-tised as being of the same strain of thinking & belonging naturally to-gether." He had *A Traveler from Altruria* reissued in a fifty-cent paper edition in the Franklin Square Library of Harper and Brothers. And in 1895, when Keir Hardie asked permission to republish one of Howells's social essays, Howells eagerly responded with an offer of four such essays. Hardie intended to publish them first in his *Labour Leader*, then in penny-pamphlet form, and finally in a shilling volume with others, making them fully available to the average workman in England, whose "opportunities for reaching good current literature are all too limited."

As he made this effort to widen his audience, and as he pondered in the 1880s and early 1890s the power of the pen, Howells began to have res-ervations about his choice of literary medium. That he chose to symbolize his humanistic effect by Maxwell's newspaper article rather than by "lit-erature" is a significant sign. He continued to make excursions into the slum areas of the city, visiting, for example, on November 23, 1892, the Tombs prison (which he found "heartbreaking"), a Chinese temple, a dime museum, and the Bowery. He did this both to collect material and for the reason given by Lindau in *A Hazard of New Fortunes* and by Denton in *The World of Chance*, who states, "The more we see and feel the misery around us, the better"; it is too easy to live in luxury and shut our eyes to it. As Howells wrote in "Tribulations of a Cheerful Giver":

> The whole spectacle of poverty, indeed, is incredible. As soon as you cease to have it before your eyes — even when you have it before your eyes — you can hardly believe it, and that is perhaps why so many people deny that it exists, or is much more than a superstition

of the sentimentalist. When I get back into my own comfortable
room, among my papers and books, I remember it as I remember
something at the theatre. It seems to be turned off, as Niagara does,
when you come away.[14]

The "spectacle" and simile indicate his sense of how stunning American poverty had become. As he made his excursions, he wondered how to
bring this sight and its implications more effectively before the people.

This desire was certainly heightened by the labor disturbances and
economic upheavals of the late 1880s to the mid-1890s. The year 1892
brought the distressing Homestead Affair; and 1893 to 1897 were the
years of America's most severe depressions — the years of Coxey's Army,
of the "Black Winter" of '94, of the Pullman Affair with all its violence. It
was a time of panic and discouragement, a time, in Robert H. Wiebe's
picture of it, of accumulated bitterness and fear on all sides, of a search
for a recognizable enemy and viable battle lines, of "nationwide crisis."
The country, according to Richard Hofstadter, was "profoundly shak-
en," and men's vision of what America meant was significantly altered.

In his 1894 essay "Are We a Plutocracy?" Howells, with the pungency
of his increasingly, if not constantly, outspoken criticism, drew this grim
picture:

> The tramps walk the land like the squalid spectres of the laborers
> who once tilled it. The miners have swarmed up out of their pits, to
> starve in the open air. In our paradise of toil, myriads of working-
> men want work; the water is shut off in the factory, the fires are cold
> in the foundries. The public domain, where in some sort the poor
> might have provided for themselves, has been lavished upon cor-
> porations, and its millions of acres have melted away as if they had
> been a like area of summer clouds.

Yet American wealth was steadily increasing, some of the rich were
growing richer, many of them making profits from the hardships of
others, and these difficult years would be brought to an end by the prosperity accompanying an unjust war, the conflict with Spain, which
Howells would actively oppose. It was easy enough for the inhuman
laissez-faire economist or the unbroken millionaire to brush aside the
temporary ill effects, and Howells wrote, with heavy irony,

. . . it is true that we still have the trusts, the syndicates, the combinations of roads, mines, and markets, the whole apparatus. If there is much cold and hunger, the price of food and fuel is yet so high as to afford a margin to the operators in coal and grain and meat. The great fortunes in almost undiminished splendor, remain the monuments of a victory that would otherwise look a good deal like defeat, and they will be an incentive to the young in the hour of our returning prosperity. The present adversity cannot last forever; and if there are many thousands of men and women who cannot outlast it, or live to see the good time which is coming back, this has been the order of events from the beginning of the world, and we must not shut our eyes to the gain because it involves a great deal of loss.[15]

The question, then, was how could he bring people face to face with the facts of poverty in such a way that they would not forget them? How could he do what, later, Upton Sinclair would try to do in his *Jungle* and what Sinclair's orator would try to do with his audience of workingmen, vividly challenging their complacency with detailed scenes of war and poverty, pleading with them to tear off the rags of custom and convention and "realize it, *realize* it!"

Howells was far from sanguine. While he could believe that "if rich and cultivated men had to go down manholes in sewers we should have a different system of drainage presently," he also knew, as he had David Hughes argue in *The World of Chance*, that if the beggars should come out from their cellars and garrets until every rich man's doorstep had a beggar on it, it would be to no avail. The rich man would give to the first two or three, then realize that to give continually would be to beggar himself: "He would harden his heart; he would know as he does now, that he must not take the chance of suffering for himself and his family by relieving the suffering of others. He could put it" — and here Hughes points a finger at Howells's most consistent rationalization — "on the highest moral ground." The poverty of the egoistic young P. B. S. Ray, in the same novel, was without care, for no one else shared it,

. . . and those spectres of want and shame which haunt the city's night, and will not always away at dawn, but remain present to eyes that have watched and wept, vanished in the joyous light that his youth shed about him, as he hurried home with the waltz music beating in his blood. A remote sense, very remote and dim, of something all wrong attended him at moments in his pleasure; at moments it seemed even he who was wrong. But this fled before his analysis; he could not see what harm he was doing. To pass his leisure in the company of well-bred, well-dressed, prosperous, and handsome people was so obviously right and fit that it seemed absurd to suffer any question of it.[16]

If Howells could only, somehow, make such Americans confront poverty and care about it and think about it even to the limited extent that he had...

Out of this need to jar his readers, then, Howells began to de-emphasize his fiction in favor of his Altrurian work and his direct, argumentative, sometimes ironic essays on behalf of economic and social equality, each of which was an attempt to bring about "realization" by taking a different persuasive tack. These essays included "Equality as the Basis of Good Society" — with its assertion that good society with its politeness and its internal equality could serve as the model for equality throughout society — "Are We a Plutocracy?," "Who Are Our Brethren?," and "The Nature of Liberty." Between 1895 and 1897, Howells also wrote a number of sketches in the manner of his earlier "Police Report," which he now revised slightly and published with some of the new sketches in *Impressions and Experiences*. In a style both personal and revealing, the sketches discuss individual American experiences and approaches to the problem of poverty, and they bear such titles as "An East-Side Ramble," "Tribulations of a Cheerful Giver," "Worries of a Winter Walk," and "The Midnight Platoon."[17]

In this last sketch, which appeared in *Harper's Weekly* for May 4, 1895, Howells tells of the experience recounted to him, he says, by a friend who during Christmas week had driven past a long line of ill-clad men waiting for a midnight handout of bread. The friend was dressed, like Angus Beaton (and like Howells), in a fur overcoat, in which he had wrapped himself up to the chin as a duty to his family, "with a conscience against taking cold and alarming them for his health." He had been told about this bread line before, had imagined it very dramatic, and was thrilled at his great luck in coming upon it. Although there seems to be no reason for a man to delight in seeing his fellow men in midwinter waiting for a dole of bread that might be their only meal in forty-eight hours, still

...the mere thought of it gave him pleasure, and the sight of it, from the very first instant. He was proud of knowing just what it was at once, with the sort of pride which one has in knowing an earthquake, though one has never felt one before. He saw the double file of men stretching up one street, and stretching down the other from the corner of the bakery where the loaves were to be given out on the stroke of twelve, and he hugged himself in a luxurious content with his perspicacity.

He practiced "self-denial," however, allowing his driver to go rapidly past this spectacle so that he could retrieve his child from the Christmas party on time, but he promised himself a slow return.

Upon his return the line was even longer, and his heart beat with glad anticipation: "He was really to see this important, this representative thing to the greatest possible advantage." He imagined that coffee sometimes was given out with the bread and, when he later learned that it was so, he was proud of his acuity. He thought of descending from his coupé to speak with the men and ask them about themselves, and "at the time it did not strike him that it would be indecent." He made a fine literary comparison between the platoon and the galley slaves whom Don Quixote released. He smiled at this and then had some decent, "conscientious" thoughts:

> He thought how these men were really a sort of slaves and convicts — slaves to want and self-convicted of poverty. All at once he fancied them actually manacled there together, two by two, a coffle of captives taken in some cruel foray, and driven to a market where no man wanted to buy. He thought how old their slavery was; and he wondered if it would ever be abolished, as other slaveries had been. Would the world ever outlive it? Would some New-Year's day come when some President would proclaim, amid some dire struggle, that their slavery was to be no more? That would be fine.

Seeing that none of them wore any sort of overcoat, he reflected on that too and was pleased and interested in the "celerity, the simultaneity of his impressions, his reflections." He tested this excellent state of mind further, taking note of the "fine mass of the great dry-goods store on the hither corner . . . and of the Gothic beauty of the church beyond," unconsciously failing the test, however, through his inability to catch the irony in these juxtapositions. He next thought to ask himself appropriate questions: How early did the lines begin to form? Did the men joke away the weary hours of waiting? Did they quarrel over precedence? And how was it with them when word went to the rear that the supply was exhausted?

> My friend did not quite like to think. Vague, reproachful thoughts for all the remote and immediate luxury of his life passed through his mind. If he reformed that and gave the saving to hunger and cold? But what was the use? There was so much hunger, so much cold, that it could not go around.

The platoon turned about and faced his too slowly moving coupé like soldiers under review about to salute a superior. This brought him a sudden awareness, not so much of the responsibility suggested as of the fact that

> ... he stood to these men for all the ease and safety that they could never, never hope to know. He was Society: Society that was to be preserved because it embodies Civilization. He wondered if they hated him in his capacity of Better Classes. He no longer thought of getting out and watching their behavior as they took their bread and coffee. He would have liked to excuse that thought, and protest that he was ashamed of it; that he was their friend, and wished them well — as well as might be without the sacrifice of his own advantages or superfluities, which he could have persuaded them would be perfectly useless.

And he told the trembling girl beside him, "You musn't mind. What we are and what we do is all right. It's what they are and what they suffer that's all wrong." This, he tells Howells, in recounting his experience, seems to be the only way out. Howells replies, "It's an easy way, and it's an idea that ought to gratify the midnight platoon."

If Howells's criticism during this period could be pungent and sarcastic, a look at his own relation to the conditions he was attacking left him uneasy and frustrated. Basil March, David Hughes, the exceedingly sorrowful young man who in Howells's poem "Parable" (1895) dreams he gives all and then watches the poor wildly misuse it, and Howells, the troubled reader of Tolstoy in the late 1880s and 1890s — all with valid objections to social action that would deprive them and their families and ultimately do no good — are represented by the friend's statement "There was so much hunger, so much cold, that it could not go around." Howells's dissatisfaction with such unassailable, intangibly hypocritical and evasive reasoning, with the selfishness of his position, is there in his friend's wishing the poor well — "as well as might be without the sacrifice of his own advantages or superfluities, which he could have persuaded them would be perfectly useless." And Howells's frustration with all individual effort, literary or other, in face of the overwhelming spectacle of long bread lines and proliferating tenements is reflected with mockery in his friend's speculation that it would be fine if some New Year's Day "some President would proclaim, amid some dire struggle, that their slavery was to be no more."

This frustration and dissatisfaction, if not new, were far from his joy in the critical reaction to *A Hazard of New Fortunes* and from the relative optimism with which, three years earlier, he had approached the more direct didacticism of the essay form. Inspired at that time by Bellamy's success in reaching a far-flung and responsive audience with *Looking Backward*, he had chosen, first of all, a variation on the utopian mode.[18]

V

The visitor from Altruria, who began to appear in the *Cosmopolitan* for November 1892, puzzles Mr. Twelvemough, his host in the country resort hotel. His direct, annoying, troubling questions about American civilization are delivered in a sincere, open manner, but Twelvemough experiences now and again a "cold doubt of something ironical in the man." He finds it difficult to credit such innocence as seems to prompt Homos's inquiries; his repeated questions about matters already "explained" to him seem sometimes malicious or stupid — Twelvemough is not certain which. And Twelvemough is not the only one puzzled and disturbed: Homos himself notices "that I seem to affect you all with a kind of misgiving." All the people in his presence speak very frankly, possibly because they are anxious to explain America to a foreigner, or, as Twelvemough suspects, because Homos exerts a "mysterious control." Twelvemough tells Mrs. Makely, "I find him quite as incredible as you do. There

are moments when he seems so entirely subjective with me, that I feel as if
he were no more definite or tangible than a bad conscience." A great deal
of strong and even bitter truth is told at the Camps' home, where Mrs.
Makely and Twelvemough have taken Homos to see the natives, and
Twelvemough narrates:

> I glanced at the Altrurian, sitting attentive and silent, and a sudden
> misgiving crossed my mind concerning him. Was he really a man, a
> human entity, a personality like ourselves, or was he merely a sort of
> spiritual solvent, sent for the moment to precipitate whatever sin-
> cerity there was in us, and show us what the truth was concerning
> our relations to each other? It was a fantastic conception.[19]

Fantastic conception or not, Homos is Howells's literary method and
purpose embodied in a semiallegorical figure. Homos makes people uncomfortable and leads them to consider contemporary economic conditions and their relation to them. He does it directly, verbally testing the
imperfect against the perfect, whereas the central conflicts in Howells's
fiction up through *A Hazard of New Fortunes* and beyond had been
expressed mainly in action and in the characters' minds. *The Quality of
Mercy* and *The World of Chance* carry somewhat more open discussion of
Howells's social ideas than the earlier fiction, and this final embodiment
of Howells's method in a character is the culmination of his frustration
over the limited effect of more subtle techniques.

This work, which gives considerable space to undercutting the flag-
waving, complacent, evasive romancer Mr. Twelvemough, as well as
other well-to-do defenders of the status quo, repeats and develops earlier
Howellsian attacks on American civilization. It also introduces a new
Howellsian portrait, the disarming and sinister banker Mr. Bullion, who
recognizes the rottenness in his nation and coldly reaffirms it. The work
culminates in Homos's speech on Altruria, which is delivered before a
huge assembly of all classes and occupations in an open space near the
hotel. This space, in Twelvemough's romantic prose, takes on some of the
lineaments and sounds of a cathedral, placing the speech in the tradition
of sermons preached by such major figures as David Sewell and Mr. Peck.

America, Homos discloses, could become the new Altruria. The
democratic ideals expressed in its Declaration of Independence and the
basic goodness and generosity of its citizens underlie its stifling accretions

of self-centered materialism. Altrurians are true followers of Christ, and Altruria intentionally resembles the earliest Christian (socialist) communities: Everything is owned in common, and every man takes care of every other. Altruria has taken advantage of its valuable industrial machinery and great monopolies and trusts and operates them for the general good. It has destroyed most of its railroads and has returned to a simple, close-to-the-earth existence in which there is neither city nor country and in which all men spend some hours each day tilling the soil. Under these changed conditions, human nature is changed and perfected. Because all people have true individualities to develop and express as they wish, all desire to dedicate themselves in special ways to the general good. All men and women of Altruria are true nobility because their first thoughts are for others. Possession of great gifts brings a sense of humane responsibility, and great men have no ambition to distinguish themselves from those less fortunate but, rather, wish to identify themselves with the great mass of men.

The similarities between American and Altrurian ideals and the similarity between American economic practice and that of Altruria before the Evolution prophesies a new Altruria, on American soil. Altruria's bloodless Evolution took place during a state of affairs more desperate even than that of America, although America's conditions approach those. The Accumulation failed to trouble itself over the vote, and suddenly men united, like the Populists in the West, and voted government ownership of communications, transportation, industry, and land, that is, voted in a socialist society.[20]

After the speech, Reuben Camp announces that Homos will stay at his house for the next week, and he invites the enthusiastic laborers and farmers to come visit. When a member of the construction gang asks about travel to Altruria, Homos replies, "Ah, you mustn't go to Altruria! You must let Altruria come to you." "'Yes,' shouted Reuben Camp, whose thin face was red with excitement, 'that's the word! Have Altruria right here and right now!'" Luckily, in a nation where the men on top argue for continuation of things as they are and where men who rise assume similar attitudes, there are men like Reuben Camp in the working class who assess the situation and tell the truth about subsistence farm life, about taxes, about the economic structure, about class division from the point of view of the poor, and about American individuality — this last by evoking a picture of mill hands returning home in droves after a

day's work. Reuben is that rare American spirit Howells is continually
seeking, the spirit that carries on the idealism that fought the Civil War —
Reuben is identified with his father, who fought slavery and felt the war
had not yet abolished it.[21] Most important, Reuben is the key to the basic
optimism of *A Traveler from Altruria*. He represents a working class that
knows enough and cares enough to wish to vote Altruria into existence in
America, that can respond to the words of Howells-Homos. His response
is ideal, and Howells implies that his and his fellow laborers' eagerness
will soon vote in an ideal, Christian Socialist America. This hopeful conclusion, deriving partly from Howells's aspirations for his new genre, is in
tone and attitude a world apart from the conclusion of the subsequent
Altrurian series.

VI

Letters of an Altrurian Traveller, which came immediately on the
heels of *A Traveler from Altruria* in *Cosmopolitan*, appearing from
November 1893 to September 1894, was stereotyped by Howells's brother
Joe under the title *The Eye of the Needle*, but it was not published separately as a whole during Howells's lifetime, very probably because of the
conservatism of Harper and Brothers.[22] Its narrative method differs from
that of *A Traveler from Altruria*, for Mr. Homos now makes direct obser-
vations and reflections in letters to a friend back in Altruria, and Howells
is even further from fiction than he had been in the previous book. The
sketches Basil March had intended to do for *Every Other Week* and that
the Harper and Brothers organization had once proposed to Howells
because of his altruism[23] are now written by Homos, as he describes the
New York streets, slums, tenement interiors, and homes and lives of the
well-to-do and reflects on their significance. Neither the shift to New
York, however, nor the shift to Homos as narrator accounts for the sharp
change in tone of this book; the turnabout can be traced only to the
American economic climate. By the time these essays were written, the
1893 panic had taken a firm hold, and the resulting misery and despera-
tion made optimism less easy for Howells.

Letters of an Altrurian Traveller is not lacking in hopefulness, however. While New York's architectural diversity, ugliness, and lack of planning — as well as the noise and squalor of its streets — reveal the soul and

structure of egoistic American life, the cooperatively constructed classical buildings of the Columbian Exposition of 1893 symbolize the Altrurian logical, harmonious spirit. And Central Park, at the heart of New York, serves, like the Exposition's White City on the Chicago shore, to typify the generosity and justness of common effort and common ownership. It is the "token, if not the pledge, of happier things," and it is there Mr. Homos constantly retires to for relief from the miseries of New York life. He takes comfort in the fact that "the potentialities of goodness implanted in the human heart by the Creator forbid the plutocratic man to be what the plutocratic scheme of life implies." And, Homos reports, there are Americans who courageously do good despite the threat of harm to one's own prosperity and family that the system imposes on self-sacrifice. (Howells possibly had in mind Governor Altgeld of Illinois, who at the cost of his political life had recently pardoned the three living Haymarket anarchists.) If change is to come, it will come not from the working class but from the middle class, which will prevent the impending "wild revolt of the poor against the rich" by a "quiet opposition of the old American instincts" and ideals "to the recent plutocratic order of things." The middle class may at present be bent mainly upon providing for themselves, but some of its members are beginning to reflect on their environment — some of them, Howells would probably wish to believe, as the result of certain kinds of reading.

But the picture is grim. Poverty is omnipresent: The "great trouble, here," Homos writes, is that "you cannot anywhere get away from the misery of life," and after the first letter, little is said about the potential of the middle class. His language grows troubled; his figures of speech, galling and painful. As he walks through New York, he finds that "business and poverty are everywhere slowly or swiftly eating their way into the haunts of respectability and destroying its pleasant homes"; poverty "festers in the squalid houses and swarms day and night in the squalid streets." The slums are "leprous," and Homos is deeply affected:

> When I come home from these walks of mine, heart-sick, as I usually do, I have a vision of the wretched quarters through which I have passed, as blotches of disease upon the civic body, as loathsome sores, destined to eat deeper and deeper into it; and I am haunted by this sense of them, until I plunge deep into the Park, and wash my consciousness clean of it all for a while.

The only respite from such things is to be found in shutting them out.

> . . . you must ignore a thousand facts, which, if you recognize them,
> turn and rend you, and instil their poison into your lacerated soul.
> In your pleasures you must forget the deprivation which your in-
> dulgence implies; if you feast, you must shut out the thought of
> them that famish; when you lie down in your bed, you cannot sleep
> if you remember the houseless who have nowhere to lay their heads.
> You are everywhere beleaguered by the armies of want and woe,
> and in the still watches of the night you can hear their invisible
> sentinels calling to one another, "All is ill! All is ill!" and hushing
> their hosts to the apathy of despair.[24]

Howells had seldom before, and never so overwhelmingly, written
such passages as these.

The tenor of these letters is unremittingly pessimistic. With all the financial instability, poverty, and misery, with all the distancing of poverty
by the well-to-do to a matter of statistical knowledge and lurid gossip,
Howells was wondering, what difference would utopian criticism and the
Altrurian vision make? What difference had his novels and essays made?
What are words on a page before the massive, immovable fact of the economic unfairness of a huge nation? Were Americans growing kinder
through reading humanistic fiction, if they were reading it at all? What
difference would any action of his make? What effective steps were
Americans taking to remedy the situation Mr. Homos so vividly presents?
Americans, unfortunately, as Homos remarks, seemed to believe that
misery on the vast scale that their financial convulsions bring testifies to
national greatness, and that the panic will bring only slight alteration.
Homos must acknowledge that his meditations on the socialistic implications of Central Park and its indictment, by comparison, of the rest of the
city probably never enter the poor man's thoughts: "The poor are slaves
of habit, they bear what they have borne, they suffer on from generation
to generation, and seem to look for nothing different." Even compassionate people who desire to do good find they can accomplish nothing and
only harm themselves and find themselves growing callous and evasive.
The vote is no longer a source of optimism, for "without economic
equality there can be no social equality, and, finally, there can be no
political equality; for money corrupts the franchise, the legislature and

the judiciary here." The result of all this, for an American who cares, is an "anguish of impotency."²⁵

This anguish is most fully portrayed in Eveleth Strange, the young American widow and "altruistic plutocrat" with whom Homos falls in love. When the men emerge from their after-dinner smoke at the Makelys's, they learn that Eveleth has been asking the women to acknowledge the many people within five minutes' walk who have had no dinner at all. When, however, a facetious gentleman asks, "What does she propose to do about it?" Eveleth can only answer, "Nothing. What does any one propose to do about it?" She cannot escape the thought of it, however, and to demonstrate her feeling she quotes six despairing quatrains from Longfellow's "The Challenge," about the "numberless, starving army, / At all the gates of life":

> And whenever I sit at the banquet,
> Where the feast and song are high,
> Amid the mirth and the music
> I can hear that fearful cry . . .
>
> For within there is light and plenty,
> And odors fill the air;
> But without there is cold and darkness,
> And hunger and despair.

As she later tells Homos, she has come to the end of her tether: "I have tried, as truly as I believe any woman ever did, to do my share, with money and with work, to help make life better for those whose life is bad, and though one mustn't boast of good works, I may say that I have been pretty thorough, and if I've given up, it's because I see, in our state of things, *no* hope of curing the evil."

As Homos reflects on Eveleth, he comes to describe someone very much like the Howells who was writing in such despair of America. He recognized from the first, he writes, her "deep and almost tragical seriousness," which she "masked with a most winning gaiety, a light irony, a fine scorn that was rather for herself than for others." She "had thought herself out of all sympathy with her environment; she knew its falsehood, its vacuity, its hopelessness; but she necessarily remained in it, and of it . . . she could not set herself up as censor of things that she must keep on doing as other people did." She has come to grips in a familiar way with a familiar biblical passage: "We *know* that Christ was perfectly right, and that he was perfectly sincere in what he said to the good young millionaire; but we all go away exceeding sorrowful, just as the good young millionaire did. We have to, if we don't want to come on charity ourselves." With no vocation for the religious life, she cannot renounce the world, and, in fact, with all her gifts, all her generosity and magnanimity, she is "without that faith, that trust in God, which comes to us from living His law, and which I wonder any American can keep." She continues mechanically to practice charity but no longer attempts to do good from her heart, for she had always the "ironical doubt that she was doing harm."

Having agreed to marry Homos, she opposes his plans to return to Altruria for the remainder of their lives. When, in response to her opposition, he decides that they will come back after a year to work together for an Altrurian America, she asserts that they must retain her money and her house as a base of operation. He replies that they cannot come "as prophets to the comfortable people, and entertain nicely," that they must sell all and renew the evangel "in the life and spirit of the First Altrurian," that "we must come poor to the poor . . . we must be simple and humble as the least of those that Christ bade follow Him," and he offers her a choice between himself and her money. And then, finally and dramatically, in the last chapter, entitled "A Plutocratic Triumph," she embodies Howells's omnipresent passage from Luke and turns sorrowfully away.[26]

The ultimate limitation of action, stance, and point of view in Atherton, David Sewell, Annie Kilburn, and Basil March, with their inevitable attachment to security and comfort, is reaffirmed in the helplessness of Eveleth Strange to be anything other than a creature of her conditions. The impossibility of valid escape from American conditions and the ineffectiveness of any effort to remedy them reflect the pessimistic conclusion of a work written in the hope of suggesting change. They reveal Howells's frustration and disappointment with his own life and his efforts as an artist and with the direction he saw his country taking. If he was not overwhelmed by this and did not live with it constantly, the fact that it emerges in so much of his writing at this time tells how substantial a part of him it had become.

VII

In a story that began to appear in *Cosmopolitan* two months after *Letters of an Altrurian Traveller* concluded there, Howells reveals his sense of age and weariness, his sense of the thinness and meaninglessness of life. Writing out of a need to confirm and justify, however shakily, Eveleth's position, he dealt with another parting. To do so, he returned to a case of which he had first learned in the mid-1870s, and which may have haunted him ever since. In this story, "A Parting and a Meeting," Roger Burton and Chloe Mason, engaged to be married, visit a Shaker village near the home of her grandfather. There, Roger is intrigued to learn that the Shakers think of themselves as antiegoists similar to the early Christians. As he and Chloe start for home, he argues that the Shakers have found the kingdom of heaven on earth, while "all the rest of the world is at war." He urges Chloe to accompany him in joining the celibate sect, and she in her grief and honesty tells him to return alone to the Shaker (in 1894 we can read, "Altrurian") village, which he does, for life.

The "meeting" comes sixty-odd years later, when Chloe returns to the village and solicits a talk with the nearly ninety-year-old Roger. She had married Ira Dickerman, Roger's rival, a year after the parting, and Ira had made a good deal of money and had been, for the most part, a good husband to her. She had "been through it all"; she had "had the best that earth could give, and I've seen my children round me, and now my grandchildren." And yet, a wondering Eveleth, he says to her Homos:

I don't know, Roger, but what I'd have done as well to stay here with you that day. What do you think? . . . You've been here ever since, and you've lived the angelic life, and you've had peace. You've escaped all the troubles of this world. You haven't had a wife to pester you; and you haven't had to go down into the grave with your children, and want to stay there with them, when they died before you. You haven't seen your partner die by inches before your eyes. Your days have flowed right on here, with no sorrow and no trouble; you've done what you thought was right, and you've had your reward. Do you think I'd better have stayed with you that day?

Throughout the story we learn little about Roger, and our respect for him is qualified though not undermined by others' conceptions of him. He is reputed to be serious but unpractical, a poetry-writing schoolteacher, moony, with a vagueness always in his eyes. His mind is dim now, and he is mainly preoccupied with the mistakes the Shaker Sisters make in preparing his bed. His life between the parting and the meeting Howells evasively glosses over. Roger here arrives at a moment of lucidity and replies to Chloe's question, "Yes, I've lived the angelic life, as you say, and it's been all I ever expected. I've had peace, I don't deny that, and I haven't had any sorrow or trouble; and still, I'm not sure but I'd have done about as well to go with *you*, Chloe."

In "A Shaker Village" (1876), a kindly treatment of the community at Shirley, Massachusetts, a younger, highly successful, more optimistic Howells had looked upon the village as principally a refuge for the "disabled against fate, the poor, the bruised, the hopeless" and had emphasized the unhealthy appearance of the Shakers. In his brief sketch of this "parting" there, he clearly condemned the character on whom Roger is based: "Perhaps in an affair like that, a girl's heart had supreme claims." And he concluded his article by telling how, while the Howellses were visiting, a married sister of a Shaker woman came to spend the night. Her baby ended up on the knees of one of the brothers, while the celibate sisters gathered around, the mother standing outside the group with complacently folded hands. "Somehow the sight was pathetic. If she were right and they wrong, how much of heaven they had lost in renouncing the supreme good of earth!"

But Chloe is that woman aged, and Howells at fifty-six no longer has confidence in his 1870s point of view. Pursuit of worldly things had not brought all he imagined ("But, oh dear me! Life a'n't what we used to think it was, Roger, when we were young"). Yet living like Christ or Tolstoy or Homos, detached from the world's life, is not so satisfactory either. The choice is an indifferent one, indifferent to oneself and to the world: One's basic character might not change, and decay leads on to death. With this attitude, Howells hoped to reach a certain finality, hoped that he had done with the Homos-Eveleth dispute within himself, for as old Roger Burton gets stiffly to his feet, the "old lady" tells her impatient granddaughter she is coming: "I guess Roger and I have about got through."[27]

Of course, it was not to be so easy, but neither were the meaninglessness of experience recorded in "A Parting and a Meeting" and the despair of *Letters of an Altrurian Traveller* to be permanent attitudes in Howells. Indeed, the poems of this period show glimmers of brighter possibilities, and in 1894 Howells was working out the solution contained in "A Circle in the Water." His later essays have their notes of hope: The young millionaire in the later "Parable," with his disturbing dream vision of society, still believes he can be effective, and the sketches, even with the self-satire and sense of having reached a dead end in "The Midnight Platoon," continue to probe the psyche and conscience of America.

VIII

Fortunately, Howells was not, amidst all his discouragement, without encouragement. The general response to *A Traveler from Altruria* was favorable. In a judicious, appreciative review in the *Atlantic*, Sophia Kirk tied the utopian novel together with *The Minister's Charge, Annie Kilburn*, and *A Hazard of New Fortunes* and stated that "no such attempt" as Howells's "has ever been made to unravel the divers threads of our social life; to reveal mind to mind and class to class; to show the part of ignorance in human failings, of kindliness in human virtue." This was real understanding, and on the whole Howells thought the reception very good. His mail contained more laudatory letters than he had ever received — letters, he told Marrion Wilcox, from all sorts of people: working people, men of fortune, distinguished professional men. "Not that these correspondents always wholly believed in Altrurian doctrines, but they were interested, and hoped for something." To such people his was clearly a voice speaking out in troubled times, a stimulus to some of them in their own search for solutions. His corner newspaperman showed him Abraham Cahan's Yiddish translation of portions of the book "in a Hebrew workingman's paper," and because of the book, editors of such magazines as the *North American Review* and the *Forum* were to solicit from him more social essays. Reformers such as Frances Willard and Edward Bellamy were pleased, and in 1898 the *American Fabian* wrote that Howells's services "to the Socialist movement call for the warmest eulogy. ... He has pictured for us our own time, the struggle of mankind ... the obligation of brotherhood"; he "attacks the whole economic framework of modern society" and is the "high-minded American gentleman."

All of this he might have added with pride and satisfaction to the kind of response his novels had received in the past, especially to the high praise accorded *A Hazard of New Fortunes*. And he might have added the accolades from the young writers of the 1890s, among them Stephen Crane, Frank Norris, Brander Matthews, Paul Laurence Dunbar, Howard Pyle, Hamlin Garland, and Stuart Merrill, and even from writers of the succeeding generation, from Robert Frost, W. E. B. Du Bois, Edgar Lee Masters, Ellen Glasgow, and others, despite the reaction that produced less favorable comment.

Howells continued to lend his voice to protest efforts — against American involvement in Venezuela in 1895, against the war in the Philippines and the expansionism it represented. He continued to lend support to Russian revolutionists, wrote President Roosevelt in support of his stand on income and inheritance taxes, took part in the founding of the NAACP, protested the English executions of Irish prisoners taken during the Easter Uprising of 1916, and, in an unfinished novel begun in 1916, he recorded in a powerful passage the brutality of a lynching in the South and its effect on a white man who overhears it from nearby.[28]

From *A Hazard of New Fortunes* he had gone onward, despite his personal and artistic frustrations and despite his anguished outlook on life after Winny's death. He continued to write and act, *as well as he could,* with sincerity, concern, and purpose, and the plaudits from some readers and fellow writers indicated that his writing was having some effect. *The Landlord at Lion's Head,* which would begin to appear in July 1896, would be of equal quality with his best previous work, and his fiction in general, whatever his doubts, would continue to be humanistic in aim and method, if less frequent and direct in its attacks on economic and social injustice.

Howells received negative criticism from some of his contemporaries and has taken more from later generations with radically different literary standards. With all his excursions into slum areas and tenements, he did not live among the poor or know them intimately, he did not probe evil or care to concern himself much with the "guilty passions," and he had no deep, intense tragic vision. Yet his great self-awareness, his integrity, and his strong sense of moral principle led him, beyond most American writers of the 1880s, to a troubled, unremitting social conscience. These qualities made him painfully aware of the ambivalent motivations of the prosperous citizen and successful author who wished to better the disturbing social conditions of his country. This consciousness, coupled with his humanistic purpose of making individuals, making *us*, increasingly self-aware and compassionate, permeated all of his work, imparting to it a tough fiber of care, insight, and purpose that make it a vital and permanently relevant body of literature.

The average student of American literature has been trained to think of Theodore Dreiser as the writer who rescued America from its age of genteel literature, and there is some truth in this. It is much less well known that Dreiser in 1902 saw his literary goals as continuous with those of at least one American writer of the older generation. He wrote to Howells that year, probably after Howells had told him he did not like *Sister Carrie*, a significant letter of appreciation, before "it be too late," an attempt to convey his "spiritual affection" for Howells, "to offer my little tribute and acknowledge the benefit I have received from your work." Dreiser had clipped a number of poems from Howells's *Stops of Various Quills* when they first appeared, he said, and he had often turned to them in "need of fellowship" when he could "no longer feign to believe that life has either a purpose or a plan." Thomas Hardy and Count Tolstoy had also provided him with some of this "spiritual fellowship."

> Of you three however I should not be able to choose, the spirit in each seeming to be the same and the large, tender kindliness of each covering all of the ills of life and voicing the wonder and yearning of this fitful dream, in what to me seems a perfect way. I may be wrong in my estimate of life, but the mental attitude of you three seems best — the richest, most appealing flowering-out of sympathy, tenderness, uncertainty, that I have as yet encountered.

He wished Howells had expressed a higher estimate of Hardy, for he thought Howells and Hardy reached out to each other: "the same sympathetic solicitude for life, sorrow for suffering — care for the least and the greatest even to the fall of a sparrow, which is so marked a feature of both of your natures." Howells, who had written in 1877 that Lowell in one line had summed up the best that America means for the race when he said, "None can breathe her air nor grow humane," was here being told that he had passed on this impulse to a writer of a radically different background, temperament, and literary method.[29] Perhaps Howells was pleased to think that his life as expressed in his work had in some degree carried through the dark age of post-Civil War America the earlier American idealism on which he had been raised. And perhaps he was able, accordingly, to feel himself a potent factor in the evolution that must eventually emancipate the new American slave on whose behalf he had pleaded.

Notes

The following abbreviations are used throughout:

ES	"Editor's Study," *Harper's Monthly*
Kirk and Kirk	Howells, *Criticism and Fiction and Other Essays,* ed. Clara and Rudolf Kirk (New York: New York University Press, 1959)
LL	*Life in Letters of Wiliam Dean Howells,* ed. Mildred Howells (Garden City, N.Y: Doubleday, 1928)
MS-H	Manuscript at Houghton Library, Harvard University

CHAPTER 1

1. W. C. Brownell, *The Nation*, 31 (July 15, 1880), 50. Unpublished letter from James to Howells, July 22, 1879, MS-H. *The Letters of Henry James*, ed. Percy Lubbock (New York, 1920), I, 73, January 31, 1880.

2. Scudder, *Atlantic Monthly*, 50 (November 1882), 710. *The Critic*, 2 (October 21, 1882), 278-79. Hay, unpublished letter, November 30, [1881], MS-H. King, unpublished letter (n.d.), MS-H.

3. Mabie, "A Typical Novel," *Andover Review*, 4 (November 1885); in *Documents of Modern Literary Realism*, ed. George J. Becker (Princeton, 1963), p. 298. Gosse, letter to Howells, August 30, 1882, in *Transatlantic Dialogue*, ed. Paul F. Mattheisen and Michael Millgate (Austin, Texas, 1965), p. 97.

4. Gilder, unpublished letter, March 27, 1882, MS-H.

5. Younger realists: see Olov Fryckstedt, *In Quest of America* (Cambridge, Mass., 1958), p. 265. Garland, *North American Review*, 176 (March 1903), 338. Fryckstedt, pp. 9, 226. See also Edwin Cady, *The Road to Realism* (Syracuse, N.Y., 1956), p. 216, and Lionel Trilling, *The Opposing Self* (New York, 1955), p. 82.

6. Higginson, *Literary World*, 10 (August 2, 1879), 249-50; in *Howells: A Century of Criticism*, ed. Kenneth E. Eble (Dallas, 1962), pp. 13-15. Resignation: unpublished letter to Houghton, January 14, 1881, MS-H. Reid, *LL*, I, 304, November 29, 1881. Jackson, unpublished letter, February 9, 1881, MS-H. Salary: unpublished letter to father, February 13, 1881, MS-H. Tired: same letter to father, and letter to Scudder, February 8, 1881, *LL*, I, 294-95. Jump out: same letter to Scudder. Criticism: see Fryckstedt, *In Quest of America*, pp. 240, 255. James, unpublished letter, dated Tuesday, 1881, MS-H.

7. Turgenev: Rutherford B. Hayes to Howells, December 22, 1879, *LL*, I, 280. Yale and Europe: *LL*, I, 298 (July 2, 1881), 341 (May 6, 1883), 351 (July 30, 1883). "Henry James, Jr.," *Century*, 25 (November 1882), 25-29. James, unpublished letter, November 27, 1882, MS-H.

8. Letter and reply: *ES*, 74 (April 1887), 824-26; also in *Criticism and Fiction* (New York, 1891), pp. 92-96. Haggard, *ES*, 75 (July 1887), 318. Falsehood over truth: *North American Review*, 196 (October 1912); also in Kirk and Kirk, p. 98.

9. Moral universe: *ES*, 81 (October 1890), 804; *Atlantic Monthly*, 30 (August 1872), 244; *ES*, 76 (March 1888), 641; *Century*, 28 (May 1884) (Kirk and Kirk, p. 244). Lines 301-2 from Browning's "Fra Lippo Lippi." Russians: "Five Interviews with William Dean Howells," ed. George Arms and William M. Gibson, *Americana*, 37 (April 1943), 291.

10. Manner in which we live: *Frank Leslie's Weekly*, 74 (March 17, 1892), 118. Take thought of ourselves: *Harper's Weekly*, 39 (April 13, 1895), 342 (Kirk and Kirk, p. 161). Dickens: *ES*, 74 (January 1887), 322-23. Ibsen: *Harper's Weekly*, 39 (April 13, 1895), 342 (Kirk and Kirk, p. 161).

11. Vogüé, in Preface to his *Le Roman Russe* (1886); in Becker, *Documents*, pp. 324-34. Russians: *ES*, 73 (September 1886), 639-40. Truth itself: *ES*, 76 (January 1888), 321. Hughes, *ES*, 80 (February 1890), 481.

12. See the author's article, "Howells, Eliot, and the Humanized Reader," *Harvard English Studies* (Cambridge, 1970), I, 149–70.

13. Eliot: *My Literary Passions* (New York, 1895), p. 185. Turgenev: *Atlantic Monthly*, 32 (September 1873), 370. Goldoni: *Atlantic Monthly*, 40 (November 1877), 601–2, 604.

14. Longfellow: Arms and Gibson, "Five Interviews," p. 267, and *ES*, 73 (June 1886), 156. Emerson: *ES*, 76 (February 1888), 478. Curtis: *Harper's Weekly*, 36 (September 10, 1892), 868, 870, and *North American Review*, 172 (April 1901) (Kirk and Kirk, pp. 325–26). Lowell: same reference in *NAR*, and *Atlantic Monthly*, 39 (March 1877), 374 ("An Ode for the 4th of July 1876").

15. Humane and democratic equated: *Prefaces to Contemporaries*, ed. George Arms, William M. Gibson, and F. C. Marston, Jr. (Gainesville, Fla., 1957), p. 82 (1898). Material of democracy: Arms and Gibson, "Five Interviews" (1914), p. 292. Equality: *ES*, 72 (January 1886), 323–24, and 81 (July 1890), 318. Claim upon America: 75th-birthday speech, Kirk and Kirk, p. 372. See also *ES*, 80 (February 1890), 482. Gods: *ES*, 77 (July 1888), 317–18.

16. Trilling, *The Opposing Self*, pp. 77, 82–84, 87. Garland, *North American Review*, 176 (March 1903), 345.

CHAPTER 2

1. Broken Promise: *LL*, I, 188. For Howells's political, social, and economic thinking in this period, see Everett Carter, *Howells and the Age of Realism* (Philadelphia, 1954), p. 177; Cady, *The Road to Realism* (Syracuse, N.Y., 1956), pp. 180–81; Fryckstedt (on the isolation of Cambridge), *In Quest of America* (Cambridge, Mass. 1958), pp. 84–85, 192–93, 198–201; *Atlantic Monthly*, 41 (April 1878), 550–51; Robert L. Hough, *The Quiet Rebel* (Lincoln, Neb., 1959), pp. 20–27. Lloyd's "Story of a Great Monopoly" appeared in 47 (March 1881), 317–34.

2. Howells, *A Modern Instance* (New York, 1964), pp. 386–87.

3. Howells generally dissociates himself from his characters, although he also believed in writing from direct observation and experience. A Chicago paper in October 1899 (clipping among Howells papers at Harvard) has him saying his characters "emanate largely from my own self, for no author can know other persons better or as well as he knows himself." He has a habit of undercutting characters closest to his own point of view, although this is precisely because he is aware of tensions and contradictions in himself. See *LL*, II, 301, for his at least partial identification with Bartley.

4. Ben's torment over his well-concealed love for Bartley's wife (and Atherton's condemnation of him for allowing himself to love her) and the contortions he goes through over it are not very universal; it is hard to identify with this situation, which is a great weakness in the book. His case is somewhat more complex than I am presenting it here, because in him Howells is also studying the results of New England over-conscientiousness; see p. 257.

5. *A Modern Instance*, p. 387.

6. Norton letter, February 6, 1874, in Kermit Vanderbilt, *Charles Eliot Norton* (Cambridge, Mass., 1959), p. 150. See also unpublished letter to Annie Fréchette, July 22, 1877, MS-H. Concord Avenue: unpublished letters to Marie Marguerite Fréchette, January 19, 1873, and to Henry James, August 26, 1873, MSS-H. Ad to sell house: among 1880 clippings in notebook at Harvard. Middle-age: James to Howells, October 15, 1882, MS-H.

7. He had often been quick to note any such arrogant foibles in himself and in his characters. See, for instance: *Venetian Life* (Boston, 1872), pp. 37, 134; *Suburban Sketches* (New York, 1871), pp. 181, 182-83, 191; *Their Wedding Journey* (Boston, 1872), pp. 252-53; *Atlantic Monthly*, 40 (November 1877), 607, and 45 (June 1880), 848.

8. Worldly success: unpublished letter to father, April 18, 1869. Restless ambition: unpublished letter to Annie Howells, December 2, 1864. Family in Ohio: unpublished letters to father, December 13, 1868, and January 17, 1869. Children: unpublished letters to father, January 15, 1872, March 30, 1873, and July 21, 1878. All in MSS-H. Squirrel story: clipping in notebook at Harvard; the fair took place in December 1880. Halleck: *A Modern Instance*, p. 355; also pp. 338-39.

9. In the humor: *Impressions and Experiences* (New York, 1896), p. 45. Dayton and Danville: letters to Elinor Howells, April 29, 1881, *LL*, I, 297, and May 5, 1881, unpublished, MS-H. Ashtabula and Cincinnati: *My Literary Passions* (New York, 1895), pp. 80, 165-66. No room: *Impressions and Experiences*, p. 80.

10. *A Modern Instance*, p. 69. Howells's portrayal of the good sides of the Hubbards, his placement of some of the responsibility for the bad on their upbringing, and Atherton's concluding words, "Ah, I don't know! I don't know!" are examples of his effort to depict merciful judgment in this book.

11. *Impressions and Experiences*, p. 82.

12. Ibid., p. 73.

13. *New York Tribune*, January 25, 1880, p. 3. Cady, *The Road to Realism*, pp. 202-3. Godkin, quoted ibid., p. 117. Mabie, "A Typical Novel," *Andover Review*, 4 (November 1885); in George J. Becker, ed., *Documents of Modern Literary Realism* (Princeton, 1963), p. 300. An observation about Howells's writing, this is also an idealist's argument against the detachment, scientific coldness, and lack of emotion in realistic fiction.

14. Black Maria: *Atlantic Monthly*, 49 (January 1882), 16. The article ends with this, adding only "But this is perhaps pessimism." I cite the *Atlantic* here since the text in *Impressions and Experiences* emends "by which some of our adoptive citizens propose to disable English commerce" to "sometimes employed by the Enemies of Society," because Howells by then was ashamed of anti-immigrant sentiments he had felt in 1882 and because Enemies of Society was more up to date. Private trials: *Impressions and Experiences*, pp. 89-90: "The public shame seemed purely depraving both to those who suffered it and to those who saw it."

15. Venice: "Letters from Venice—XXIII," *Boston Advertiser*, June 25, 1864, p. 2. *A Chance Acquaintance* (Boston, 1873), p. 58. *A Modern Instance*,

pp. 201, 392. Kingsley, in Introduction to *Living Truths from the Writings of Charles Kingsley* (Boston, 1882), p. 4.

16. Plans: unpublished letters to Charles Fairchild, October 6, 1881, and to father, October 23, 1881, MSS-H. Illness: *LL*, I, 303. Seven weeks: unpublished letter to Charles Dudley Warner, April 2, 1882, MS-H. Well again: *LL*, I, 309-10.

17. Kermit Vanderbilt, in *The Achievement of William Dean Howells* (Princeton, 1968), pp. 81-82, suggests that pressure had built up from Howells's struggle with the contradiction between freedom and fate in *A Modern Instance*. Strain probably developed too over having given up a secure salary to earn his living entirely by writing. The title of his first long story after his "emancipation" from the *Atlantic*, "A Fearful Responsibility" (1881), may have had more than one meaning for him. A number of his books written while he was contemplating freedom and after he had gained it deal with heroes who did not quite make it, with a woman who gave up for marriage her attempt to establish a successful medical practice in *Doctor Breen's Practice* (1881), and with people from the country who for one reason or another could not make their way in Boston (*A Modern Instance, The Rise of Silas Lapham* [1885], and *The Minister's Charge* [1887]).

18. Much older: unpublished letter to Warner, April 2, 1882, MS-H; also *LL*, I, 310. Weakened heart: unpublished letters to Fairchild, January 2, 1882, and March 3, 1882, MSS-H. "Niagara Revisited, Twelve Years After Their Wedding Journey," *Atlantic Monthly*, 51 (May 1883), 598-610.

19. "Lexington," *Longman's Magazine*, 1 (November 1882), 41-61; later published in *Three Villages* (Boston, 1884).

20. Gymnasium: Cady, *The Road to Realism*, p. 217. Letters of 1881 call her condition nervous prostration, MSS-H. Burden on heart: unpublished letter to father, July 17, 1881, MS-H. Bathed and rubbed: unpublished letter to Annie Fréchette, August 14, 1881, MS-H. Adverse effects: *Mark Twain–Howells Letters*, ed. Henry Nash Smith and William M. Gibson (Cambridge, Mass., 1960), I, 373, September 11, 1881. Improvement and invalidism: unpublished letters to Professor Child, October 15, 1881, and to Charles Fairchild, October 6, 1881, MSS-H. What she might do in literature: *Winifred Howells* [Boston, 1891], p. 10.

21. Harlots: London notebook, MS-H. Elinor Howells reported that "Edmund Gosse of London & Will have struck up a great friendship," unpublished letter to Victoria Howells, November 28, 1882; see also Howells to Fairchild, October 23, 1882, MSS-H. John Hay was in London too, and Howells was taken to many choice places by "Hutton, who is writing a 'Literary Guide to London,'" (letter from Elinor to Annie Howells, London (n.d.), MS-H. Dreadful purlieu: *London Films* (New York, 1906), p. 107.

22. Unpublished letter to James, October 4, 1882, MS-H. These reflections probably derive in part from his difficulty with *A Woman's Reason* (Boston, 1883), which was taking shape "very slowly and reluctantly." This novel, which I do not intend to discuss, is an interesting study in the stops, starts, and hesitations of Howells to go further than he does. He sends the Butlers away, wrecks Robert

Fenton on an atoll and has his death published to the world, takes Helen's $5,000 from her, yet never makes her position seem finally desperate. Able to learn little: *A Little Swiss Sojourn* (New York, 1892), p. 76. Socialism: unpublished letter to father, October 7, 1882, MS-H. Pauperism, politics, etc.: both in his 1882 Switzerland notebook, MS-H, and in *A Little Swiss Sojourn*.

23. Realistic portrait: *Tuscan Cities* (Boston, 1886), p. 122. *Tuscan Cities* first appeared in the *Century*, 29-30 (February, April, June, August, September, and October 1885). Police court: *Tuscan Cities*, p. 108. (He also says, p. 4, that he originally meant to write about all aspects of the city.) See Joseph Pennell, *The Adventures of an Illustrator* (Boston, 1925). Enraging and insubstantial: unpublished letters to father, January 14 and 28, 1883, MSS-H. What follows is in both *Tuscan Cities* and Howells's notebook used in Florence, MS-H.

24. Stunned: Venice notebook, April 21, 1883, MS-H. To Twain: *LL*, I, 340. John: unpublished letter to father, April 22, 1883, MS-H. Shock: *LL*, I, 340. Head stopped: *LL*, I, 341, May 6, 1883.

25. Birth and miracle: *Winifred Howells*, pp. 3-4. Miserable experience elsewhere: unpublished letters to father, January 28 and April 22, 1883, MSS-H; *LL*, I, 340; *Winifred Howells*, p. 4. Romantic soul: unpublished letter to father, April 22, 1883, MS-H.

26. Leaving Italy: unpublished letters to father, May 27 and June 3, 1883, MSS-H. Warner and Perry: March 4 and 13, 1883, *LL*, I, 337-38. Dickens: *Atlantic Monthly*, 29 (February 1872), 240-41.

27. On second thought: letter to Osgood quoted by Rudolf and Clara M. Kirk, *Essays in Literary History*, ed. Rudolf Kirk and C. F. Main (New Brunswick, N.J., 1960), p. 183. Intended article: letter to Gosse, November 16, 1882, in *Transatlantic Dialogue*, ed. Paul F. Mattheisen and Michael Millgate (Austin, Texas, 1965), p. 105. Johns Hopkins: letter to President Gilman, December 3, 1882, *LL*, I, 330-31. The offer was renewed in the summer of 1883, and Howells was again seriously tempted (*LL*, I, 351).

28. Auction: *A Woman's Reason*, pp. 2, 101. *Minister's Charge* in mind: letters to Osgood, November 28, 1883, and May 12, 1884, *LL*, I, 356, 361, and December 6, 1883, unpublished, MS-H; Osgood to Howells, May 16, 1884, unpublished, MS-H. Mead was editor of the *New England Magazine*, long a friend of Howells and a sympathizer with the laboring class. Howells had also meant to go "a-prisoning and a-hospitalling" with a Professor Hall that fall (unpublished letter to S. Weir Mitchell, December 19, 1883, manuscript at University of Pennsylvania, quoted by permission of the Charles Patterson Van Pelt Library, University of Pennsylvania). The two excursions are recorded in the Venice notebook, MS-H. Tear up stories: unpublished letter to father (n.d.), MS-H. Mrs. Butler: *A Woman's Reason*, p. 209.

29. Gilder, unpublished letter, August 14, 1883, MS-H.

30. Gilder, unpublished letter, January 3, 1884, MS-H. To Hay: *LL*, I, 357-58. Troubling himself: *LL*, I, 358. Unpopular assertion: Samuel Eliot Morison and Henry Steele Commager, *The Growth of the American Republic* (New York, 1962), II, 231-32. Hay's opinion: "And when a labor spokesman tried

to remonstrate with his picture of the growing union movement, Hay replied that if his work had succeeded in preventing one honest workman from joining a labor organization, he felt it had been worth while," in Everett Carter, *Howells and the Age of Realism* (Philadelphia, 1950), p. 176.

31. Alden and *Indian Summer*: unpublished letter, March 17, 1884, MS-H. *Minister's Charge*: see note 28 above. Osgood, unpublished letters, November 17, 1882, and April 2, 1883, MSS-H. James, *The Letters of Henry James*, ed. Percy Lubbock (New York, 1920), I, 104-5, February 21, 1884. Works: "The Register," "A Sea Change," and a collaboration on "Colonel Sellers" with Mark Twain. Tragical: *LL*, I, 361. To Howe, April 16, 1884, in *The Story of a Country Town* (Cambridge, Mass., 1961), pp. xii-xiii. To Twain, in Smith and Gibson, *Mark Twain–Howells Letters*, II, 484, April 10, 1884.

32. Cambridge: Mattheisen and Millgate, *Transatlantic Dialogue*, p. 142, May 20, 1884. Cady, *The Road to Realism*, p. 223. In 1877, Howells hoped receipts from his play *A Counterfeit Presentment* would enable Winny to attend a private school in Boston — "a well-known preliminary step necessary to establish a young lady in the proper circles of the Boston social world," in Vanderbilt, *Achievement*, p. 104. To Twain, in Smith and Gibson, *Mark Twain–Howells Letters*, II, 494. (C. B. & Q.: the Chicago, Burlington and Quincy Railroad). The house cost $21,000, which Howells believed "a very good investment, for it will rent for a handsome sum when I want to leave it" (unpublished letter to father, June 22, 1884, MS-H).

33. To Elinor, unpublished letter, August 10, 1884, MS-H. To Twain and father, *LL*, I, 363-65. To James, ibid., p. 366, August 22, 1884. Ten days: unpublished letter to Scudder, August 28, 1884, MS-H. Wister, "William Dean Howells," *Atlantic Monthly*, 160 (December 1937), 71; this incident probably took place in the summer or fall of 1884. These were the Harvard Class Races, which could be held in any season. See Howells, *My Mark Twain* (Baton Rouge, La., 1967), for the prevention of a woman's suicide attempt in November or the following March, the times of Twain's two visits to 302 Beacon.

34. "Fourth Annual Report of the Associated Charities of Boston, November 1883," *Associated Charities of Boston* (Boston, 1879-87), pp. 22-23. Mrs. James T. Fields, *How to Help the Poor* (Boston, 1884), pp. 2, 12. The archives of the Family Service Association of Boston, according to Mrs. Elinor Zaki, give no evidence either way. To Norton, unpublished letter, January 21, 1884, MS-H. "Tribulations": see *Impressions and Experiences*, pp. 175-76, 184, 187.

35. Blush: to Henry James, August 22, 1884, *LL*, I, 366. Widow: Smith and Gibson, *Mark Twain–Howells Letters*, II, 499, August 10, 1884. Double standard: ibid., p. 503, September 4, 1884. Sheep: unpublished letter to John Hay, September 17, 1884, MS-H. Perry, unpublished letter, August 12, 1884, MS-H. Smith and Gibson, *Mark Twain–Howells Letters*, II, 508. Harlot: quoted by Edwin Cady, *The Realist at War* (Syracuse, N.Y., 1958), p. 124. On Blaine: unpublished letters to father, September 27 and 28, and October 19, 1884, MSS-H.

36. To Gosse, January 2, 1884, in Mattheisen and Millgate, *Transatlantic*

Dialogue, p. 127; italics mine. Smith and Gibson, *Mark Twain–Howells Letters*, II, 508. Criticism of Hayes, Garfield, and Arthur: unpublished letters to father, November 8, 1874, October 14, 1877, July 25, 1880, and July 3, 1881, MSS-H. Parallels: *Sketch of the Life and Character of Rutherford B. Hayes* (Boston, 1876), pp. 114, 162, 174, 182–83, 185–86; "Garfield," *Atlantic Monthly*, 48 (November 1881), 707–8. Vanderbilt argues the point about the Irish in *Achievement*, p. 140.

37. The November *Century* appeared in October; see October 20 and 23 letters in Smith and Gibson, *Mark Twain–Howells Letters*, II, 512. Lapham: *The Rise of Silas Lapham* (New York, 1964), p. 2. Monroe, *Lippincott's*, 39 (January 1887), 128. Smith, "An Hour with Howells," *Frank Leslie's Weekly*, 74 (March 17, 1892), 118.

38. Interview: Marrion Wilcox, "Works of William Dean Howells (1860–96)," *Harper's Weekly*, 40 (July 4, 1896), 656. Bottom dropped out: "Every nerve had to be strained to patch the hole and get the water back in the canal before almost irreparable damage followed" (Cady, *The Road to Realism*, pp. 243–44). Gosse and Howells went to Concord on December 19 (Mattheisen and Millgate, *Transatlantic Dialogue*, p. 13). Gosse to Howells, February 15, 1885, ibid., p. 166. Howells to Gosse, March 9, 1885, ibid., p. 168. Masque: MS-H. *Lapham*, pp. 256, 380.

39. Unpublished letters to father, October 19 and November 9, 1884, and January 18, 1885; same on carpentry and father's troubles, September 27 and July 1, 1884; all in MSS-H. Howells to Parton, March 27, 1885, and Parton to Howells, April 6, 1885, MSS-H. His work load included constant correspondence over rights, translations, new editions, payment negotiations, and articles, and with writers, would-be-writers, and readers.

40. Shocking prices: to Bliss Perry, unpublished letter, April 9, 1907, MS-H. Failure of dramatic works, Winny's first party: unpublished letters to father, November 9 and September 7, 1884, and March 29, 1885, MSS-H.

41. Unpublished letter to father, November 9, 1884, MS-H.

42. To Gosse, December 24, 1884, in Mattheisen and Millgate, *Transatlantic Dialogue*, p. 158. Gosse, "The Passing of William Dean Howells," *Living Age*, 306 (July 10, 1920), 99–100.

43. Howells wrote Gosse on December 24, 1884, "I have been working like a beaver since you left, and am getting Silas well on to disaster. He is about to be 'squeezed' by a railroad, in a trade," Mattheisen and Millgate, *Transatlantic Dialogue*, p. 158. The dinner scene is in Chap. 14, the turning point for the Lapham fortunes. Chaps. 15 through 19, fifty-two pages, concern the revelation of Tom Corey's love for Penelope. In Chap. 20, Lapham sees the railroad could squeeze him. In Chaps. 15 through 19 we learn Lapham is getting "deeper" in with Rogers. Sometime before January 23 Gilder had the dinner chapter in his hands; Gilder to Howells, unpublished letter, MS-H. It is possible the crisis occurred during the writing of the dinner chapter, close to the time of Gosse's arrival, and that Howells either wrote a bit of the following chapters (not crucial to the novel's larger problems — though see Vanderbilt, *Achievement*, pp. 135ff.)

during Gosse's stay or, "working like a beaver," wrote all of Chaps. 15 to 20 between Gosse's departure and his letter to Gosse on December 24.

44. Vanderbilt, *Achievement*, pp. 96-143. The reply to the editor of the *American Hebrew* is quoted by Vanderbilt, p. 122. Smith to Howells, unpublished letter, February 18, 1885, MS-H.

45. Rogers: *Lapham*, p. 49. Smith to Howells, March 21 and 24, 1885, MSS-H. The row of bricks tumbling, *Lapham*, pp. 392-93, may suggest the factors involved in Howells's crisis. Sewell's words two paragraphs later might suggest the strengthening of character Howells felt he had derived from the crisis. I owe these suggestions and the one cited on p. 42 to conversations with Kenneth Lynn.

46. Winny: unpublished letter to Aurelia Howells, December 20, 1885, MS-H, and Mattheisen and Millgate, *Transatlantic Dialogue*, p. 179, October 26, 1885. See *Lapham*, p. 380. The Howellses were not leaving 302 Beacon Street permanently at this point. Putnam: unpublished letter from Howells to Mitchell, October 20, 1885, manuscript at the University of Pennsylvania. Improving: unpublished letter to Aurelia, December 20, 1885, MS-H.

47. Father and brother: in October 1885 he began to send home $25 a month, raised to $50 in January 1888. This did not include "irregular supplies," which were numerous. Unpublished letters to Aurelia Howells, December 20, 1885, and to father, January 2, 1891, MSS-H. Harpers: see Cady, *The Realist at War*, pp. 1-3. Young banker: *Brooklyn Magazine*, November 1885, p. 78. James O'Donnell Bennett of the Chicago *Journal* wrote on October 26, 1899: "Seeing him in company and making a guess at his walk in life you would say he was a very rich and well-groomed banker—probably retired" (p. 4). To Mitchell, October 20, 1885, manuscript at the University of Pennsylvania.

48. Readings: Smith and Gibson, *Mark Twain-Howells Letters*, II, 528n. Believe in it: *LL*, I, 362, May 12, 1884. To Twain, *Mark Twain-Howells Letters*, II, 532. July 1 and 2: *Indian Summer* notebook, MS-H. Defoe: to Twain, August 9, 1885, *LL*, I, 371.

49. *ES*, 74 (May 1887), 987.

50. *Munsey's Magazine*, 17 (April 1897); in Kirk and Kirk, p. 98.

51. On James: *Century*, 25 (November 1882), 28. *ES*, 75 (September 1887), 639.

52. Pérez Galdós: *Prefaces to Contemporaries*, ed. George Arms, William M. Gibson, and F. C. Marston, Jr. (Gainesville, Fla., 1957), pp. 56-57 (1896); hereafter *Prefaces*.

53. Great lesson: *Harper's Weekly*, 39 (April 13, 1895); in Kirk and Kirk, p. 163. Own time and place: *Atlantic Monthly*, 33 (March 1874), 369-70. Microcosm: Arms et al., *Prefaces*, p. 184. Majority of people: see *ES*, 75 (October 1887), 803; 77 (November 1888), 966; and 72 (May 1886), 973.

54. Authorial intrusion: *ES*, 75 (November 1887), 963, and *Century*, 25 (November 1882), 26. Absent and impartial: *ES*, 77 (October 1888), 801; *Munsey's Magazine*, 17 (April 1897) (Kirk and Kirk, p. 99); and *My Literary Passions*, p. 254. Living before you: *My Literary Passions*, p. 254. No comment:

Atlantic Monthly, 33 (June 1874), 745. Turgenev: *Atlantic Monthly*, 31 (February 1873), 239.

55. Plot: *My Literary Passions*, p. 68; *North American Review*, 75 (November 1902) (in Arms et al., *Prefaces*, pp. 89–102); *ES*, 76 (February 1888), 479, and 82 (March 1891), 641. Character: *LL*, I, 361 (1884); *ES*, 72 (May 1886), 972, and 76 (May 1888), 966; *Atlantic Monthly*, 35 (April 1875), 493, and 45 (February 1880), 283; *Century*, 25 (November 1882), 27; *Frank Leslie's Weekly*, 74 (March 17, 1892), 118. Twenty characters: Howells quoted by Cady, *The Realist at War*, p. 62. Eddies: *ES*, 83 (July 1891), 318.

56. Little space: *Atlantic Monthly*, 25 (April 1870), 512; reference is to Bjornstjerne Bjornson's *Fisher-Maiden*. Pity: *ES*, 76 (January 1888), 321.

57. To Higginson, September 17, 1879; quoted by Cady, *The Road to Realism*, p. 189. *A Modern Instance*, pp. 154–59.

58. *The Minister's Charge* (Boston, 1887), pp. 33–34, 12, 22–23, 406–7, 431–35. Also pp. 298, 299. These points are essential to Howells: The best people can do insensitive things and commit subtle wrongs.

59. *The Minister's Charge*, pp. 252–53, 393–94.

60. Ibid., pp. 130–31, 175–76, 275, 37.

61. Ibid., pp. 457–59.

62. Holmes: *LL*, I, 368, February 5, 1885. The Holmes *Portfolio* he refers to is in *Atlantic Monthly*, 55 (February 1885), 248ff. Interview: *Good Housekeeping*, 1 (July 11, 1885), 2. Simple purpose: to James, *LL*, I, 387, December 25, 1886.

63. *In War Time*: *ES*, 72 (January 1886), 323. *The Minister's Charge*, p. 320. *Mark Rutherford*: *ES*, 72 (February 1886), 485–86.

64. Bennett, *George Eliot* (Cambridge, England, 1948), pp. 77–78.

65. George Eliot, *Adam Bede*, Chap. 15.

66. *ES*, 75 (July 1887), 318, and 72 (January 1886), 323.

67. Frankness: to James, *LL*, I, 387, December 25, 1886. De Forest to Howells, unpublished letter, December 6, 1886, MS-H. Limp bundle: ibid., p. 56.

68. To the top: *ES*, 72 (February 1886), 482–83. *Rutherford*, ibid., pp. 485–86. In cell: *The Minister's Charge*, p. 71. Sewell: ibid., pp. 129–30.

69. *The Minister's Charge*, pp. 129, 100, 240–41. The critics: see *The Critic*, 2 (October 21, 1882), 278, and 3 (December 22, 1883), 518, and *Lippincott's*, 39 (February 1887), 352–54. Robert Louis Stevenson thought Howells had suppressed his natural tastes and natural narrative propensities in paying homage to his Lemuel Barkers: "A Humble Remonstrance," *The Travels and Essays of Robert Louis Stevenson* (New York, 1895), Vol. 13, 257–58.

70. Jail visitors: *The Minister's Charge*, pp. 68–70. Sewell waking up and at lodge: pp. 110–30.

71. The Coreys: ibid., pp. 366–67, 382. Cosmos: p. 36. Question the attitude: Miss Vane argues with Sewell, p. 36. Also pp. 22, 38–39, 276.

CHAPTER 3

1. Masters, in Tribute Book, Howells Collection at Harvard.

2. James, unpublished letter, November 27, 1882, MS-H; *Harper's Weekly,* 30 (June 19, 1886), 394-95 (in *The American Essays of Henry James,* ed. Leon Edel [New York, 1956], p. 152). Mabie, "A Typical Novel," *Andover Review,* 4 (November 1885); in *Documents of Modern Literary Realism,* ed. George Becker (Princeton, 1963), pp. 297-98. Robertson, *The Westminster Review,* n. s., 132 (October 1884), 347-75; in *Essays Towards a Critical Method* (London, 1889), p. 157. Scudder, *Atlantic Monthly,* 52 (November 1883), 706, and 57 (June 1886), 855. Garland, *North American Review,* 176 (March 1903), 341, 346-47.

3. Brooks, *World's Work,* 18 (May 1909), 11547-49; also in "Five Interviews with William Dean Howells," ed. George Arms and William M. Gibson, *Americana,* 37 (April 1943), 283. Brooks at this time had read only one Howells novel, according to Cady, *The Realist at War* (Syracuse, N.Y., 1958), pp. 256-57. Parrington, *The Beginnings of Critical Realism in America* (New York, 1930), p. 251. Berthoff, *The Ferment of Realism* (New York, 1965), pp. 53, 57.

4. "Old Cambridge," *Literature,* n. s., I (June 9, 1899), 506.

5. Whitman: I take this from Olov Fryckstedt, *In Quest of America* (Cambridge, Mass., 1958), p. 28 (Fryckstedt is citing Howells's "Bardic Symbols," *Ohio State Journal,* 23 [March 28, 1960]). August 25, 1864 letter to father, *LL,* I, 88. Lowell to Howells, November 2, 1865, unpublished letter, MS-H. Lowell, *North American Review,* 103 (October 1866), 611-12.

6. Clippings are in a notebook at Harvard. The first is from the *St. Louis Globe—Democrat* in late 1881 or early 1882. The second, on "Novelists and Their Subjects, " by M.T., is from an unidentified paper, dated February 21, 1882. Unpublished letter to father, April 20, 1873, MS-H. Howells tells, with some ambivalence, of how the *Atlantic* became more American and less Eastern during his time in "Recollections of an Atlantic Editorship," *Atlantic Monthly,* 100 (November 1907), 600-602.

7. Extol Boston: quoted in Van Wyck Brooks's *Howells: His Life and World* (New York, 1959), p. 9.

8. Time and quality: Kirk and Kirk, pp. 379, 381 (from *The House of Harper: A Century of Publishing in Franklin Square* [New York, 1912]); *LL,* II, 138 (letter to Thomas Bailey Aldrich, November 4, 1900). Forum: *ES* (January 1886), 321. To Gosse, January 24, 1886, *Transatlantic Dialogue,* ed. Paul F. Mattheisen and Michael Millgate (Austin, Texas, 1965); p. 184. *Mark Twain–Howells Letters,* ed. Henry Nash Smith and William M. Gibson (Cambridge, Mass., 1960), II, 532.

9. Howells came to Tolstoy in time for Tolstoy to influence the last chapters of *The Minister's Charge* (Boston, 1887). *Cossacks: My Literary Passions* (New York, 1895), p. 253. *Anna Karenina:* letter to Thomas S. Perry, October 30, 1885, *LL,* I, 373. Unpublished letter to father, January 17, 1886, MS-H. To Norton, unpublished letter, July 13, 1886; MS-H. Revelation: "Lyof N. Tolstoy," *North*

American Review, 188 (December 1908), 851-52. Ethics and concluding passage: *My Literary Passions*, pp. 250, 258.

10. Completion of sketch: unpublished letter to father, September 13, 1885; MS-H. *My Year in a Log Cabin* (New York, 1893) was first published in *Youth's Companion*, 60 (May 12, 1887), 213-15.

11. False starts: unpublished letter to father, June 27, 1886, MS-H. Beginning *April Hopes*: unpublished letters to Osgood, June 2 and July 17, 1886, MSS-H. Marrion Wilcox, "Works of William Dean Howells —(1860-96)," *Harper's Weekly*, 40 (July 4, 1896), 655. Combating sentimental notions: letter to Hamlin Garland, March 11, 1888, *LL*, I, 410.

12. *April Hopes* (New York, 1888), pp. 129-31.

13. To Norton, unpublished letter, May 22, 1886, MS-H. *ES* (April 1886), 808.

14. Thinking: *ES*, 73 (August 1886), 480. Grant: ibid., p. 476. Goethe: *ES*, 73 (June 1886), 154. Guerrazzi, *Modern Italian Poets* (New York, 1887), pp. 2-3; the Introduction was probably composed toward the end of 1886.

15. Smith, unpublished letter, March 17, 1885, MS-H. Attentive to strikes: see Cady, *The Realist at War*, p. 69. Sources used on the Haymarket Affair are: ibid., pp. 69-80; Everett Carter, *Howells and the Age of Realism* (Philadelphia, 1954), pp. 179-85; and Henry David, *The History of the Haymarket Affair* (New York, 1936).

16. Smiling aspects: *ES*, 73 (September 1886), 641-42. Cady, *The Realist at War*, p. 134. Before trial: Cady, ibid., pp. 134-35; Carter, *Howells and the Age of Realism*, pp. 187-88.

17. "Mark Twain," *Century*, 24 (September 1882), 782. Dostoievsky: *ES*, 73 (September 1886), 642.

18. *ES*, 73 (June 1886), 154.

19. Henry, Swedenborg, and Lowell mills: unpublished letters to father, February 13 and 20, 1887, MSS-H.

20. Sale of house, etc.: unpublished letter to father, March 27, 1887, MS-H. Pleasure in possession spoiled: same, April 17, 1887. Auburndale: Hamlin Garland, *Roadside Meetings* (New York, 1930), pp. 57-58.

21. Under trees: unpublished letter to father, May 29, 1887; MS-H. Albany: Edward E. Hale, Jr., *The Life and Letters of Edward Everett Hale* (Boston, 1917), II, 328; May 28, 1887. Interview: *New York Tribune*, July 10, 1887, p. 12.

22. Pp. 13-19 of manuscript at Harvard. The back of p. 1 indicates the manuscript was written at the Gilmore Cottage, June 28, 1887; this is where the Howellses were staying at Lake George.

23. *Sebastopol* Introduction: *Prefaces to Contemporaries* (1882-1920), ed. George Arms, William M. Gibson, and F. C. Marston, Jr. (Gainesville, Fla., 1957), pp. 3-10. Luke 18: 18-30; Tolstoy uses the passage twice in *Que Faire?* (*ES*, 75 [July 1887], 316-17).

24. Last year and a half: unpublished letters to father, February 21 and June 13, 1886, and March 6, 1887, MSS-H. Not so well, better, wit's end: same, June 26, July 17, and August 7, 1887. Little better: unpublished letter to Aurelia Howells, August 14, 1887, MS-H. Wretched summer: unpublished letter to Thomas Bailey

Aldrich, October 25, 1887, MS-H. Poem and long ebb: *Winifred Howells* [Boston, 1891], pp. 8-9, 18. The first two stanzas only are included in the book, and probably Boott set no more to music; I have not been able to locate a copy of the song. The third stanza is in a manuscript closed in Aldrich's copy of the book at Harvard. Sanatorium: unpublished letters to father, September 18 and 27, 1887, and to Aldrich, October 25, 1887, MSS-H.

25. Tolstoy, *Que Faire?*: quotation from Aylmer Maude translation, *What Then Must We Do?* (New York, 1925), pp. 324-29. To Curtis, August 10, 1887, MS-H. Curtis and editorial policy: Clara and Rudolf Kirk, "William Dean Howells, George William Curtis, and the 'Haymarket Affair,'" *American Literature*, 40 (January 1969), 492-93. Curtis, unpublished letter, August 12, 1887, MS-H. Lum's pamphlet, undated, published by the Socialistic Publishing Society, Chicago. The second pamphlet Howells sent Curtis was possibly *Was It a Fair Trial?: An Appeal to the Governor of Illinois* by Gen. M. M. Trumbull, "on behalf of the condemned anarchists." Curtis returned at least one pamphlet, and there is a copy of this in the Howells "anarchist file" at Harvard. But the Kirks argue convincingly in their article for the Lum pamphlet. September 1 letter, MS-H. Letters of September 23, 25, 27, 26, MSS-H.

26. Whittier, September 24, 1887, *The Letters of John Greenleaf Whittier*, Vol. 3, 1861-92, ed. John B. Pickard (Cambridge, Mass., 1975), p. 538. Also see Howells/Whittier 1888 exchange, ibid., pp. 561-62. To Pryor, September 25, 1887, *LL*, I, 393. To Whittier, November 1, 1887, quoted by John A. Pollard, *John Greenleaf Whittier* (Boston, 1949), p. 315. Whittier's reply: David, *History of the Haymarket Affair*, p. 398. David's source and the quotation source are Albert Mordell, *Quaker Militant: John Greenleaf Whittier* (Port Washington, N.Y., 1933), pp. 261-62.

27. Curtis, Philisteria: unpublished letter, March 5, 1887, MS-H. Curtis, fairness doubtful: August 12, 1887, same. Both Whittier letters, March 18 and 23, 1886, are in *LL*, I, 380-81, and in Pickard, *Letters*, pp. 523-24. On Curtis: *Harper's Weekly*, 36 (September 10, 1892), 868. Pre-war spirit: In *Annie Kilburn*, Colonel Marvin, who had fought in the Civil War, would be the businessman to treat his workers fairly. The anarchists' speeches before and during the trial emphasized their concern with slavery. Later Howells could philosophize the defection of these older men; see *Literary Friends and Acquaintance* (New York, 1900), pp. 135-36 (from November 1895), and Kirk and Kirk, pp. 371-72.

28. Pryor, unpublished letters and telegram, September 24 and October 12, 1887, MSS-H; October 3 and November 1 letters in *LL*, I, 394-95, 397-98. In manuscript "now" is above the line.

29. Browne, unpublished letter, dated Thursday — 6 P.M. MS-H. Reid, unpublished letter, November 8, 1887, MS-H. The petition carried eight signatures and was sent from Dansville, New York, according to a clipping in Howells's "anarchist file." Quotation from *Tribune* letter: *LL*, I, 398-99. Clipping with Howells letter as published was included in an unpublished letter from Browne, November 8, 1887, MS-H. Clement, unpublished letter, November 7, 1887, MS-H.

30. Maine paper: clipping sent by Charles E. Allen to Howells, unpublished letter, November 14, 1887, MS-H. Other examples in Cady, *The Realist at War*, pp. 72-73. Letters of praise: Mead, November 8, 1887; Palmer, December 10, 1887; Smith, November 11, 1887; Noble, November 8, 1887; Aveling n.d.; all unpublished, MSS-H. Howells quotes Spofford in a letter to his father, November 13, 1887, *LL*, I, 403.

31. Letter in Cady (except for the opening paragraph, which I quote here), *The Realist at War*, pp. 73-77. A number of drafts are at Harvard. The *Tribune* never named Howells, although on the day following publication of his letter, it printed a summary of the Illinois Supreme Court decision, entitled "What the Anarchists Did. Facts for Sentimentalists to Consider" (November 7, p. 3). Its editorial that day, entitled "Facts vs. Gush" (p. 4), asked that "all persons, whose faith in the justice of the conviction of these men may have been shaken by the loud talk of socialist demagogues, and the soft-hearted appeals of sentimentalists, to read it. These people have had most of the talk to themselves, while the great patient public has been silent." An editorial on the same subject followed on November 8 (p. 4): "The Mistake of Cowardice."

32. Cady, *The Realist at War*, pp. 77-78.

33. Record of trial: letters from Courtlandt Palmer (December 10), William M. Salter (November 22 and 27), Albert Leffingwell, a Dansville resident (December 3), William P. Black, attorney for the anarchists (February 8), and Hale (November 25), and letter to father (December 1), MSS-H. Discouragement: Joseph W. Harper to Howells, unpublished letter, December 2, 1887, MS-H. For later "interference," see Alden to Howells, unpublished letter, November 13, 1888, MS-H. This rightly contradicts Howells's disclaimer in *House of Harper*, in Kirk and Kirk, pp. 379-80.

34. Lea: *ES*, 76 (March 1888), 640-41. Emerson: *ES*, 76 (February 1888), 477-78.

35. *Harper's Weekly*, 32 (January 14, 1888), 23. Manuscript in the Boston Public Library, quoted by courtesy of the Trustees of the Boston Public Library. There is no telling who decided the Anarchist aside should be dropped from the published letter.

36. To Browne, November 11, 1887, *LL*, I, 402. Bellew, unpublished letter, November 12, 1887, MS-H. Gronlund, *The Cooperative Commonwealth* (Cambridge, Mass., 1965), p. 8.

37. To Annie Fréchette, *LL*, I, 403-5. Winny's cure: unpublished letter to father, November 13, 1887, MS-H.

38. To know our kind: *ES*, 75 (September 1887), 638-39. Thanet's "The Communist's Wife" in *Knitters in the Sun*, *ES*, 76 (January 1888), 321. Realism: ibid., p. 321. Tolstoy's sympathy: ibid., p. 320; and limitations: *ES*, 76 (February 1888), 479.

39. To Stedman, February 4, 1888, *LL*, I, 410. His reading: Cady, *The Realist at War*, p. 81. Unpublished letter to father, January 22, 1888, MS-H. To Garland, *LL*, I, 407-8. Gronlund and Ely: *ES*, 76 (April 1888), 801-3. Sugar-coat: Howells wrote to Stedman on February 4, "People take me so viciously awry, and think (or

say) that I have no serious meaning when my whole trouble has been to sugarcoat my medicinal properties," *LL*, I, 409. On Bellamy: *ES*, 78 (June 1888), 154-55. Bellamy to Howells, unpublished letter, June 17, 1888, and Howells to Bellamy, same, July 31, 1888, MSS-H.

40. Excursions: notebook entries February 26, 1888, MS-H; there are entries for the 29th also. Reluctance to invest: unpublished letter to Annie Fréchette, June 2, 1887, MS-H. To Twain, *LL*, I, 411. "Was There Nothing to Arbitrate?" *Harper's Weekly*, 32 (April 21, 1888), 286. Howells regretted that the strike became violent, changing the general sentiment, but he did not ask his readers to refer to their just feelings against the strikers, as he had in 1884.

41. Reports from sanitorium: letters to father, November 27, 1887, and February 26, 1888, and to Aurelia Howells, March 11, 1888, MSS-H. Other news: unpublished letters to father, March 25, April 1, April 15, April 29, and May 5, 1888, MSS-H.

42. Wide verandah: to James, October 10, 1888, *LL*, I, 417. Garland, *Roadside Meetings*, p. 64; Garland misdates this as 1886. Dining room and confidence: Garland, *Boston Evening Transcript*, May 22, 1920, pp. 4-5. Reports on Winny: unpublished letters to father, June 17 and July 1 and 8, 1888, MSS-H. Invitation: to Hjalmar Boyesen, July 19, 1888, manuscript in the W. D. Howells Collection, Barrett Library, University of Virginia. In retrospect: *Winifred Howells*, pp. 24, 25, 14.

43. Garland, Boston *Evening Transcript*, May 22, 1920, pp. 4-5. Unpublished letter to father, July 1, 1888, MS-H. Grim story: unpublished letter to Mildred Howells, April 18, 1913, MS-H. Van Dyke, "Public Meeting Held at the Stuart Gallery, New York Public Library, New York, March 1st, 1921, in Memory of William D. Howells," *American Academy Proceedings*, July 1, 1921, II, 1-21. In Alden's hands: unpublished letter from Alden, August 14, 1888, MS-H.

44. *Annie Kilburn* (New York, 1889), pp. 13-18; hereafter *AK*. There may be some self-criticism in the Victory: Howells wrote concerning Civil War monuments in 1866 that "the ruling sentiment of our time is triumphant and trustful." Kenneth Lynn, *William Dean Howells* (New York, 1971), p. 185.

45. *AK*, pp. 47, 62, 76.

46. *AK*, pp. 47, 164, 130, 147-50. Conditions all wrong: p. 62; these are Annie's words. *AK*, pp. 94, 93-94, 81-84, and 86-87. Putney: pp. 204, 93.

47. Peck: *AK*, pp. 61, 65, 140, 169.

48. *AK*, pp. 130-32, 257-58.

49. Juxtapositions: for instance, Annie's inexplicable displeasure at hearing Peck has been married, p. 19, his presence in her house, her attempt to befriend his daughter, and the speculation that rises in the minds of the townspeople. Limitations: the "Study" could have been written in December 1887; the letter to his sister was written November 18, 1887. Although these sides to Peck were evident earlier, it need not mean they were in the manuscript until a late stage in the writing. Morrell and Annie, not married in *AK*, are so in *The Quality of Mercy* (New York, 1892). The dinner scene through the walk home with Dr. Morrell is pp. 125-44.

50. Amused voice: *AK*, p. 95. Sincere and serious is consistent with Howells's theory of humor. It is kindly humor, without cynicism, in which there is something better than mere humor, humor which is based upon a serious outlook on life; Mabie, "A Typical Novel," *Andover Review*, November 1885; in *Documents of Modern Literary Realism*, ed. George J. Becker (Princeton, 1963), p. 300. Annie's annoyance: *AK*, pp. 97, 139, 141, 142, 266. Undercut: pp. 298-99. The relationship is somewhat more complex than this, but the complexity does not alter Howells's standpoint. Annie is often overwrought, and she shares with a number of other Howellsian women, like Grace Breen of *Doctor Breen's Practice* (Boston, 1881), the nervousness and other unsound characteristics which her Puritan background has planted in her. Dr. Morrell's treatment of her, when seen in this light, is consciously therapeutic (p. 259), although it is not only that, as his playing with the large ivory paper-knife during his visits indicates (p. 260). Howells, by projecting his problems of personal commitment into the character of a highly nervous New England woman, as by turning Morrell's humor on them, may be seen as distancing himself from them, perhaps attempting to alleviate whatever torment they caused him by viewing them through such a medium.

51. To Garland, November 6, 1888, *LL*, I, 419. Kenneth Lynn suggested to me the guilt that lies behind the reply. See Lynn, *William Dean Howells*, pp. 294-95, for one biographical interpretation of *AK* along these lines. Sermon: *AK*, pp. 239-42.

52. *AK*, pp. 266-83.

53. Peck done with preaching: *AK*, pp. 288, 291. Annie volunteers: pp. 291-93. In no wise exegetic: p. 317.

54. First paragraph with direct quotations: *AK*, pp. 320, 322-25, 324. Second paragraph: pp. 326-27. Third paragraph: pp. 326-27, 328, 329.

55. To Hale, *LL*, I, 416. Norton to Curtis, December 29, 1889, *Letters of Charles Eliot Norton*, ed. Sara Norton and M. A. DeWolfe Howe (Boston, 1913), II, 194. Ex-President Hayes: "It is the doctrine of the Declaration of Independence, and of the Sermon on the Mount," *Diary and Letters of Rutherford Birchard Hayes*, ed. Charles Richard Williams (The Ohio State Archaeological and Historical Society, 1925), IV, 434-35.

56. Literary precedents: Hollingsworth in *The Blithedale Romance* and Mrs. Jellyby in *Bleak House*. To James, October 10, 1888, *LL*, I, 417. Of course, Tolstoy's money remained in the family; they would not be deprived of medical care. Winthrop is also the surname of the first governor of Massachusetts Bay. It is tempting to suggest a connection for Howells between social irresponsibility on his part and damage to his family (Winthrop became crippled when his father dropped him on the stairs while drunk); he may now have been dimly seeing Winny's illness as some sort of punishment visited upon him. Winthrop also seems to serve as a goad to Putney's conscience. The reader will recall how Henry ceased jouncing Howells in the latter's dreams once he had visited the Lowell mills. See also p. 127 in this volume for another example of Howells's relating his behavior to a family member's view of him.

57. Common sense: Cady, Carter, and Van Wyck Brooks have suggested this

reason; Cady, *The Realist at War*, pp. 78, 91; Carter, *Howells and the Age of Realism*, pp. 195–96; Brooks, *Howells: His Life and World*, pp. 187–88. Zola: "Emile Zola," *North American Review*, 175 (November 1902); in Arms et al., *Prefaces to Contemporaries*, pp. 102, 96.

CHAPTER 4

1. Lewisohn, *Mid-Channel* (New York, 1929), p. 14.

2. Roosevelt, in Tribute Book, Howells Collection at Harvard.

3. Johnson, *Remembered Yesterdays* (Boston, 1923), pp. 355–56. Dreiser, "Five Interviews with William Dean Howells," ed. George Arms and William M. Gibson, *Americana*, 37 (April 1943), 277. Dreiser's interview appeared in *Ainslee's Magazine*, 5 (March 1900), 137–42.

4. Harriet Earhart Monroe, "Statesman and Novelist: A Talk Between Senator Ingalls and Mr. Howells," *Lippincott's*, 39 (January 1887), 130. To James, December 25, 1886, *LL*, I, 389. Not a new note: Samuel Pierpont Langley, unpublished letter to Howells, August 3, 1885, and Howells letter to father, June 27, 1886, MSS-H. Age restrictions: to T. S. Perry, April 14, 1888, *LL*, I, 413.

5. To James, October 10, 1888, *LL*, I, 417. Beaton in *A Hazard of New Fortunes* would guiltily buy a fur-lined overcoat rather than send money to his needy father. To Hale, October 10, 1888, *LL*, I, 418–19. Alice Rollins: *ES*, 77 (October 1888), 801–2. To Hale, August 30, 1888, *LL*, I, 416. *A Hazard of New Fortunes* (New York, 1890), I, 88. Tolstoy, *ES*, 78 (December 1888), 158–60. October 10 letter to Hale.

6. House: unpublished letters to father, September 29 and October 7, 1888, and to Annie Fréchette, October 12, 1888, MSS-H. Sad story: unpublished letter to father, August 25, 1889, MS-H. Doctors: unpublished letter to father, September 10, 1888, MS-H.

7. James: "Emile Zola," *Atlantic Monthly*, 92 (August 1903), 209. To Hale, October 10, 1888, *LL*, I. 418–19. *ES*, 77 (November 1888), 973; compare pp. 75–76 of present text. Christmas literature: *ES*, 78 (December 1888), 158–60.

8. Five hundred pages: unpublished letter to father, December 23, 1888, MS-H. Hale, unpublished letter (n.d.), MS-H. Mission: *ES*, 78 (December 1888), 159.

9. No vote and Republican vote: unpublished letters to father. November 4 and July 8, 1888, MSS-H. To Perry, April 14, 1888, *LL*, I, 414.

10. "Mr. Howells and the Anarchist Meeting," *Harper's Weekly*, 32 (November 24, 1888), 887. Alden to Howells, unpublished letter, November 13, 1888, MS-H. Letter to editor: unpublished, November 23, 1888, MS-H. Howells refers to the newspaper articles in his reply but does not identify the newspaper. Bellamy to Howells, unpublished letter, June 17, 1888, MS-H.

11. Cahan, *Workman's Advocate*, April 6, 1889; cited from Rudolf and Clara M. Kirk, "Abraham Cahan and William Dean Howells: The Story of a Friendship," *American Jewish Historical Quarterly*, 52 (September 1962), 29.

Bennett, *The Realism of William Dean Howells; 1889–1920* (Nashville, 1973), pp. 40–43. Bennett has a provocative argument and some good insights into weaknesses in *A Hazard of New Fortunes*.

12. One observer ("an occasional correspondent of the *Tribune*"): "The New Socialism: Boston's Two Nationalist Societies and What They Aim to Accomplish," *New York Tribune*, October 6, 1889, p. 15. This is the source of the information throughout the paragraph. Relief works were to be established by states, cities, and towns, where the unemployed would have work; homes were to be built and sold at cost to working people; job training should be provided; free technical education; the eight-hour day; enfranchisement of women, and so forth: "The New Socialism," *The Nation*, 48 (June 13, 1889), 478. Hostile critic: Nicholas Paine Gilman, *Socialism and the American Spirit* (New York, 1893), p. 197. Cahan, op. cit., p. 56. For general background relevant to these groups, see Robert H. Wiebe, *The Search for Order* (New York, 1967), Chaps. 2 to 4.

13. *ES*, 79 (August 1889), 479.

14. Lecture: *LL*, I, 421–22. McGlynn: unpublished letter to father, January 19, 1889, MS-H. (The letter should be dated the 20th because Howells usually wrote his father on Sunday and McGlynn did not speak on the 19th but addressed a packed meeting at the Cooper Union on the 20th, on "Church and State.") To Newton, unpublished letter, January 27, 1889; quoted by Clara and Rudolf Kirk, "Howells and the Church of the Carpenter," *New England Quarterly*, 32 (June 1959), 193.

15. Information from beginning of section V through hope for temporary invalidism comes from unpublished letters to father, November 18 and 25, December 2 and 23, 1888, January 6, 19, and 27, February 3, 10, and 17, 1889, MSS-H. To Gosse, February 28, 1889, in *Transatlantic Dialogue*, ed. Paul F. Mattheisen and Michael Millgate (Austin, Texas, 1965), p. 213. Death and funeral: unpublished letters to father, March 4 and 10, 1889, MSS-H, and unpublished letter to Mitchell, March 7, 1889, manuscript at University of Pennsylvania; quoted by permission of the Charles Patterson Van Pelt Library, University of Pennsylvania. Greatest sorrow: "Mr. Howells's Paper," *The House of Harper: A Century of Publishing in Franklin Square* (New York, 1912); in Kirk and Kirk, p. 382. Garland, "William Dean Howells's Boston: A Posthumous Pilgrimage," Boston *Evening Transcript*, May 22, 1920, pp. 4–5.

16. Memoir, *Winifred Howells* (Boston, 1891), pp. 4, 6–7. To Mitchell, unpublished letter, March 7, 1889, manuscript at University of Pennsylvania. The reliving was, he wrote his father on March 22, "anguish, anguish that rends the heart and brain," unpublished letter, MS-H. See also *LL*, I, 424–25.

17. Kinder to all: unpublished letter to father, March 31, 1889, MS-H. To Alice James, April 26, 1889, *LL*, I, 426. *Winifred Howells*, p. 25. In the past: see present text, pp. 76–77, 109–10, and 130, also p. 184 n. 56, above.

18. To Gosse, February 28, 1889, in Mattheisen and Millgate, *Transatlantic Dialogue*, p. 213. To John: unpublished letter, June 15, 1889, MS-H. Manuscripts for effects are among business papers at Harvard. The figures after 1889 do not include the $800 rent from the Cambridge house or the $2000–$2500 royalties from his copyrighted books.

19. Fat optimism: *ES*, 78 (May 1889), 985. Also *ES*, 78 (January 1889), 319–20; 79 (July 1889), 317; and 79 (August 1889), 480. Carlyle: *ES*, 79 (August 1889), 480–81.

20. Optimism: *ES*, 78 (March 1889), 660, 663. Movement: *ES*, 79 (August 1889), 479–80. Sharp: *ES*, 79 (September 1889), 641.

21. Completed *Hazard*: unpublished letter to father, September 29, 1889, MS-H. Sorrow: "Autobiographical," *A Hazard of New Fortunes* (Bloomington, 1976), p. 509. Slow then fast pace: "Author's Preface," *A Hazard of New Fortunes* (New York, 1952), p. xxiii. To Hay, June 10, 1890, *LL*, II, 5. The novel needs the concentration of his earlier work; this would give it more impact without loss of New York's size and variety. Interrelationships are too coincidental, and there is much extraneous material.

22. For Tolstoy's replies to his critics, see *What Then Must We Do?* (New York, 1925), trans. Aylmer Maude, pp. 362–72. The wolf: *Hazard*, I, 82. Mind to Lindau: I, 126. No children: II, 151. Consequences: II, 137–38, 140, 148–49.

23. Description of March: *Hazard*, I, 180. In a May 17, 1890, letter to Howells, MS-H, James identifies the four Marches with the four Howellses; this portion of the letter is not in the Lubbock edition of James's letters. The names of the children, Bella and Tom, sound like those of Howells's two surviving children, Pilla (for Mildred) and John. Weakness: *Hazard*, I, 138. In "Autobiographical" (op. cit., p. 507), Howells found March's "ambitions and experiences ... so much more like my own, in revision, than I realized when I imagined them."

24. First paragraph: *Hazard*, I, 26–28. Theater: I, 88. Not real suffering: I, 86. Fine turn and outburst: I, 255–56. Rhetoric: I, 257. Conrad and March: I, 194–95.

25. Ease of mind: *Hazard*, I, 254; II, 66–67. Examples of humor: I, 120, 253, 258; II, 44, 122; I, 86; II, 67–68. Laugh: II, 75.

26. Squalid streets: *Hazard*, I, 89. New growth: see March on Dryfoos, II, 319.

27. Pensive and discomfort: *Hazard*, I, 241–44. Complicity: II, 74. Dinner: II, 106–27. Lindau and theater: II, 150–52. Perhaps Howells was comparing this to his not pursuing the anarchist affair further and not sending off his fierce letters.

28. Arbitrate: *Hazard*, II, 213. Battle, etc.: II, 251–54. The flirting with naturalism implied in "conditions *make* character" is not entirely new; it is especially strong in *A Modern Instance*. Utopia: *Hazard*, II, 251. Loving kindness: II, 276.

29. Cranks: *Hazard*, II, 68, 145, 151, 254. Murders: II, 232–34.

30. Hugo: *ES*, 78 (December 1888), 160. Vanderbilt, *The Achievement of William Dean Howells* (Princeton, 1968), pp. 163–64. Paternalism, disorder: *Hazard*, II, 126, 272. High-minded: I, 198. Humanists: *ES*, 73 (September 1886), 642. All figures: *Hazard*, I, 141. Old German: "Autobiographical," op. cit., p. 505. Civil War and pension: *Hazard*, I, 255–56. Shuffling evasion, etc.: II, 57–58; I, 80. Tenderness: "Autobiographical," p. 505.

31. Conrad is denied a pulpit partly by his own weak will, by his buckling to his father's demands. Howells may be suggesting, from experience, the potential weakness and ambiguity of moral arguments and socialist ideas preached by those who have not sufficiently cut their ties with capitalism.

32. Devotion: *Hazard*, II, 39. Preacher: II, 286. Kingdom of heaven: II, 133-34. Suffered more: "Autobiographical," op. cit., pp. 508-9.

33. James quoted by F. O. Mattheissen, *The James Family* (New York, 1947), p. 508. Hale, unpublished letter (n.d.), MS-H. Bellamy, unpublished letter, October 17, 1889, MS-H. Twain, February 11, 1890, *Mark Twain-Howells Letters*, ed. Henry Nash Smith and William M. Gibson (Cambridge, Mass., 1960), II, 630. Lowell to Thomas Hughes, April 20, 1890, *Letters of James Russell Lowell*, ed. Charles Eliot Norton (New York, 1894), II, 399. A few days before this, Lowell had written Howells that he thought the anarchists "well hanged"; ibid., pp. 394-95. Robertson James, unpublished letter, December 8, 1889, MS-H. Parton to Howells, December 30, 1889, and January 5, 1890, and Howells to Parton, January 3, 1890, unpublished letters, MSS-H. Curtis to Howells, unpublished letter, December 24, 1889, MS-H. "The Editor's Easy Chair," *Harper's Monthly*, 80 (January 1890), 313-14.

CHAPTER 5

1. *LL*, II, 158-59.

2. *LL*, II, 316.

3. Markham, Tribute Book, Howells Collection at Harvard.

4. Description of decline: see Everett Carter, *Howells and the Age of Realism* (Philadelphia, 1954), pp. 223, 226, and Larzer Ziff, *The American 1890s* (New York, 1966), pp. 39-40, 47-49. George Bennett, *The Realism of William Dean Howells 1889-1920* (Nashville, 1973). Parallels: *ES*, 82 (March 1891), 640, and ibid. (April 1891), 806; also *Harper's Weekly*, 39 (August 31, 1895), 820.

5. Aware: "The Man of Letters as a Man of Business," *Scribner's*, 14 (October 1893); in *Literature and Life* (New York, 1902), pp. 34-35. Slackening inspiration: Carter, *Howells and the Age of Realism*, p. 226, and Edwin Cady, *The Realist at War* (Syracuse, N.Y., 1958), pp. 177, 223, 233. "The Country Printer," *Scribner's*, 13 (May 1893), 539-58; *Impressions and Experiences* (New York, 1896), p. 44. Overwork: unpublished letter to Aurelia Howells, October 21, 1892, MS-H. Readership: "I think it is a pity if an author disappoints even the unreasonable expectation of the reader, whom his art has invited to love him." *Harper's Monthly*, 94 (December 1896), 134.

6. Autobiographical urge: this began in 1885 with the log-cabin sketch and set in in earnest in the 1890s with *A Boy's Town* (New York, 1890), "The Country Printer," *My Literary Passions* (New York, 1895), *Literary Friends and Acquaintance* (New York, 1900), and the editing of his father's memories of life in early Ohio. Strange mood: unpublished letter to father, November 24, 1889, MS-H. To Parton, unpublished letter, January 3, 1890, MS-H. Why: unpublished letter to father, June 15, 1890, MS-H. Howells's brother died while Howells was in Venice in 1864, and his sister died painfully in his presence, of malaria, in December 1886. Young couple: unpublished letter to father, May 3, 1891, MS-H. "Bride Roses," *The Complete Plays of W. D. Howells*, ed. Walter J. Meserve (New York, 1960),

pp. 431-37; first in *Harper's Monthly*, 87 (August 1893), 424-30. Memoir: *Winifred Howells* (Boston, 1891), pp. 26, 25. Pyle to Howells, unpublished letters, December 29, 1890, and February 15, 1891, MSS-H. The poem is "What Shall It Profit?" published in *Harper's Monthly*, 82 (February 1891), 384. Birthday: unpublished letter to father, March 1, 1891, MS-H. To Mitchell, unpublished letter, April 2, 1891, manuscript at University of Pennsylvania; quoted by permission of the Charles Patterson Van Pelt Library, University of Pennsylvania. "Mortality," *Harper's Monthly*, 82 (May 1891), 848-49, "Life," ibid. (March 1891), 608. Choice of life: unpublished letter to father, March 29, 1891, MS-H. Shocks: unpublished letter to Aurelia Howells, August 27, 1895, MS-H. See Kenneth Lynn's interesting discussion of Howells's philosophical disillusionment at a slightly earlier point: *William Dean Howells* (New York, 1971), pp. 294-96.

7. Smouldering rage: cited by Edward Wagenknecht, *William Dean Howells: The Friendly Eye* (New York, 1969), p. 40. "A Circle in the Water," *A Pair of Patient Lovers* (New York, 1901), pp. 285-386.

8. Associated Charities: see Clara Kirk, *W. D. Howells, Traveler from Altruria 1889-1894* (New Brunswick, N.J., 1962), p. 26; Margaret Rich, *A Belief in People* (New York, 1956), p. 34; Howells, "Tribulations of a Cheerful Giver," *Impressions and Experiences*, p. 184. Howells continued to send a monthly check — up to $75 in late 1891 — home and to pay doctors' and other bills for his father and some of his siblings. Though preferring "not to be one of his hands," Howells was very pleased with his friendship with Andrew Carnegie: Carnegie to Howells, unpublished letter, November 27, [1891], unpublished letters to father, February 7, 1892, and August 5, 1894, MSS-H. A & T stock: unpublished letter to father, November 16, 1890, MS-H. *A Boy's Town*, p. 177. Aristocrats: to father, February 2, 1890, *LL*, II, 1. Vanity: to Hale, May 6, 1890, *LL*, II, 4. William James: *ES*, 83 (July 1891), 315. Pit: unpublished letter, February 28, 1892, MS-H.

9. "I Talk of Dreams," *Impressions and Experiences*, pp. 103, 107-9, 98-99, 117-18, 99-100; first published in *Harper's Monthly*, 90 (May 1895), 836-45. Years 1902 and 1912: see first two epigraphs, p. 140. "Peonage," *Harper's Monthly*, 82 (March 1891), 609. See also "Temperament" and "Some One Else," ibid. James. March 27, 1912, *LL*, II, 318-19.

10. See Louis J. Budd, "Twain, Howells, and the Boston Nihilists," *New England Quarterly*, 32 (September 1959), 351-71. Also *LL*, II, 12-14, 36, and unpublished letters, Edward R. Pease to Howells, December 12, 1890, Howells to father, January 18, 1891, and March 19, 1893 (his vow), Sergei Stepnyak to Howells, April 18, 1891, MSS-H.

11. Balestier to Howells, unpublished letters, December 20, 1890, and February 18, 1891, MSS-H. *Cosmopolitan:* see Cady, *The Realist at War*, 178-79, 187-89; Clara and Rudolf Kirk, "Introduction," *The Altrurian Romances* (Bloomington, 1968), pp. xix-xxi; D. M. Rein, "Howells and the *Cosmopolitan*," *American Literature*, 21 (March 1949), 49-55; Hamlin Garland, "Mr. Howells's Plans," *Boston Evening Transcript*, January 1, 1892, p. 6; *LL*, II, 19-20, 24; unpublished letters to father, December 13, 1891, and June 15, 1892, MSS-H. Romance: *Harper's Bazaar*, 27 (June 16, 1894), 475. Letters, etc.: *Boston Evening*

Transcript, January 7, 1893, p. 6. *Harper's Weekly,* 39 (September 7, 1895), 844; "Niagara, First and Last," *The Niagara Book* (Boston, 1893), pp. 1-27.

12. Pyle to Howells, unpublished letters, October 22 and November 5, 1893, MSS-H. The newspapers referred to the Altrurian work. Reply: October 29, 1893, *LL,* II, 40. Crane, "Five Interviews with William Dean Howells," ed. George Arms and William M. Gibson, *Americana,* 37 (April 1943), 272-73.

13. *The Quality of Mercy* (New York, 1892), pp. 151-72.

14. *Annie Kilburn* and *Hazard:* John F. Phayre to Howells, unpublished letter, September 17, 1890, MS-H. *Traveler:* Harper & Brothers to Howells, unpublished letter, December 1, 1894, MS-H. Hardie to Howells, unpublished letters, December 10, 1895, and January 8, 1896, MSS-H. In *A Boy's Town* he preached democratic relations to his young readers, and in 1893 he published a volume of children's stories, *Christmas Every Day and Other Stories* (New York, 1893), which included two tales with the Howellsian message, "Christmas Every Day" (1886) and "Turkeys Turning the Tables" (1893). Excursions: unpublished letter to father, November 23, 1892, MS-H. See also "An East-Side Ramble" and "Tribulations of a Cheerful Giver," *Impressions and Experiences,* pp. 129ff, 184. Denton: *World of Chance* (New York, 1893), p. 182. Spectacle: *Impressions and Experiences,* p. 163.

15. Robert H. Wiebe, *The Search for Order* (New York, 1967), pp. 76-81. Richard Hofstadter, *The Age of Reform* (New York, 1955), p. 166. "Are We a Plutocracy?" *North American Review,* 158 (February 1894), 194. See also Howells's 1895 poems, "Society," "Vision," "Statistics," "The King Dines," and "Labor and Capital," all in *Stops of Various Quills* (New York, 1895).

16. Sinclair, *The Jungle* (New York, 1946), p. 301. Drainage: Marrion Wilcox, "W. D. Howells's First Romance," *Harper's Bazaar,* 27 (June 16, 1894), 475. Hughes: *World of Chance,* pp. 183-84. Ray: ibid., p. 217.

17. "Equality as the Basis of Good Society," *Century,* 51 (November 1895), 63-67. "Who Are Our Brethren?" *Century,* 51 (April 1896), 932-36. "The Nature of Liberty," *Forum,* 20 (December 1895), 401-9. "An East-Side Ramble" and "Tribulations of a Cheerful Giver" (the latter first published in *Century,* 50 [June-July 1895]) "Worries of a Winter Walk" (*Harper's Weekly,* 41 [April 3, 1897]) and "The Midnight Platoon" (*Harper's Weekly,* 39 [May 4, 1895]), in *Literature and Life.*

18. "Parable," *Harper's Monthly,* 91 (September 1895), 519; in *Stops of Various Quills.* The passage [XVIII: 18-30] from Luke would continue to appear in his writing: see, for example, his 1906 reference to Carnegie, *LL,* II, 169; the title of his second published utopian romance, *Through the Eye of the Needle* (New York, 1907), comes from the same passage; and see "Are the Americans Bible Readers?" *Literature,* n.s.1 (June 30, 1899), 585. Reader of Tolstoy: *My Literary Passions,* pp. 250-52, 257; *Harper's Weekly,* 39 (April 13, 1895), 342; "Lyof Tolstoy," in *A Library of the World's Best Literature,* ed. Charles Dudley Warner (New York, 1897), pp. 14985-94 — the last two in Kirk and Kirk, pp. 162, 171-72. Percy Brandreth, the young publisher in *The World of Chance,* was eager to get hold of a book like *Looking Backward,* pp. 261-62. Howells also had in mind the Nationalist groups that formed in response to Bellamy's book.

19. Cold doubt: *A Traveler from Altruria*, in *The Altrurian Romances*, ed. Clara and Rudolf Kirk and Scott Bennett, p. 25; hereafter *Traveler*. It ran in the *Cosmopolitan*, 14-15 (November 1892 to October 1893), and appeared as a Harper & Brothers book in 1894. Innocence, repeated questions, misgiving: *Traveler*, pp. 29, 57-58, 92. Control, conscience: pp. 123, 92. Fantastic: p. 99.

20. Mr. Twelvemough is satirized for writing "good, old-fashioned" love stories; there is self-satire here, for Howells was writing concurrently *The Coast of Bohemia*, a "mating and marrying" story which he hoped was his last; letter from Howells to Charles Eliot Norton, December 11, 1892, *LL*, II, 29. See Kirk, *W. D. Howells, Traveler from Altruria*, for a discussion of Mr. Homos and Mr. Twelvemough as two sides of Howells. Homos's speech: *Traveler*, p. 145. The predominant literary influence for this pastoral utopia is William Morris's *News from Nowhere*, not Bellamy's *Looking Backward*.

21. Altruria here and now: *Traveler*, p. 177. Those on top: the talk of the banker, professor of political economy, minister, romancer, doctor, society lady, and manufacturer demonstrate this throughout the book. Those who rise: pp. 41, 126-27. Reuben's truth: pp. 82, 81, 97, 93-94. Slavery: p. 103.

22. Stereotyping: *LL*, II, 235. Conservatism: see Clara and Rudolf Kirk, "Introduction," *The Altrurian Romances*, pp. xxiv-xxviii. They suggest the reaction to the first Altrurian book made Harper reluctant to venture another — there was some strong negative criticism. The firm's implicit attitude during the anarchist affair was hands-off; they also told Howells he was treading delicate ground in favorably reviewing Mrs. Humphry Ward's *Robert Elsmere* and praising Zola's *La Terre* in 1888. When Letters III through V were incorporated into *Impressions and Experiences*, published by Harper & Brothers, they were very much toned down.

23. Henry Mills Alden to Howells, unpublished letter, September 14, 1888, MS-H.

24. Hopefulness: *Letters of an Altrurian Traveller, 1893-94* (Gainesville, Fla., 1961), pp. 19, 23, 33, 70-71, 73, 80; hereafter *Letters*. Exposition: *Letters*, p. 21. Central Park: pp. 39-40, 56. Potentialities: p. 85. Courage: pp. 77-78. Altgeld issued his pardon on June 26, 1893; its basis was not leniency, but his opinion that all eight men had been victims of gross injustice. Howells made a special visit to Altgeld when in Chicago in 1899: Robert Rowlette, "William D. Howells's 1899 Midwest Lecture Tour," *American Literary Realism, 1870-1910*, 10 (Spring 1977), 131. Middle class: *Letters*, pp. 17-18. Misery: p. 40. Walks: pp. 58-59. All is ill: pp. 62-63.

25. Homos himself falls prey to defensive tendencies against *realization*. He does not succumb to the American reliance on humor for refuge from the despair of conditions (pp. 26, 74-75), but does become "hardened," tending to see impoverished scenes from an aesthetic point of view (pp. 59, 62). National greatness, alteration: pp. 16, 18. Central Park: p. 40. Vote: pp. 17, 67, 52. Impotency: pp. 63-64.

26. After dinner: *Letters*, p. 105. No hope: p. 115. Homos on Eveleth: p. 120. Luke: pp. 115-16. Decision: pp. 124-27.

27. "A Parting and a Meeting" ran in the *Cosmopolitan*, 18 (December 1894 to

February 1895). The text used here is *A Parting and a Meeting* (New York, 1896). The incident appeared in brief in "A Shaker Village," *Atlantic Monthly*, 37 (June 1876), 688-710, republished as "Shirley," *Three Villages* (Boston, 1884). Citations here from pp. 74-75, 78-79, 86-87, 94-95, 112-13.

28. Sophia Kirk, "America, Altruria, and the Coast of Bohemia," *Atlantic Monthly*, 74 (November 1894), 701-4. Marrion Wilcox, *Harper's Bazaar*, 27 (June 16, 1894), 475. Editors: unpublished letter to father, January 7, 1894 (the *North American Review* was "very urgent to have me do" a paper on plutocracy), and unpublished letter from Walter Hines Page to Howells, April 1894, MSS-H. Willard and *Fabian*: Cady, *The Realist at War*, pp. 203-4, 151-52. He signed a declaration of principles against expansionism and spoke out against it during his 1899 tour. See Rowlette, "William Dean Howells 1899 Midwest Lecture Tour," op. cit., n.24, and "The Philippine Problem; How to Secure Peace. Views of William D. Howells and Judge Bischoff," New York *Evening Post* (clipping in Howells collection at Harvard). NAACP: see W. E. B. Du Bois's tribute to Howells at the latter's 75th birthday, Boston *Evening Transcript*, February 24, 1912. Lynching: "The Home-towners or, [Incident of Convalescence]," pp. 8-10; MS-H.

29. Dreiser, unpublished letter, May 14, 1902, MS-H. The letter is written from Charlottesville, Va.; Dreiser did not return to New York until February 1903, and it is likely Howells mentioned *Sister Carrie* to him before that. Neither Dorothy Dudley's nor W. A. Swanberg's biography of Dreiser gives a definite date for the incident. (Dorothy Dudley, *Forgotten Frontiers: Dreiser and the Land of the Free* [New York, 1932]; W. A. Swanberg, *Dreiser* [New York, 1965].) It is uncertain what estimate of Hardy Dreiser had read. Howells's estimate is very high in *My Literary Passions*, pp. 248-49, and in his review of *Jude the Obscure* in *Harper's Weekly*, 39 (December 7, 1895), 1156. Some of Dreiser's later critical statements on Howells are not so laudatory. All the poems Dreiser mentions appeared in *Harper's Monthly*, 86 (March 1893), 547-50, except one, "Hope," which appeared ibid., 91 (September 1895), 516, with a number of the social poems; every poem Dreiser lists is one of Howells's personal poems. Lowell's line: *Atlantic Monthly*, 39 (March 1877), 374.

Bibliography

BOOKS BY HOWELLS

The Altrurian Romances. Ed. Clara and Rudolf Kirk and Scott Bennett. Bloomington: Indiana University Press, 1968.

Annie Kilburn. New York: Harper, 1889.

April Hopes. New York: Harper, 1888.

A Boy's Town, Described for "Harper's Young People." New York: Harper, 1890.

A Chance Acquaintance. Boston: Osgood, 1873.

Christmas Every Day and Other Stories Told for Children. New York: Harper, 1893.

The Coast of Bohemia. New York: Harper, 1893.

The Complete Plays. Ed. Walter J. Meserve. New York: New York University Press, 1960.

A Counterfeit Presentiment. Boston: Osgood, 1877.

Criticism and Fiction. New York: Harper, 1891.

Criticism and Fiction and Other Essays. Ed. Clara and Rudolf Kirk. New York: New York University Press, 1959.

Dr. Breen's Practice. Boston: Osgood, 1881.

A Fearful Responsibility and Other Stories. Boston: Osgood, 1881.

A Hazard of New Fortunes. New York: Harper, 1890.

A Hazard of New Fortunes. New York: Dutton, 1952.

A Hazard of New Fortunes. Bloomington: Indiana University Press, 1976.

Impressions and Experiences. New York: Harper, 1896.

Indian Summer. Boston: Ticknor, 1886.

The Landlord at Lion's Head. New York: Harper, 1897.

Letters of an Altrurian Traveller, 1893–4; A Facsimile Reproduction. Gainesville, Fla.: Scholars' Facsimiles and Reprints, 1961.

Life in Letters of William Dean Howells. Ed. Mildred Howells. Garden City, N.Y.: Doubleday, Doran, 1928.

Literary Friends and Acquaintance: A Personal Retrospective of American Authorship. New York: Harper, 1900.

Literature and Life: Studies. New York: Harper, 1902.

A Little Swiss Sojourn. New York: Harper, 1892.

London Films. New York: Harper, 1906.

The Minister's Charge, or the Apprenticeship of Lemuel Barker. Boston: Ticknor, 1887.

A Modern Instance. New York: New American Library, 1964. Signet Classic, following 1882 edition (Boston: Osgood).

Modern Italian Poets: Essays and Versions. New York: Harper, 1887.

My Literary Passions. New York: Harper, 1895.

My Mark Twain; Reminiscences and Criticisms. Baton Rouge: Louisiana State University Press, 1967.

My Year in a Log Cabin. New York: Harper, 1893.

A Pair of Patient Lovers. New York: Harper, 1901.

A Parting and a Meeting. New York: Harper, 1896.

Prefaces to Contemporaries, 1882–1920. Ed. George Arms, William M. Gibson, and F. C. Marston, Jr. Gainesville, Fla.: Scholars' Facsimiles and Reprints, 1957.

The Quality of Mercy. New York: Harper, 1892.

The Rise of Silas Lapham. New York: Holt, Rinehart & Winston, 1964.

Sketch of the Life and Character of Rutherford B. Hayes. Boston: Hurd and Houghton, 1876.

Stops of Various Quills. New York: Harper, 1895.

Suburban Sketches. New York: Hurd and Houghton, 1871.

Their Wedding Journey. Boston: Osgood, 1872.

Three Villages. Boston: Osgood, 1884.

Through the Eye of the Needle: A Romance. New York: Harper, 1907.

Tuscan Cities. Boston: Ticknor, 1886.

Venetian Life. (New and enlarged edition.) Boston: Osgood, 1872.

Winifred Howells. Boston: privately printed, 1891.

A Woman's Reason. Boston: Osgood, 1883.

The World of Chance. New York: Harper, 1893.

REVIEWS, ARTICLES, ESSAYS, ETC., BY HOWELLS

"Are the Americans Bible Readers?" *Literature,* n.s. 1 (June 30, 1899), 585–86.

"Are We a Plutocracy?" *North American Review,* 158 (February 1894), 185–96.

"Author's Preface" (1909), *A Hazard of New Fortunes.* New York: Dutton, 1952.

"Autobiographical," *A Hazard of New Fortunes.* Bloomington: Indiana University Press, 1976.

"Bardic Symbols," *Ohio State Journal,* 23 (March 28, 1860), 2.

"Bride Roses, Scene," *Harper's Monthly,* 87 (August 1893), 424–30. Play.

"Carlo Goldoni," *Atlantic Monthly,* 40 (November 1877), 601–13.

"Christmas Every Day," *Saint Nicholas,* 13 (January 1886), 163–67. Story.

"A Circle in the Water," *Scribner's,* 17 (March–April 1895), 293–303, 428–40. Story.

"Clemency for the Anarchists, a Letter from Mr. W. D. Howells," *New York Tribune*, November 6, 1887, p. 5.

"Degeneration," *Harper's Weekly*, 39 (April 13, 1895), 342.

"The Editor's Study," monthly column in *Harper's Monthly*, 72-84 (January 1886-March 1892).

"Emile Zola," *North American Review*, 175 (November 1902), 587-96.

"Equality as the Basis of Good Society," *Century*, 51 (November 1895), 63-67.

"Execution by Electricity," *Harper's Weekly*, 32 (January 14, 1888), 23.

"A Fearful Responsibility," *Scribner's*, 22 (June-July 1881), 276-93, 390-414. Story.

"Garfield," *Atlantic Monthly*, 48 (November 1881), 707-9.

"George William Curtis," *Harper's Weekly* (September 10, 1892), 868, 870.

"Henry James, Jr.," *Century*, 25 (November 1882), 25-29.

"Hope," *Harper's Monthly*, 91 (September 1895), 517. Poem.

Introduction to *Living Truths from the Writings of Charles Kingsley*, pp. 3-4. Boston: Lothrop, 1882.

"James's Hawthorne," *Atlantic Monthly*, 45 (February 1880), 282-85.

"The King Dines," *Harper's Monthly*, 84 (May 1892), 942. Poem.

"Labor and Capital," *Harper's Monthly*, 84 (May 1892), 942. Poem.

"Letters from Venice — XXIII," Boston *Advertiser*, June 25, 1864, p. 2.

"Lexington," *Longman's Magazine*, 1 (November 1882), 41-61.

"Life," *Harper's Monthly*, 82 (March 1891), 608. Poem.

"Life and Letters," *Harper's Weekly*, 39 (August 31, 1895), 820; 39 (September 7, 1895), 844; 39 (December 7, 1895), 1156.

"Lyof N. Tolstoy," *North American Review*, 188 (December 1908), 842-59.

"Lyof Tolstoy," *A Library of the World's Best Literature*. Vol. 27. Ed. Charles Dudley Warner. New York: International Society, 1897.

"The Man of Letters as a Man of Business," *Scribner's*, 14 (October 1893), 429-45.

"Mark Twain," *Century*, 24 (September 1882), 780-83.

"The Midnight Platoon," in "Life and Letters," *Harper's Weekly*, 39 (May 4, 1895), 416-17.

"Mortality," *Harper's Monthly*, 82 (May 1891), 848-49. Poem.

"Mr. Garland's Books," *North American Review*, 196 (October 1912), 523-28.

"Mr. Howells on Forest Preservation," Boston *Evening Transcript*, January 7, 1893, p. 6. Letter.

"Mr. Howells's Paper," *The House of Harper: A Century of Publishing in Franklin Square*. New York: Harper, 1912.

"My Favorite Novelist and His Best Book," *Munsey's Magazine*, 17 (April 1897), 18-25.

"The Nature of Liberty," *Forum*, 20 (December 1895), 401-9.

"A New Observer," *Atlantic Monthly*, 45 (June 1880), 848-49.

"Niagara, First and Last," *The Niagara Book*. Boston: Underhill and Nichols, 1893.

"Niagara Revisited, Twelve Years After Their Wedding Journey," *Atlantic Monthly*, 51 (May 1883), 598-610.

"Old Cambridge," *Literature*, n.s. 1 (June 9, 1899), 505-6.

"Oliver Wendell Holmes," *Harper's Monthly*, 94 (December 1896), 120-34.

"Parable," *Harper's Monthly*, 91 (September 1895), 519. Poem.

"A Parting and a Meeting," *Cosmopolitan*, 18 (December 1894-February 1895), 183-88, 307-16, 469-74. Story.

"Peonage," *Harper's Monthly*, 82 (March 1891), 609.

"Police Report," *Atlantic Monthly*, 49 (January 1882), 1-6.

"Professor Barrett Wendell's Notions of American Literature," *North American Review*, 172 (April 1901), 623-40.

"Recent American Novels: 'The Breadwinners,'" *Century*, 28 (May 1884), 153-54.

"Recollections of an Atlantic Editorship," *Atlantic Monthly*, 100 (November 1907), 594-606.

Reviews, *Atlantic Monthly*, 25 (April 1870), 504-12; 29 (February 1872), 236-42; 30 (August 1872), 243-44; 31 (February 1873), 237-42; 32 (September 1873), 369-70, 372-73, 375-76; 33 (March 1874), 368-71; 33 (June 1874), 745-47, 748; 35 (April 1875), 490-95; 39 (March 1877), 374-78; 41 (April 1878), 550-51.

"A Shaker Village," *Atlantic Monthly*, 37 (June 1876), 688-710.

"Society," *Harper's Monthly*, 90 (March 1895), 630. Poem.

"Some One Else," *Harper's Monthly*, 82 (March 1891), 609. Poem.

"Temperament," *Harper's Monthly*, 82 (March 1891), 608. Poem.

"Tribulations of a Cheerful Giver," *Century*, 50 (June-July 1895), 181-85, 417-21.

"A Tribute to William Dean Howells. Souvenir of a Dinner Given to the Eminent Author in Celebration of His Seventy-fifth Birthday," *Harper's Weekly*, 66 (March 9, 1912), 27-34 (Howells's speech, pp. 28-29).

"True, I Talk of Dreams," *Harper's Monthly*, 90 (May 1895), 836-45.

"Vision," *Harper's Monthly*, 91 (September 1895), 518. Poem.

"Was There Nothing to Arbitrate?" *Harper's Weekly*, 32 (April 21, 1888), 286.

"What Shall It Profit?" *Harper's Monthly*, 82 (February 1891), 384. Poem.

"Who Are Our Brethren?" *Century*, 51 (April 1896), 932-36.

"Worries of a Winter Walk," in "Life and Letters," *Harper's Weekly*, 41 (April 3, 1897), 338-39.

BOOKS BY OTHER WRITERS

BECKER, GEORGE JOSEPH, ed. *Documents of Modern Literary Realism*. Princeton: Princeton University Press, 1963.

BENNETT, GEORGE N. *The Realism of William Dean Howells, 1889-1920*. Nashville: Vanderbilt University Press, 1973.

BENNETT, JOAN. *George Eliot, Her Mind and Her Art*. Cambridge: Cambridge University Press, 1948.

BERTHOFF, WARNER. *The Ferment of Realism: American Literature 1884-1919*. New York: Free Press, 1965.

BROOKS, VAN WYCK. *Howells, His Life and World*. New York: Dutton, 1959.

CADY, EDWIN. *The Realist at War: The Mature Years, 1885–1920, of William Dean Howells.* Syracuse: Syracuse University Press, 1958.

——. *The Road to Realism: The Early Years, 1837–1885, of William Dean Howells.* Syracuse: Syracuse University Press, 1956.

CARTER, EVERETT. *Howells and the Age of Realism.* Philadelphia: Lippincott, 1954.

DAVID, HENRY. *The History of the Haymarket Affair: A Study in the American Social-Revolutionary and Labor Movements.* New York: Farrar & Rinehart, Inc., 1936.

DUDLEY, DOROTHY. *Forgotten Frontiers: Dreiser and the Land of the Free.* New York: H. Smith and R. Hass, 1932.

EBLE, KENNETH. *Howells, a Century of Criticism.* Dallas: Southern Methodist University Press, 1962.

FIELDS, ANNIE (MRS. JAMES T.). *How to Help the Poor.* Boston: Houghton Mifflin, 1885.

FRYCKSTEDT, OLOV. *In Quest of America: A Study of Howells' Early Development as a Novelist.* Cambridge: Harvard University Press, 1958.

GARLAND, HAMLIN. *Roadside Meetings.* New York: Macmillan, 1930.

GILMAN, NICHOLAS PAINE. *Socialism and the American Spirit.* New York: Houghton Mifflin, 1893.

GRONLUND, LAURENCE. *The Cooperative Commonwealth.* Cambridge: Harvard University Press, 1965.

HALE, EDWARD EVERETT, JR., ed. *The Life and Letters of Edward Everett Hale.* Boston: Little, Brown, 1917.

HAYES, RUTHERFORD B. *The Diary and Letters of Rutherford Birchard Hayes, Nineteenth President of the United States.* Vol. 4. Ed. Charles Richard Williams. The Ohio State Archaeological and Historical Society, 1925.

HOFSTADTER, RICHARD. *The Age of Reform: From Bryan to F.D.R.* New York: Knopf, 1955.

HOUGH, ROBERT. *The Quiet Rebel: William Dean Howells as Social Commentator.* Lincoln: University of Nebraska Press, 1959.

HOWE, EDGAR WATSON. *The Story of a Country Town.* Cambridge: The Belknap Press of Harvard University Press, 1961.

JAMES, HENRY. *The American Essays of Henry James.* Ed. Leon Edel. New York: Vintage, 1956.

——. *The Letters of Henry James.* Ed. Percy Lubbock. New York: Octagon Books, 1920.

JOHNSON, ROBERT UNDERWOOD. *Remembered Yesterdays.* Boston: Little, Brown, 1923.

KIRK, CLARA. *William Dean Howells, Traveler from Altruria.* New Brunswick, N.J.: Rutgers University Press, 1962.

KIRK, RUDOLF, and C. F. MAIN, eds. *Essays in Literary History Presented to J. Milton French.* New Brunswick, N.J.: Rutgers University Press, 1960.

LEWISOHN, LUDWIG. *Mid-Channel: An American Chronicle.* New York: Harper, 1929.

LYNN, KENNETH. *William Dean Howells: An American Life*. New York: Harcourt Brace Jovanovich, 1971.

MATTHEISEN, PAUL, and MICHAEL MILLGATE, eds. *Transatlantic Dialogue: Selected American Correspondence*. Austin: University of Texas Press, 1965.

MATTHIESSEN, F. O. *The James Family, Including Selections from the Writings of Henry James, Senior, William, Henry, & Alice James*. New York: Knopf, 1947.

MORDELL, ALBERT. *Quaker Militant, John Greenleaf Whittier*. Port Washington, N.Y.: Kennikat Press, 1969 (identical with 1933 edition).

MORISON, SAMUEL ELIOT, and HENRY STEELE COMMAGER. *The Growth of the American Republic*. 5th ed., rev. New York: Oxford University Press, 1962.

NORTON, CHARLES ELIOT. *The Letters of Charles Eliot Norton, with Biographical Comment by his Daughter Sara Norton and M. A. De Wolfe Howe*. Boston: Houghton Mifflin, 1913.

————, ed. *The Letters of James Russell Lowell*. New York: Harper, 1894.

PARRINGTON, VERNON L. *The Beginnings of Critical Realism, Completed to 1900 Only*. New York: Harcourt, Brace, 1930.

PENNELL, JOSEPH. *The Adventures of an Illustrator, Mostly in Following His Authors in America and Europe*. Boston: Little, Brown, 1925.

POLLARD, JOHN A. *John Greenleaf Whittier: Friend of Man*. Boston: Houghton Mifflin, 1949.

RICH, MARGARET. *A Belief in People: A History of Family Social Work*. New York: Family Service Association of America, 1956.

ROBERTSON, J. M. *Essays Toward a Critical Method*. London: T. Fisher Unwin, 1889.

SINCLAIR, UPTON. *The Jungle*. New York: Viking, 1946.

SMITH, HENRY NASH, and WILLIAM M. GIBSON with the assistance of FREDERICK ANDERSON, eds. *Mark Twain–Howells Letters: The Correspondence of Samuel L. Clemens and William Dean Howells 1872–1910*. 2 vols. Cambridge: Harvard University Press, 1960.

SWANBERG, W. A. *Dreiser*. New York: Scribner, 1965.

TOLSTOY, LEO. *What Then Must We Do?* New York: Oxford University Press, 1925.

TRILLING, LIONEL. *The Opposing Self: Nine Essays in Criticism*. New York: Viking, 1955.

VANDERBILT, KERMIT. *The Achievement of William Dean Howells: A Reinterpretation*. Princeton: Princeton University Press, 1968.

————. *Charles Eliot Norton: Apostle of Culture in a Democracy*. Cambridge: Harvard University Press, 1959.

WAGENKNECHT, EDWARD. *William Dean Howells: The Friendly Eye*. New York: Oxford University Press, 1969.

WHITTIER, JOHN GREENLEAF. *The Letters of John Greenleaf Whittier*. Vol. 3: 1861–1892. Ed. John B. Pickard. Cambridge: Harvard University Press, 1975.

WIEBE, ROBERT. *The Search for Order, 1877–1920.* New York: Hill and Wang, 1967.

ZIFF, LARZER. *The American 1890's: The Life and Times of a Lost Generation.* New York: Viking, 1966.

REVIEWS, ARTICLES, ESSAYS, ETC. BY OTHER WRITERS

ALEXANDER, WILLIAM. "Howells, Eliot, and the Humanized Reader," *Harvard English Studies.* Vol. 1. Cambridge: Harvard University Press, 1970.

BENNETT, JAMES O'DONNELL. "Howells, Teacher," Chicago *Journal,* October 26, 1899, p. 4.

Brooklyn Magazine, November 1885, p. 78.

BROWNELL, W. C. "The Novels of Mr. Howells," *The Nation,* 31 (July 15, 1880), 49–51.

BUDD, LOUIS J. "Twain, Howells, and the Boston Nihilists," *New England Quarterly,* 32 (September 1959), 351–71.

CLARK, BRYAN W. "The Literature of the Household: A Sketch of America's Leading Writer of Fiction, W. D. Howells," *Good Housekeeping,* 1 (July 11, 1885), 2–3.

CURTIS, GEORGE WILLIAM. "The Editor's Easy Chair," *Harper's Monthly,* 80 (January 1890), 313–14.

"Facts Vs. Gush." Editorial, *New York Tribune,* November 7, 1887, p. 4.

"Five Interviews with William Dean Howells," eds. GEORGE ARMS and WILLIAM M. GIBSON, *Americana,* 37 (April 1943), 257–95.

"Fourth Annual Report of the Associated Charities of Boston, November 1883," *Associated Charities of Boston, 1879–87,* pp. 22–23. Boston: Associated Charities of Boston, 1887.

GARLAND, HAMLIN. "Mr. Howells's Plans," Boston *Evening Transcript,* January 1, 1892, p. 6.

_____. "Sanity in Fiction," *North American Review,* 176 (March 1903), 336–48.

_____. "William Dean Howells' Boston: A Posthumous Pilgrimage," and "From Venice as Far as Belmont," Boston *Evening Transcript,* May 22, 1920, pp. 4, 5.

GOSSE, EDMUND. "The Passing of William Dean Howells," *Living Age,* 306 (July 10, 1920), 98–100.

HIGGINSON, HENRY WENTWORTH. "Howells," *Literary World,* 10 (August 2, 1879), 249–50.

HOLMES, OLIVER WENDELL. "The New Portfolio," *Atlantic Monthly,* 29 (February 1885), 248–58.

JAMES, HENRY. "Emile Zola," *Atlantic Monthly,* 92 (August 1903), 193–210.

_____. "William Dean Howells," *Harper's Weekly,* 30 (June 19, 1886), 394–95.

KIRK, CLARA and RUDOLF. "Howells and the Church of the Carpenter," *New England Quarterly*, 32 (June 1959), 185–206.

———. Introduction to *The Altrurian Romances*. Bloomington: Indiana University Press, 1968.

———. "William Dean Howells, George William Curtis, and the 'Haymarket Affair,'" *American Literature*, 40 (January 1969), 487–98.

KIRK, RUDOLF, and CLARA. "Abraham Cahan and William Dean Howells: The Story of a Friendship," *American Jewish Historical Quarterly*, 52 (September 1962), 25–57.

KIRK, SOPHIA. "America, Altruria, and *The Coast of Bohemia*," *Atlantic Monthly*, 74 (November 1894), 701–4.

"Literature: *A Modern Instance*," *The Critic*, 2 (October 21, 1882), 278–79.

"Literature: *A Woman's Reason*," *The Critic*, 3 (December 22, 1883), 518–19.

LLOYD, HENRY DEMAREST. "Story of a Great Monopoly," *Atlantic Monthly*, 47 (March 1881), 317–34.

LOWELL, JAMES RUSSELL. Review of *Venetian Life*, in *North American Review*, 103 (October 1866), 610–13.

MABIE, HAMILTON WRIGHT. "A Typical Novel," *Andover Review*, 4 (November 1885), 417–29.

"The Mistake of Cowardice." Editorial, *New York Tribune*, November 8, 1887, p. 4.

MONROE, HARRIET EARHART. "Statesman and Novelist: A Talk Between Senator Ingalls and Mr. Howells," *Lippincott's*, 39 (January 1887), 128–32.

"Mr. Howells and the Anarchist Meeting," *Harper's Weekly*, 32 (November 24, 1888), 887.

"Mr. Howells on Realism, a Talk with the Novelist. Rider Haggard, a Counter Current — a Russian Shakespeare," *New York Tribune*, July 10, 1887, p. 12.

"The New Socialism," *The Nation*, 48 (June 13, 1889), 478.

"The New Socialism: Boston's Two Nationalist Societies and What They Aim to Accomplish," *New York Tribune*, October 6, 1889, p. 15.

Newspaper clipping, Maine, November 1877 (found in file in Howells Collection at Harvard).

Newspaper clipping, *St. Louis Globe-Democrat*, probably 1882 (found in file in Howells Collection at Harvard).

"Novelists and Their Subjects." Unidentified newspaper, February 21, 1882 (found in file in Howells Collection at Harvard).

"Our Monthly Gossip," *Lippincott's*, 39 (February 1887), 184–86.

"The Philippine Problem: How to Secure Peace. Views of William Dean Howells and Judge Bischoff," New York *Evening Post*, n.d. (found in file in Howells Collection at Harvard).

REIN, D. M. "Howells and the *Cosmopolitan*," *American Literature*, 21 (March 1949), 49–55.

ROBERTSON, J. M. "Mr. Howells' Novels," *Westminster Review*, n.s. 132 (October 1884), 347–75.

ROWLETTE, ROBERT. "William Dean Howells' 1899 Midwest Lecture Tour," *American Literary Realism, 1870–1910*, 10 (Spring 1977), 125–69.

SCUDDER, HORACE. "The East and West in Recent Fiction," *Atlantic Monthly*, 52 (November 1883), 704-5.

_____. "James, Crawford, and Howells," *Atlantic Monthly*, 57 (June 1886), 855-57.

_____. "*A Modern Instance*," *Atlantic Monthly*, 50 (November 1882), 709-13.

SMITH, FRANKLIN. "An Hour with Howells," *Frank Leslie's Weekly*, 74 (March 17, 1892), 118-19.

STEVENSON, ROBERT LOUIS. "A Humble Remonstrance," *The Travels and Essays of Robert Louis Stevenson*. Vol. 13. New York: Charles Scribner, 1895.

VAN DYKE, HENRY. Remarks, "Public Meeting Held at the Stuart Gallery, New York Public Library, New York, March 1st, in Memory of William D. Howells," *American Academy Proceedings*, July 1, 1921, II, 1-21. Reprinted in *Campfires and Guideposts: A Book of Essays and Excursions*. New York: Scribner, 1921.

"W. D. Howells at Home," *New York Tribune*, January 25, 1880, p. 3.

"What the Anarchists Did. Facts for Sentimentalists to Consider," *New York Tribune*, November 7, 1887, p. 3.

WILCOX, MARRION, "W. D. Howells's First Romance," *Harper's Bazaar*, 27 (June 16, 1894), 475.

_____. "Works of William Dean Howells (1860-96)," *Harper's Weekly*, 40 (July 4, 1896), 655-56.

WISTER, OWEN. "William Dean Howells," *Atlantic*, 160 (December 1937), 704-13.

Index